SILVER SURFER

NEW DAWN

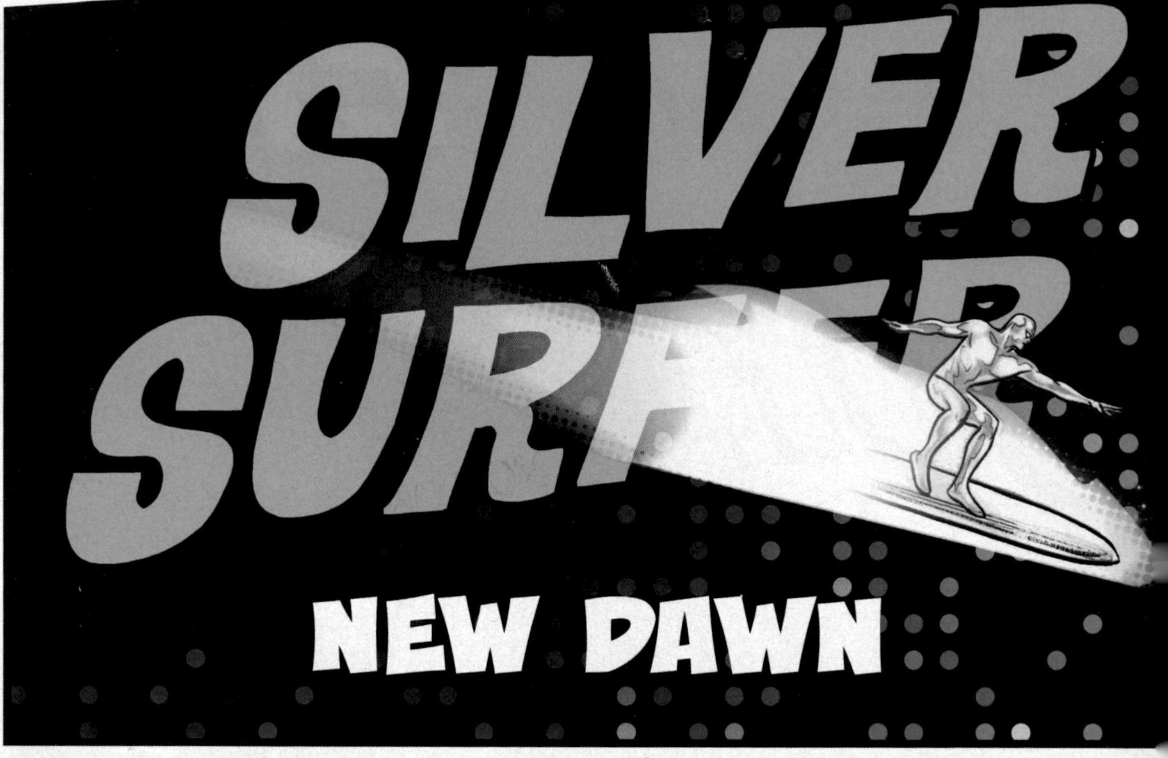
SILVER SURFER
NEW DAWN

STORYTELLERS:

DAN SLOTT & MICHAEL ALLRED

COLOR ARTIST:

LAURA ALLRED

LETTERER:

VC'S CLAYTON COWLES

COVER ART:

MICHAEL ALLRED & LAURA ALLRED

ASSISTANT EDITOR:

JAKE THOMAS

EDITOR:

TOM BREVOORT

Collection Editor: **Jennifer Grünwald**
Assistant Editor: **Sarah Brunstad**
Associate Managing Editor: **Alex Starbuck**
Editor, Special Projects: **Mark D. Beazley**
Senior Editor, Special Projects: **Jeff Youngquist**
SVP Print, Sales & Marketing: **David Gabriel**
Book Designer: **Rodolfo Muraguchi**

Editor in Chief: **Axel Alonso**
Chief Creative Officer: **Joe Quesada**
Publisher: **Dan Buckley**
Executive Producer: **Alan Fine**

SILVER SURFER VOL. 1: NEW DAWN. Contains material originally published in magazine form as SILVER SURFER #1-5 and ALL-NEW MARVEL NOW! POINT ONE #1. First printing 2014. ISBN# 978-0-7851-8878-0. Publis by MARVEL WORLDWIDE, INC., a subsidiary of MARVEL ENTERTAINMENT, LLC. OFFICE OF PUBLICATION: 135 West 50th Street, New York, NY 10020. **Printed in Canada.** ALAN FINE, EVP - Office of the President, Marvel Worldwide, Inc. EVP & CMO Marvel Characters B.V.; DAN BUCKLEY, Publisher & President - Print, Animation & Digital Divisions; JOE QUESADA, Chief Creative Officer; TOM BREVOORT, SVP of Publishing; DAVID BOGART, SVP of Operatior Procurement, Publishing; C.B. CEBULSKI, SVP of Creator & Content Development; DAVID GABRIEL, SVP Print, Sales & Marketing; JIM O'KEEFE, VP of Operations & Logistics; DAN CARR, Executive Director of Publishing Technolc SUSAN CRESPI, Editorial Operations Manager; ALEX MORALES, Publishing Operations Manager; STAN LEE, Chairman Emeritus. For information regarding advertising in Marvel Comics or on Marvel.com, please contact N Disla, Director of Marvel Partnerships, at ndisla@marvel.com. For Marvel subscription inquiries, please call 800-217-9158. **Manufactured between 8/29/2014 and 10/6/2014 by SOLISCO PRINTERS, SCOTT, QC, CANA**

10 9 8 7 6 5 4 3 2 1

1

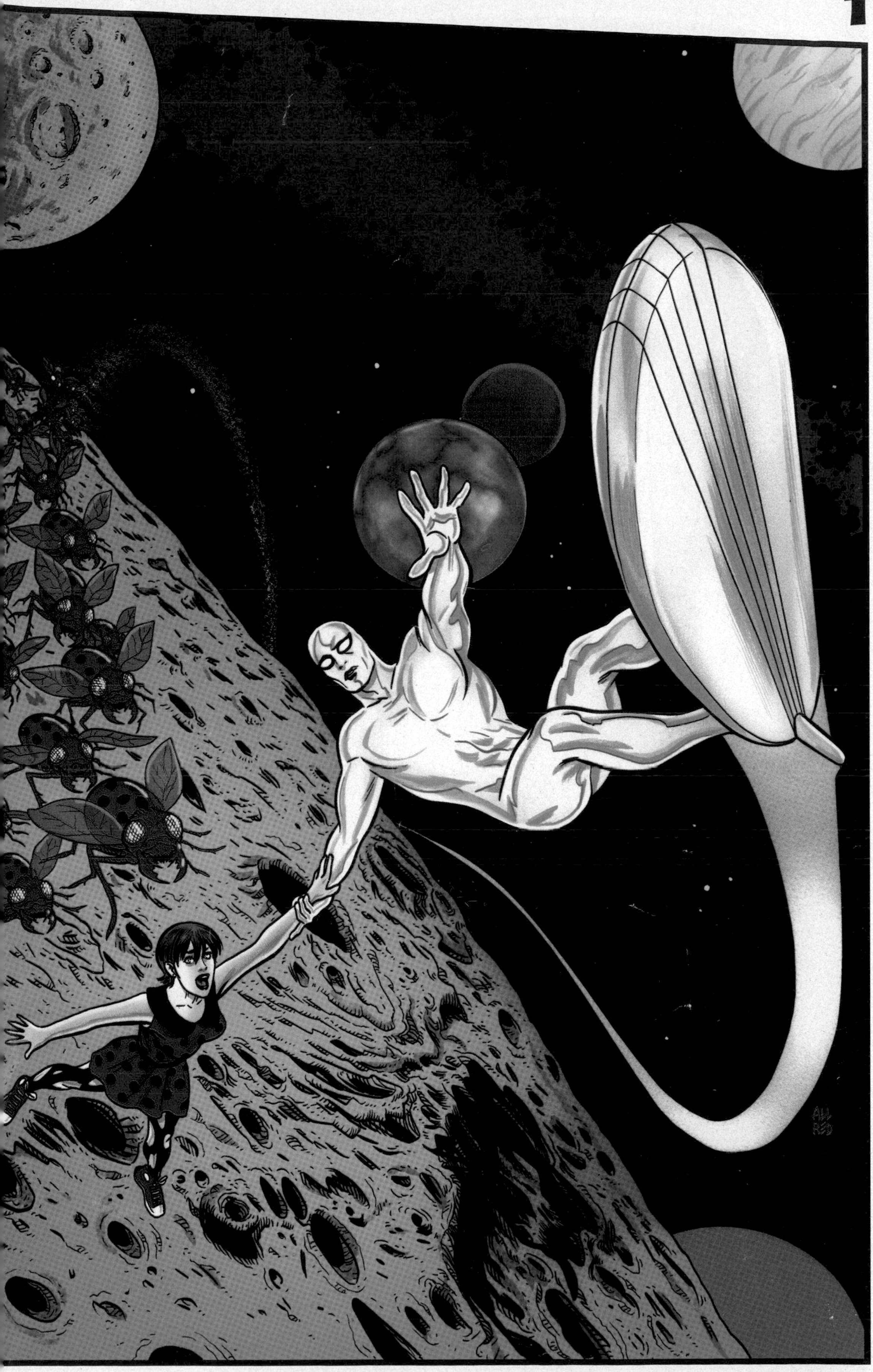

THE MOST IMPORTANT PERSON IN THE UNIVERSE

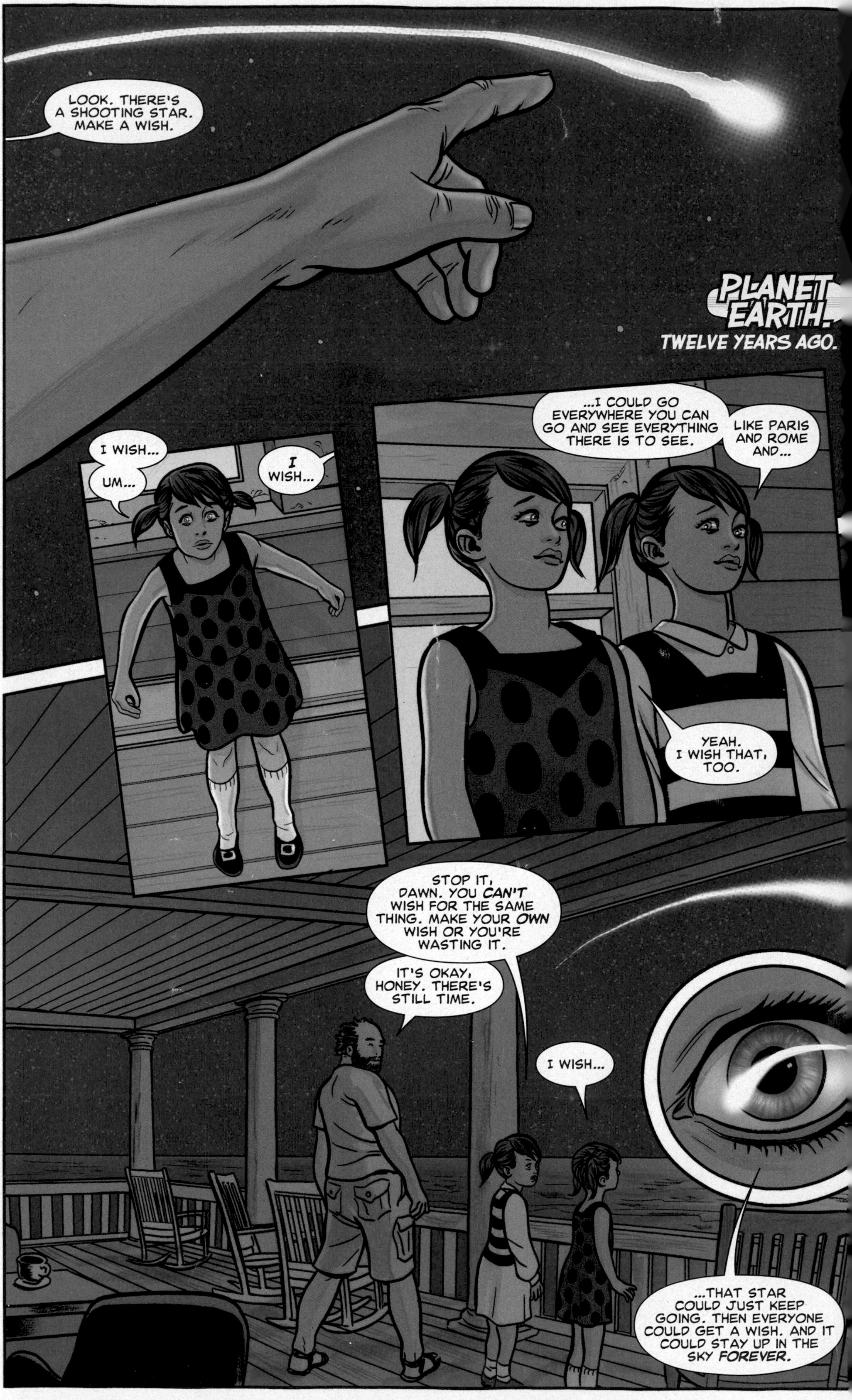
LOOK. THERE'S A SHOOTING STAR. MAKE A WISH.
PLANET EARTH.
TWELVE YEARS AGO.
I WISH...
UM...
I WISH...
...I COULD GO EVERYWHERE YOU CAN GO AND SEE EVERYTHING THERE IS TO SEE.
LIKE PARIS AND ROME AND...
YEAH. I WISH THAT, TOO.
STOP IT, DAWN. YOU CAN'T WISH FOR THE SAME THING. MAKE YOUR OWN WISH OR YOU'RE WASTING IT.
IT'S OKAY, HONEY. THERE'S STILL TIME.
I WISH...
...THAT STAR COULD JUST KEEP GOING. THEN EVERYONE COULD GET A WISH. AND IT COULD STAY UP IN THE SKY FOREVER.

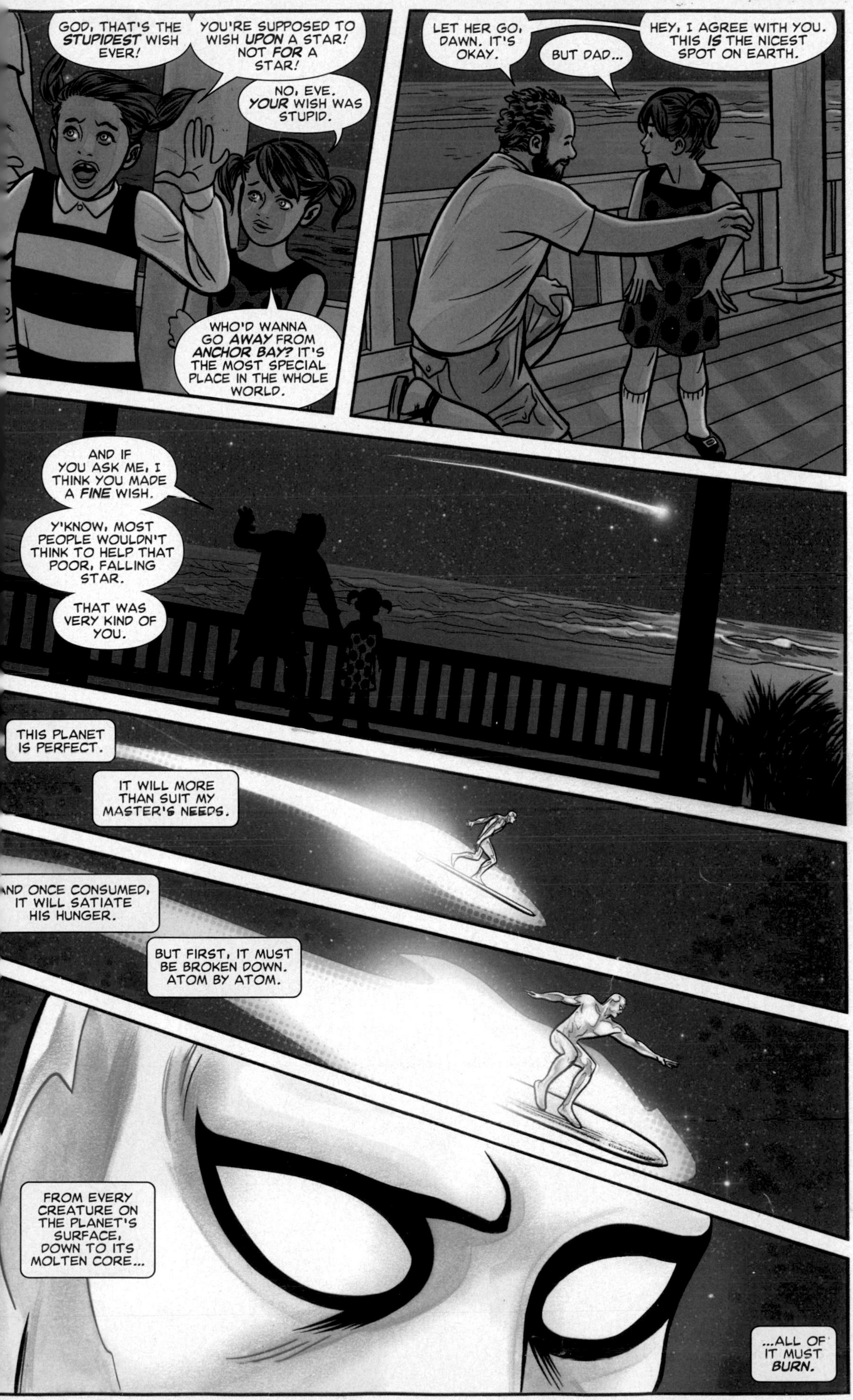
GOD, THAT'S THE STUPIDEST WISH EVER!
YOU'RE SUPPOSED TO WISH UPON A STAR! NOT FOR A STAR!
NO, EVE. YOUR WISH WAS STUPID.
WHO'D WANNA GO AWAY FROM ANCHOR BAY? IT'S THE MOST SPECIAL PLACE IN THE WHOLE WORLD.
LET HER GO, DAWN. IT'S OKAY.
BUT DAD...
HEY, I AGREE WITH YOU. THIS IS THE NICEST SPOT ON EARTH.
AND IF YOU ASK ME, I THINK YOU MADE A FINE WISH.
Y'KNOW, MOST PEOPLE WOULDN'T THINK TO HELP THAT POOR, FALLING STAR.
THAT WAS VERY KIND OF YOU.
THIS PLANET IS PERFECT.
IT WILL MORE THAN SUIT MY MASTER'S NEEDS.
AND ONCE CONSUMED, IT WILL SATIATE HIS HUNGER.
BUT FIRST, IT MUST BE BROKEN DOWN. ATOM BY ATOM.
FROM EVERY CREATURE ON THE PLANET'S SURFACE, DOWN TO ITS MOLTEN CORE...
...ALL OF IT MUST BURN.

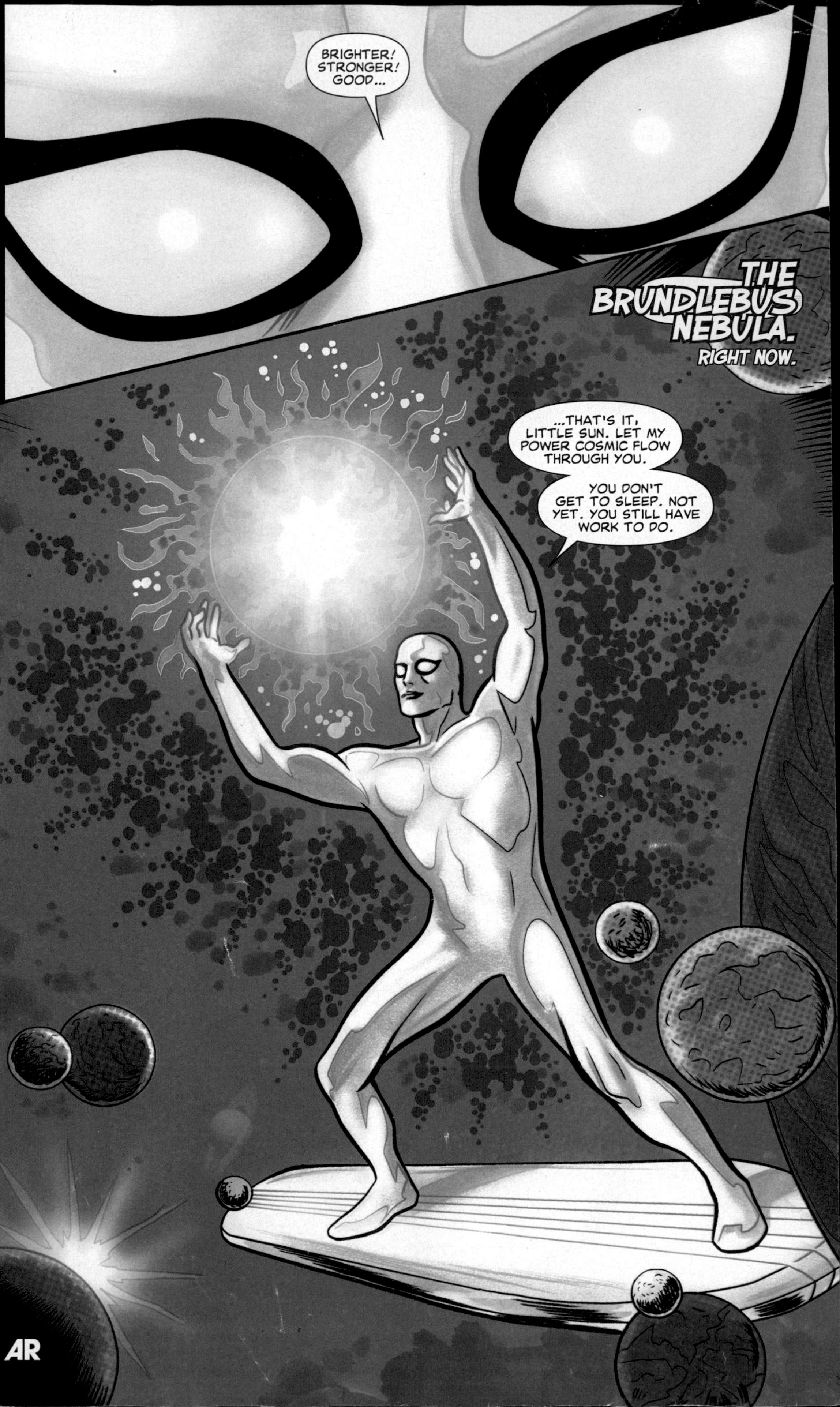
BRIGHTER! STRONGER! GOOD...
THE BRUNDLEBUS NEBULA. RIGHT NOW.
...THAT'S IT, LITTLE SUN. LET MY POWER COSMIC FLOW THROUGH YOU.
YOU DON'T GET TO SLEEP. NOT YET. YOU STILL HAVE WORK TO DO.
AR

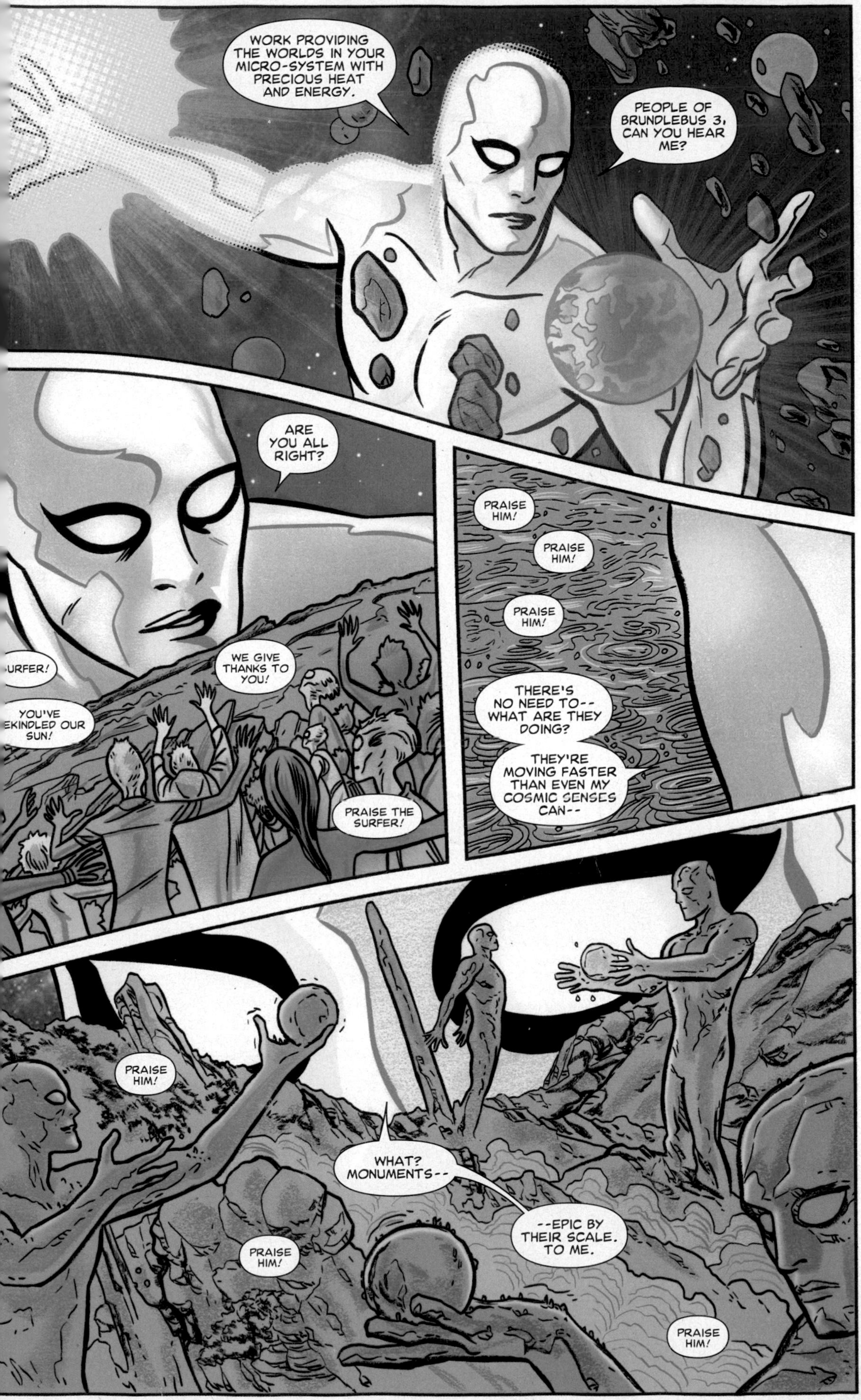
WORK PROVIDING THE WORLDS IN YOUR MICRO-SYSTEM WITH PRECIOUS HEAT AND ENERGY.
PEOPLE OF BRUNDLEBUS 3, CAN YOU HEAR ME?
ARE YOU ALL RIGHT?
SURFER!
YOU'VE EKINDLED OUR SUN!
WE GIVE THANKS TO YOU!
PRAISE THE SURFER!
PRAISE HIM!
PRAISE HIM!
PRAISE HIM!
THERE'S NO NEED TO-- WHAT ARE THEY DOING?
THEY'RE MOVING FASTER THAN EVEN MY COSMIC SENSES CAN--
PRAISE HIM!
WHAT? MONUMENTS--
--EPIC BY THEIR SCALE. TO ME.
PRAISE HIM!
PRAISE HIM!

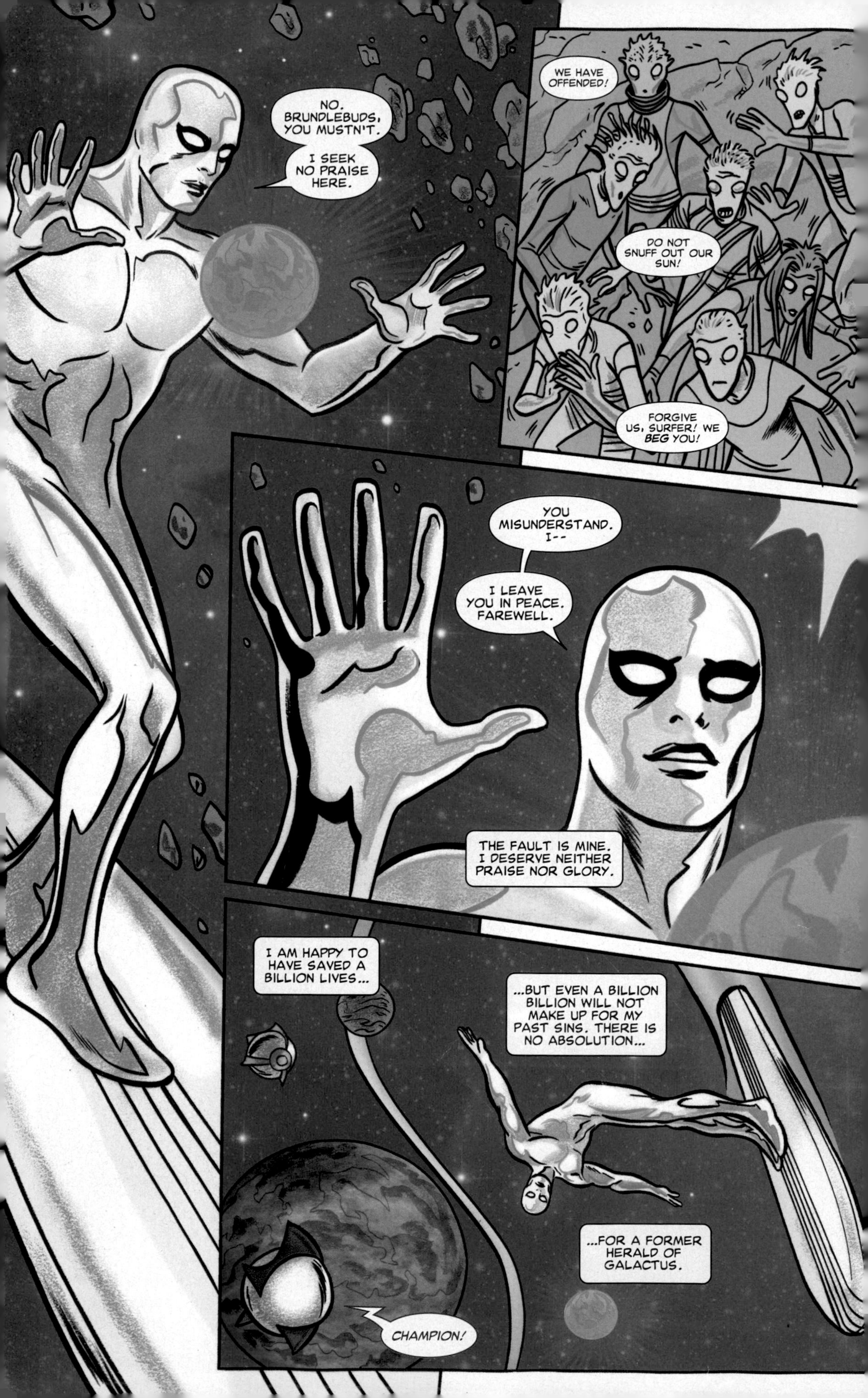
NO. BRUNDLEBUDS, YOU MUSTN'T.
I SEEK NO PRAISE HERE.
WE HAVE OFFENDED!
DO NOT SNUFF OUT OUR SUN!
FORGIVE US, SURFER! WE BEG YOU!
YOU MISUNDERSTAND. I--
I LEAVE YOU IN PEACE. FAREWELL.
THE FAULT IS MINE. I DESERVE NEITHER PRAISE NOR GLORY.
I AM HAPPY TO HAVE SAVED A BILLION LIVES...
...BUT EVEN A BILLION BILLION WILL NOT MAKE UP FOR MY PAST SINS. THERE IS NO ABSOLUTION...
...FOR A FORMER HERALD OF GALACTUS.
CHAMPION!

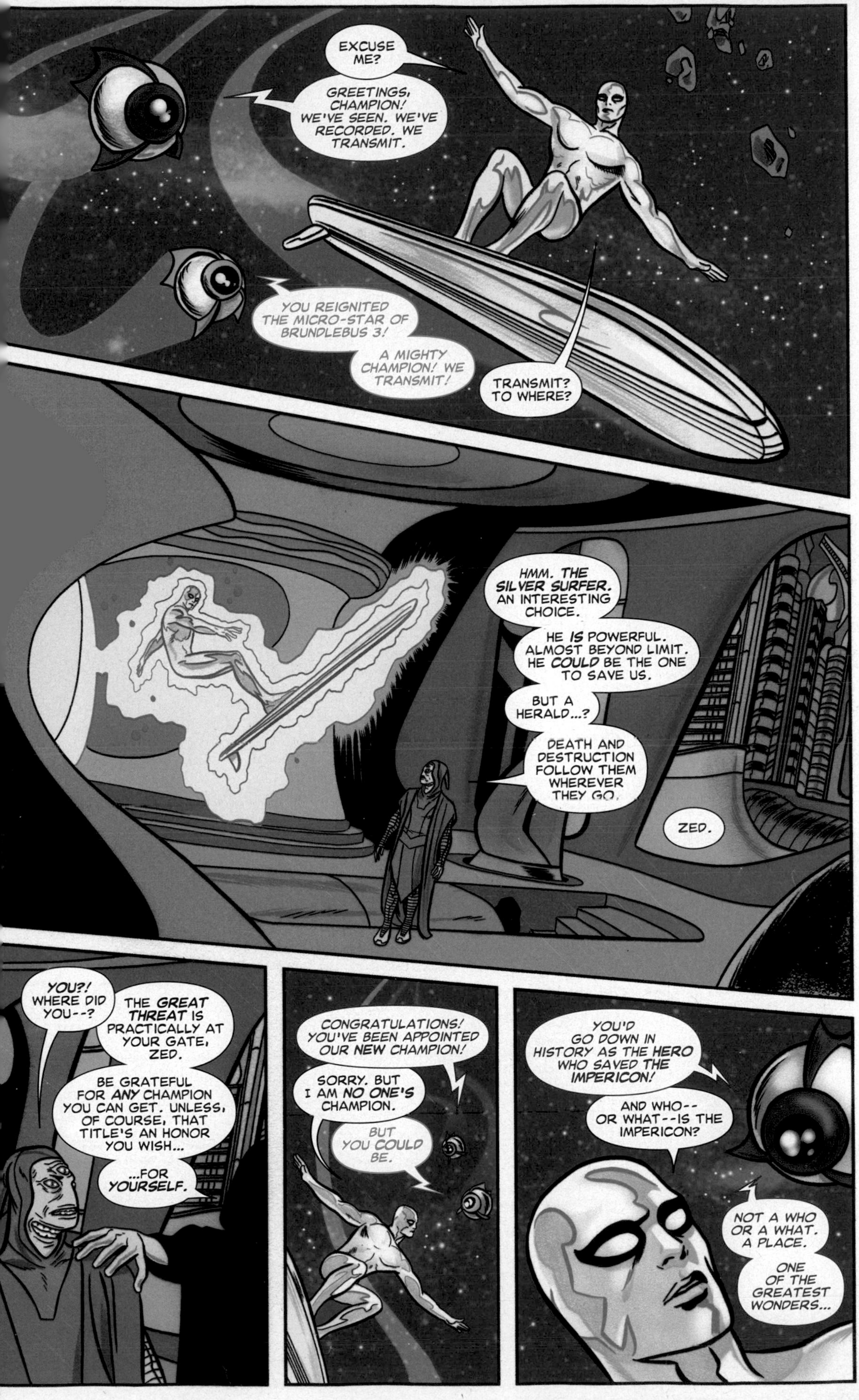
EXCUSE ME?
GREETINGS, CHAMPION! WE'VE SEEN. WE'VE RECORDED. WE TRANSMIT.
YOU REIGNITED THE MICRO-STAR OF BRUNDLEBUS 3!
A MIGHTY CHAMPION! WE TRANSMIT!
TRANSMIT? TO WHERE?
HMM. THE SILVER SURFER. AN INTERESTING CHOICE.
HE IS POWERFUL. ALMOST BEYOND LIMIT. HE COULD BE THE ONE TO SAVE US.
BUT A HERALD...?
DEATH AND DESTRUCTION FOLLOW THEM WHEREVER THEY GO.
ZED.
YOU?! WHERE DID YOU--?
THE GREAT THREAT IS PRACTICALLY AT YOUR GATE, ZED.
BE GRATEFUL FOR ANY CHAMPION YOU CAN GET. UNLESS, OF COURSE, THAT TITLE'S AN HONOR YOU WISH...
...FOR YOURSELF.
CONGRATULATIONS! YOU'VE BEEN APPOINTED OUR NEW CHAMPION!
SORRY. BUT I AM NO ONE'S CHAMPION.
BUT YOU COULD BE.
YOU'D GO DOWN IN HISTORY AS THE HERO WHO SAVED THE IMPERICON!
AND WHO-- OR WHAT--IS THE IMPERICON?
NOT A WHO OR A WHAT. A PLACE.
ONE OF THE GREATEST WONDERS...

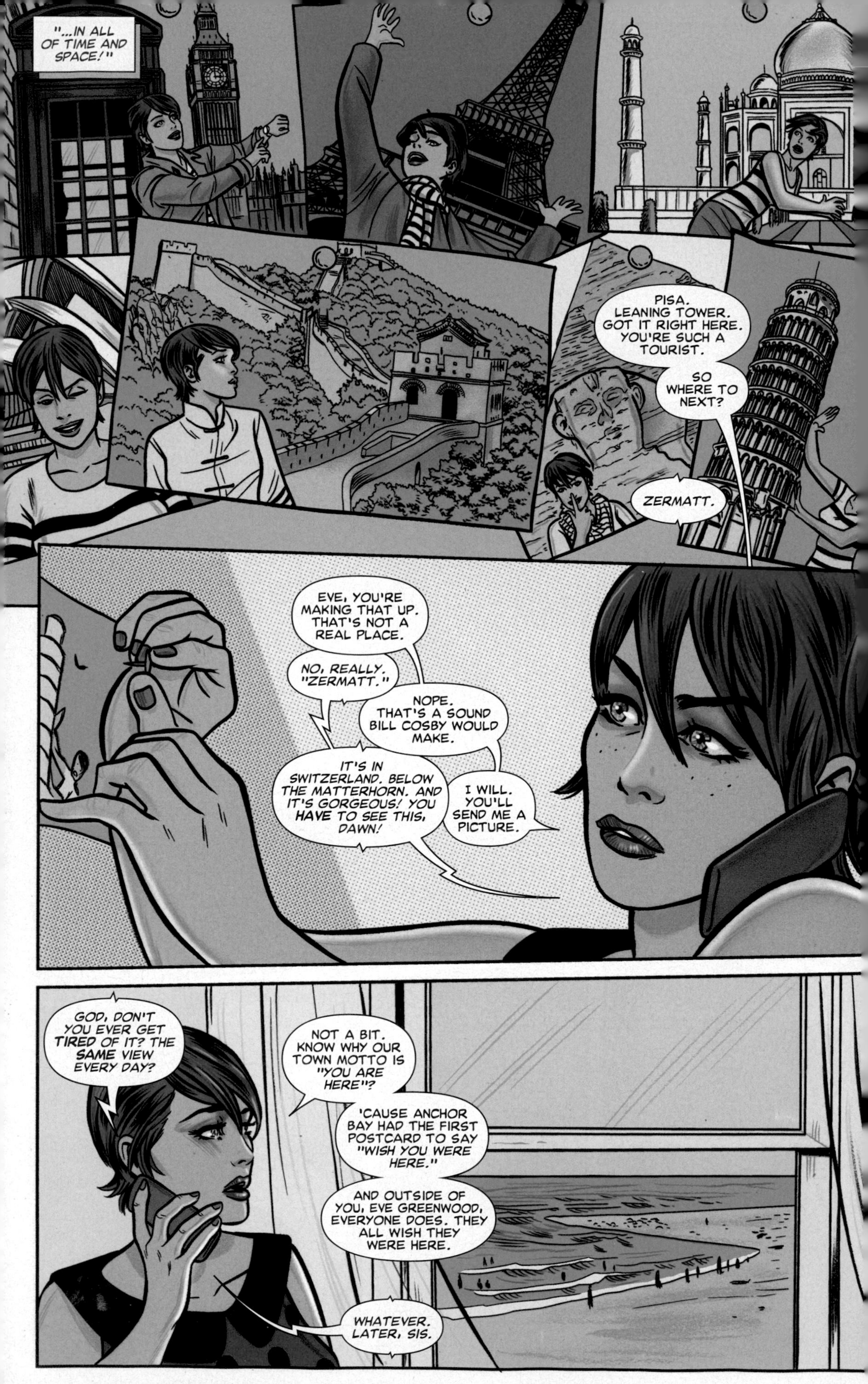
"...IN ALL OF TIME AND SPACE!"
PISA. LEANING TOWER. GOT IT RIGHT HERE. YOU'RE SUCH A TOURIST.
SO WHERE TO NEXT?
ZERMATT.
EVE, YOU'RE MAKING THAT UP. THAT'S NOT A REAL PLACE.
NO, REALLY. "ZERMATT."
NOPE. THAT'S A SOUND BILL COSBY WOULD MAKE.
IT'S IN SWITZERLAND. BELOW THE MATTERHORN. AND IT'S GORGEOUS! YOU HAVE TO SEE THIS, DAWN!
I WILL. YOU'LL SEND ME A PICTURE.
GOD, DON'T YOU EVER GET TIRED OF IT? THE SAME VIEW EVERY DAY?
NOT A BIT. KNOW WHY OUR TOWN MOTTO IS "YOU ARE HERE"?
'CAUSE ANCHOR BAY HAD THE FIRST POSTCARD TO SAY "WISH YOU WERE HERE."
AND OUTSIDE OF YOU, EVE GREENWOOD, EVERYONE DOES. THEY ALL WISH THEY WERE HERE.
WHATEVER. LATER, SIS.

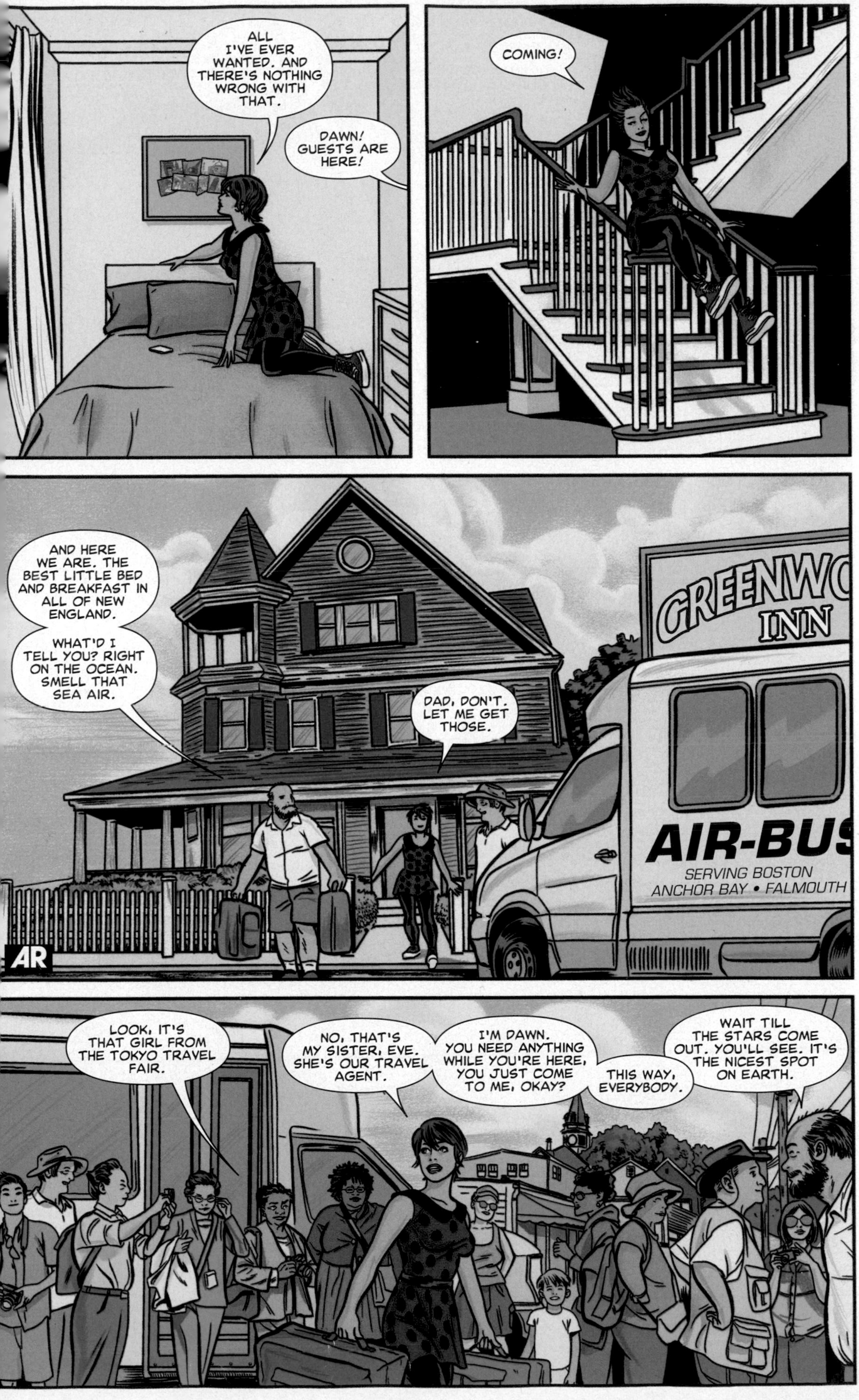
ALL I'VE EVER WANTED. AND THERE'S NOTHING WRONG WITH THAT.
DAWN! GUESTS ARE HERE!
COMING!
AND HERE WE ARE. THE BEST LITTLE BED AND BREAKFAST IN ALL OF NEW ENGLAND.
WHAT'D I TELL YOU? RIGHT ON THE OCEAN. SMELL THAT SEA AIR.
DAD, DON'T. LET ME GET THOSE.
GREENWO
INN
AIR-BUS
SERVING BOSTON
ANCHOR BAY • FALMOUTH
AR
LOOK, IT'S THAT GIRL FROM THE TOKYO TRAVEL FAIR.
NO, THAT'S MY SISTER, EVE. SHE'S OUR TRAVEL AGENT.
I'M DAWN. YOU NEED ANYTHING WHILE YOU'RE HERE, YOU JUST COME TO ME, OKAY?
THIS WAY, EVERYBODY.
WAIT TILL THE STARS COME OUT. YOU'LL SEE. IT'S THE NICEST SPOT ON EARTH.

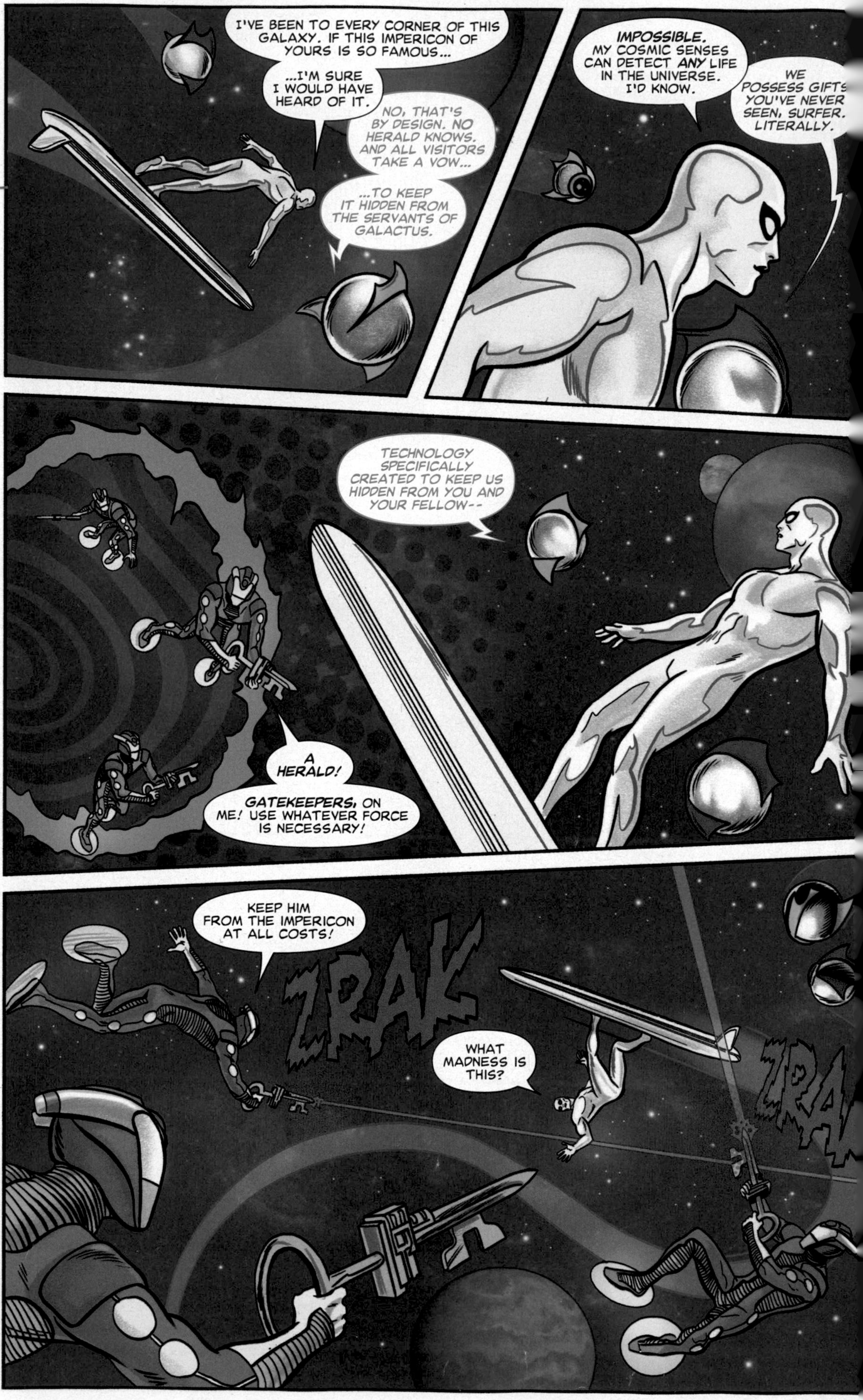
I'VE BEEN TO EVERY CORNER OF THIS GALAXY. IF THIS IMPERICON OF YOURS IS SO FAMOUS...
...I'M SURE I WOULD HAVE HEARD OF IT.
NO, THAT'S BY DESIGN. NO HERALD KNOWS. AND ALL VISITORS TAKE A VOW...
...TO KEEP IT HIDDEN FROM THE SERVANTS OF GALACTUS.
IMPOSSIBLE. MY COSMIC SENSES CAN DETECT ANY LIFE IN THE UNIVERSE. I'D KNOW.
WE POSSESS GIFTS YOU'VE NEVER SEEN, SURFER. LITERALLY.
TECHNOLOGY SPECIFICALLY CREATED TO KEEP US HIDDEN FROM YOU AND YOUR FELLOW--
A HERALD!
GATEKEEPERS, ON ME! USE WHATEVER FORCE IS NECESSARY!
KEEP HIM FROM THE IMPERICON AT ALL COSTS!
ZRAK
WHAT MADNESS IS THIS?

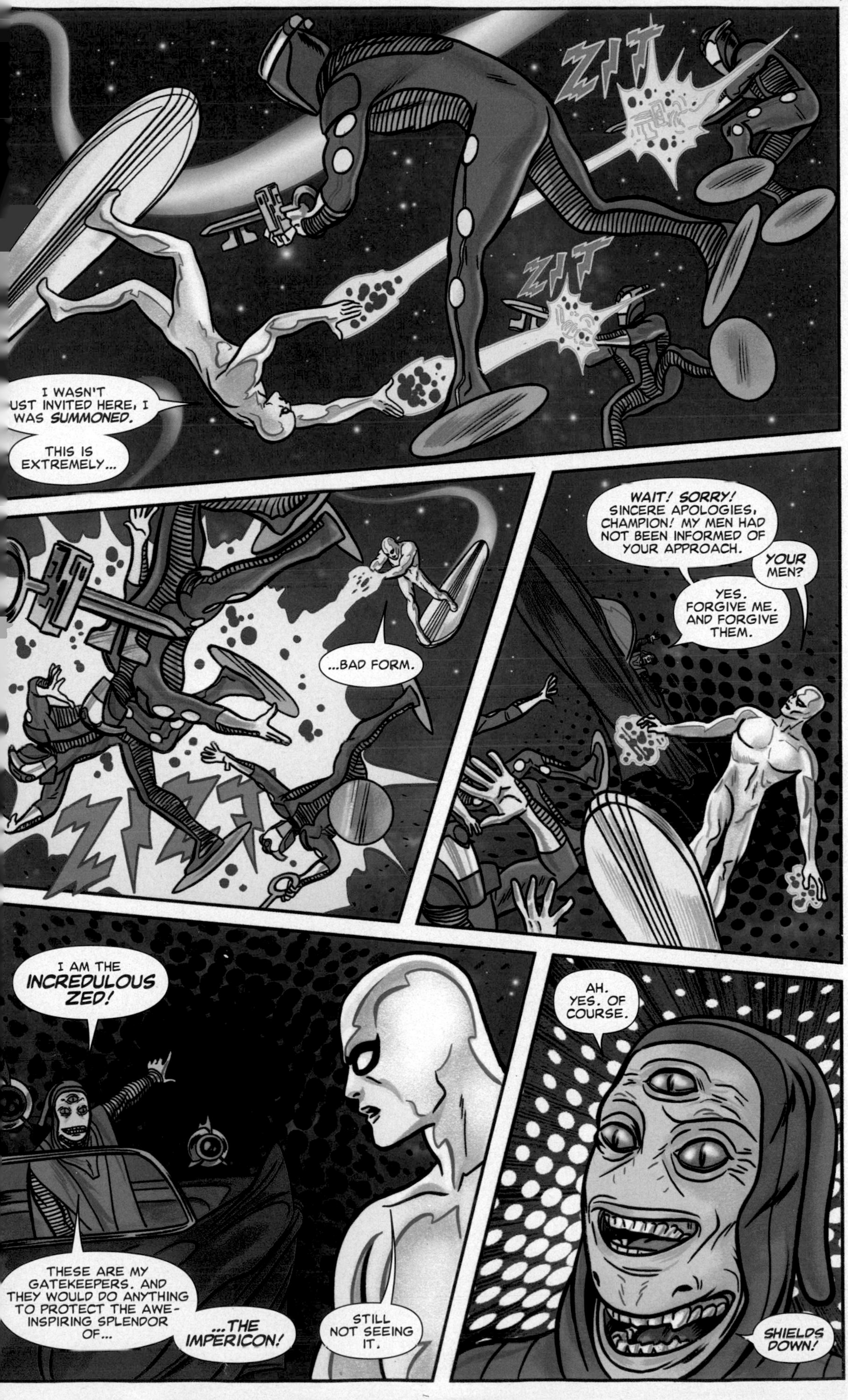
ZIT
ZIT
I WASN'T UST INVITED HERE, I WAS SUMMONED.
THIS IS EXTREMELY...
...BAD FORM.
ZZZZ
WAIT! SORRY! SINCERE APOLOGIES, CHAMPION! MY MEN HAD NOT BEEN INFORMED OF YOUR APPROACH.
YOUR MEN?
YES. FORGIVE ME. AND FORGIVE THEM.
I AM THE INCREDULOUS ZED!
THESE ARE MY GATEKEEPERS. AND THEY WOULD DO ANYTHING TO PROTECT THE AWE-INSPIRING SPLENDOR OF...
...THE IMPERICON!
STILL NOT SEEING IT.
AH. YES. OF COURSE.
SHIELDS DOWN!

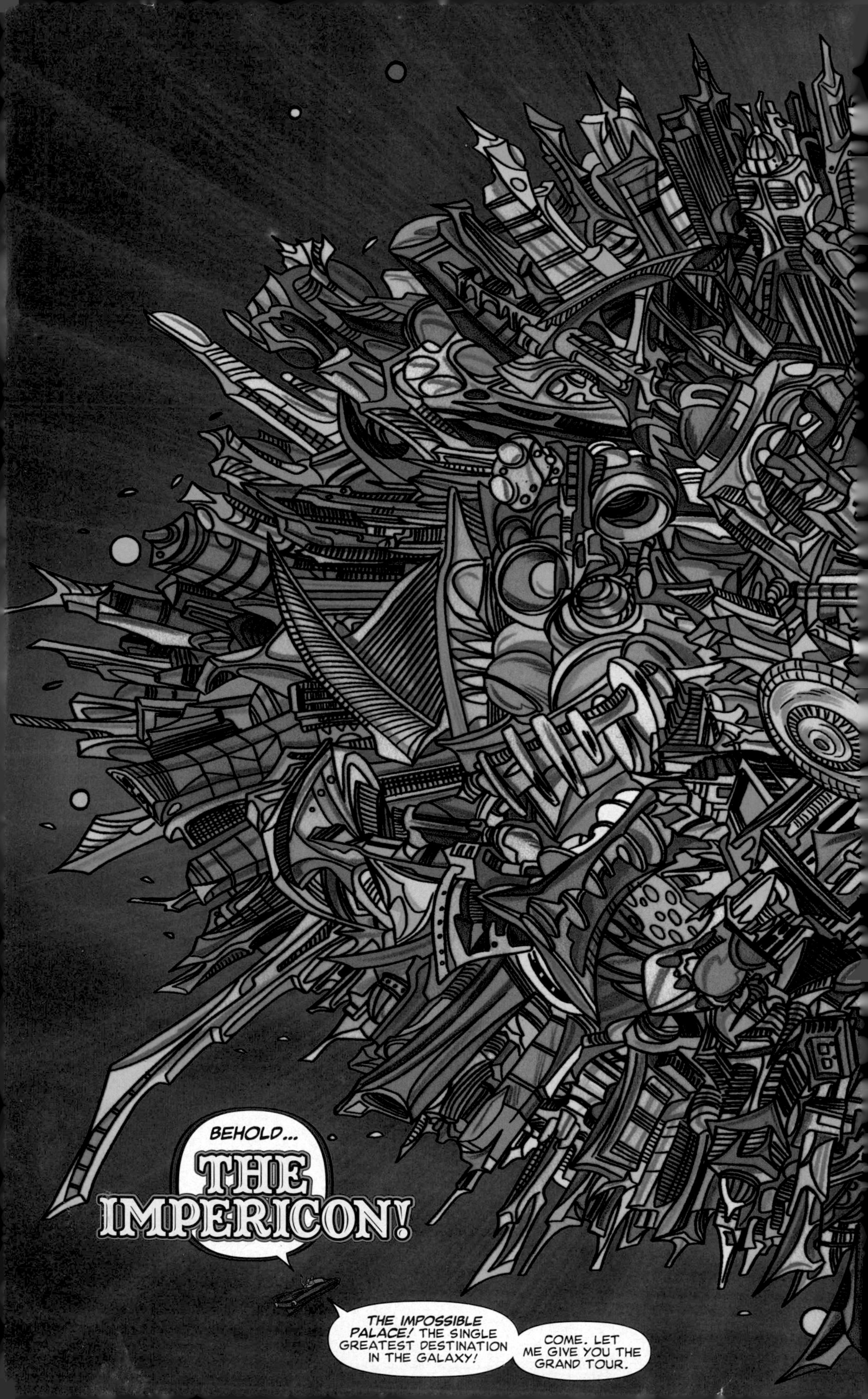
BEHOLD...
THE IMPERICON!
THE IMPOSSIBLE PALACE! THE SINGLE GREATEST DESTINATION IN THE GALAXY!
COME. LET ME GIVE YOU THE GRAND TOUR.

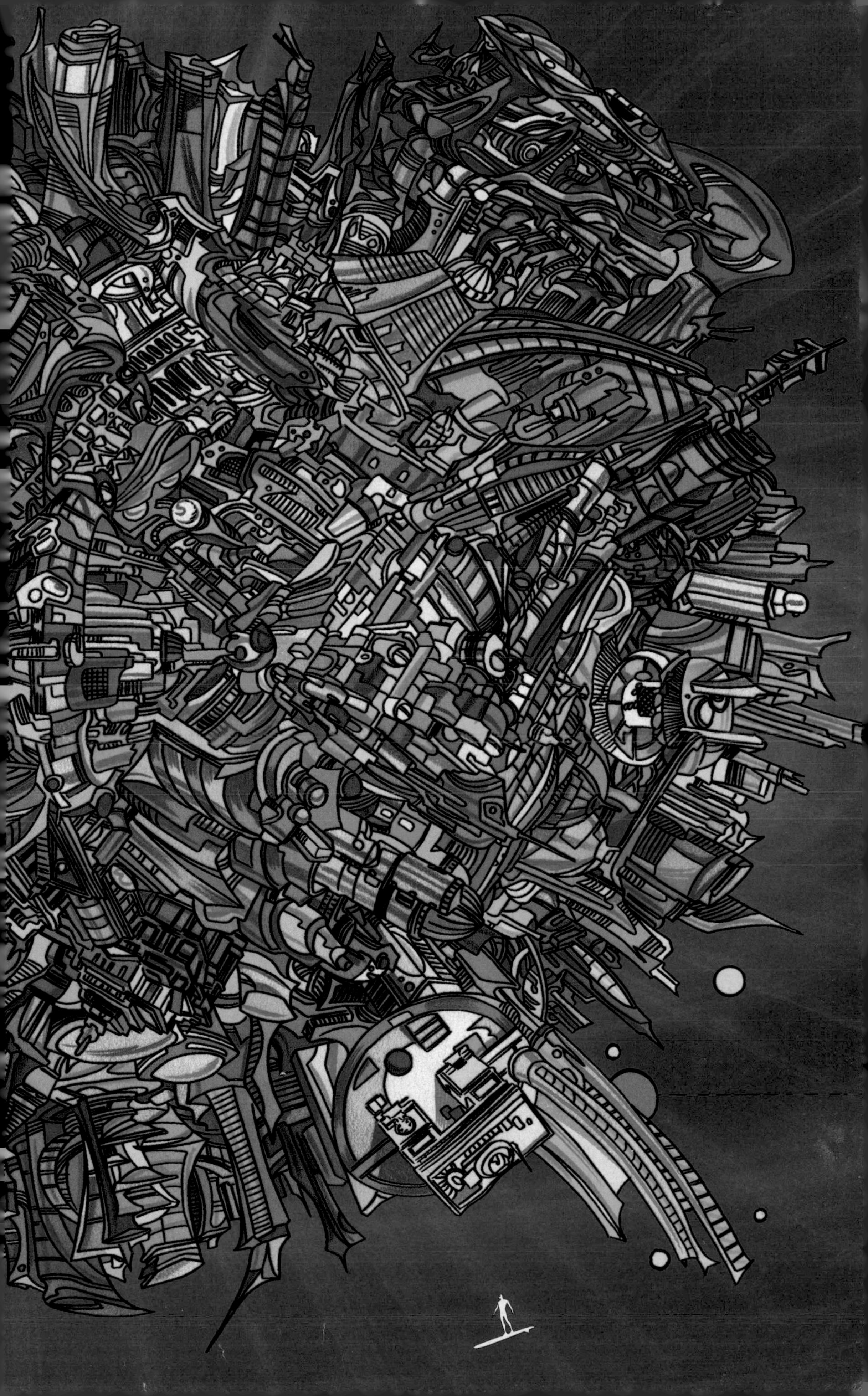

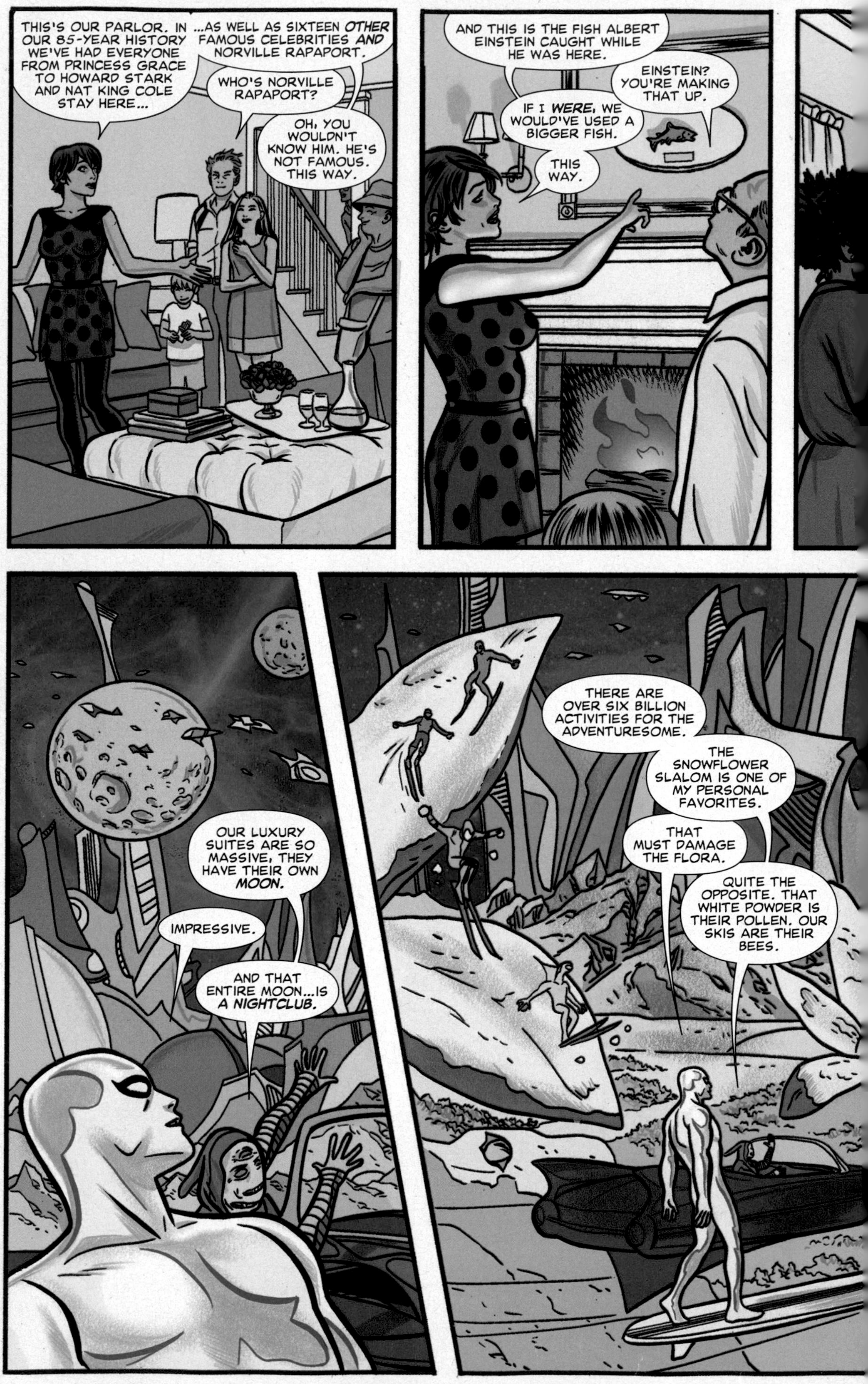
THIS'S OUR PARLOR. IN OUR 85-YEAR HISTORY WE'VE HAD EVERYONE FROM PRINCESS GRACE TO HOWARD STARK AND NAT KING COLE STAY HERE...
...AS WELL AS SIXTEEN OTHER FAMOUS CELEBRITIES AND NORVILLE RAPAPORT.
WHO'S NORVILLE RAPAPORT?
OH, YOU WOULDN'T KNOW HIM. HE'S NOT FAMOUS. THIS WAY.
AND THIS IS THE FISH ALBERT EINSTEIN CAUGHT WHILE HE WAS HERE.
EINSTEIN? YOU'RE MAKING THAT UP.
IF I WERE, WE WOULD'VE USED A BIGGER FISH.
THIS WAY.
OUR LUXURY SUITES ARE SO MASSIVE, THEY HAVE THEIR OWN MOON.
IMPRESSIVE.
AND THAT ENTIRE MOON...IS A NIGHTCLUB.
THERE ARE OVER SIX BILLION ACTIVITIES FOR THE ADVENTURESOME.
THE SNOWFLOWER SLALOM IS ONE OF MY PERSONAL FAVORITES.
THAT MUST DAMAGE THE FLORA.
QUITE THE OPPOSITE. THAT WHITE POWDER IS THEIR POLLEN. OUR SKIS ARE THEIR BEES.

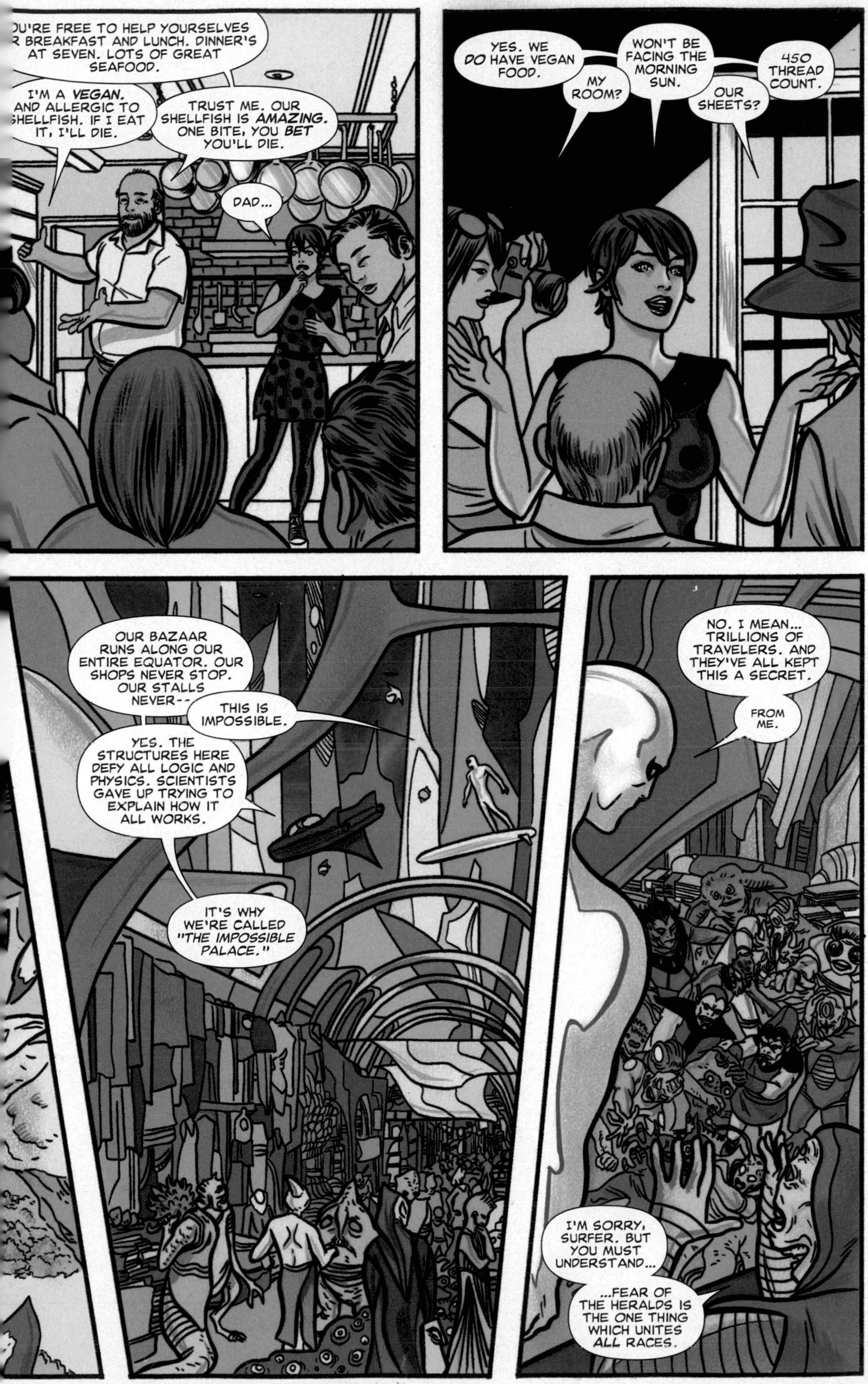

OU'RE FREE TO HELP YOURSELVES R BREAKFAST AND LUNCH. DINNER'S AT SEVEN. LOTS OF GREAT SEAFOOD.
I'M A *VEGAN.* AND ALLERGIC TO SHELLFISH. IF I EAT IT, I'LL DIE.
TRUST ME. OUR SHELLFISH IS *AMAZING.* ONE BITE, YOU *BET* YOU'LL DIE.
DAD...
YES. WE *DO* HAVE VEGAN FOOD.
MY ROOM?
WON'T BE FACING THE MORNING SUN.
OUR SHEETS?
450 THREAD COUNT.
OUR BAZAAR RUNS ALONG OUR ENTIRE EQUATOR. OUR SHOPS NEVER STOP. OUR STALLS NEVER--
THIS IS IMPOSSIBLE.
YES. THE STRUCTURES HERE DEFY ALL LOGIC AND PHYSICS. SCIENTISTS GAVE UP TRYING TO EXPLAIN HOW IT ALL WORKS.
IT'S WHY WE'RE CALLED *"THE IMPOSSIBLE PALACE."*
NO. I MEAN... TRILLIONS OF TRAVELERS. AND THEY'VE ALL KEPT THIS A SECRET.
FROM ME.
I'M SORRY, SURFER. BUT YOU MUST UNDERSTAND...
...FEAR OF THE HERALDS IS THE ONE THING WHICH UNITES *ALL* RACES.

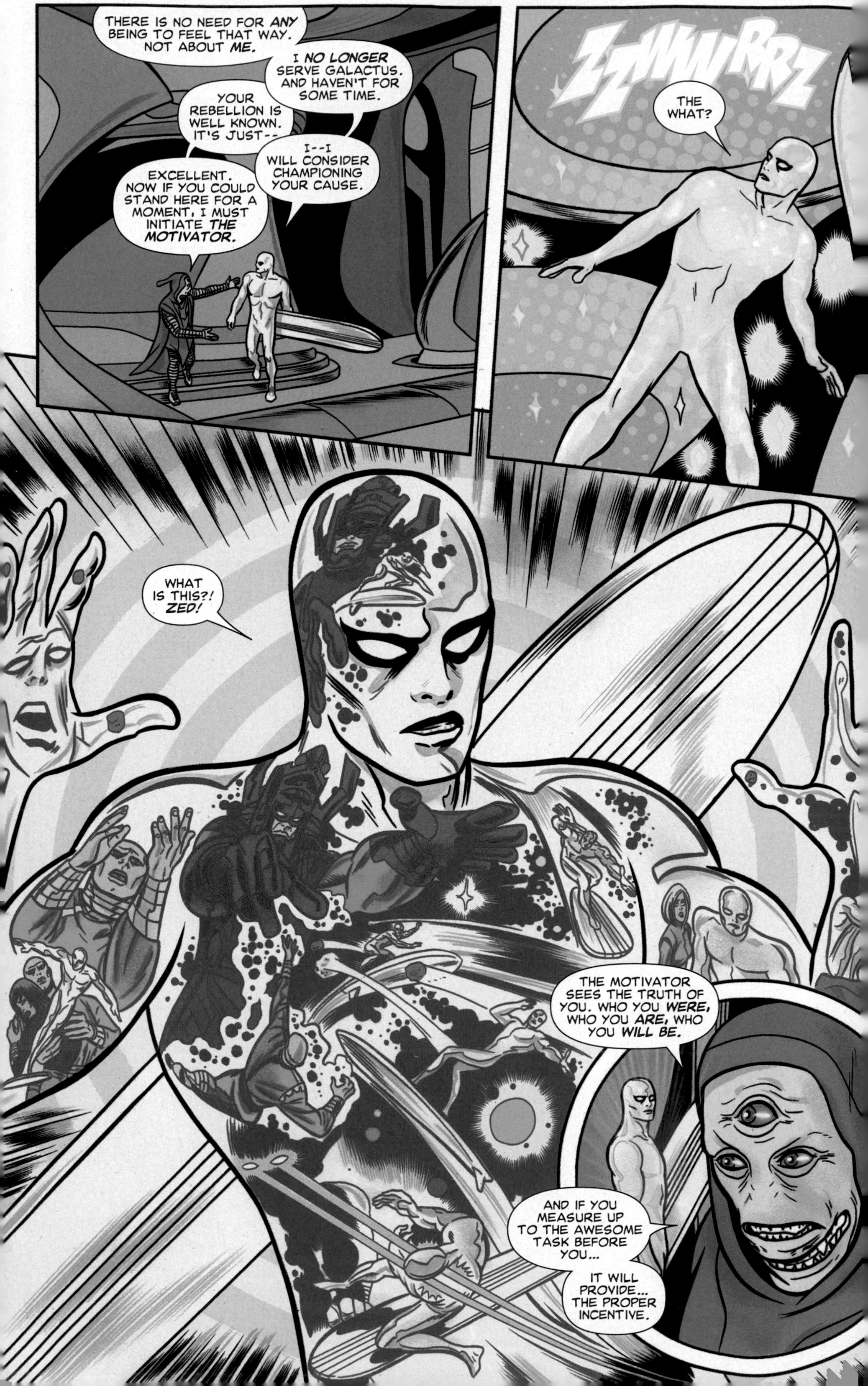
THERE IS NO NEED FOR ANY BEING TO FEEL THAT WAY. NOT ABOUT ME.
I NO LONGER SERVE GALACTUS. AND HAVEN'T FOR SOME TIME.
YOUR REBELLION IS WELL KNOWN. IT'S JUST--
I--I WILL CONSIDER CHAMPIONING YOUR CAUSE.
EXCELLENT. NOW IF YOU COULD STAND HERE FOR A MOMENT, I MUST INITIATE THE MOTIVATOR.
ZZWWRRZ
THE WHAT?
WHAT IS THIS?! ZED!
THE MOTIVATOR SEES THE TRUTH OF YOU. WHO YOU WERE, WHO YOU ARE, WHO YOU WILL BE.
AND IF YOU MEASURE UP TO THE AWESOME TASK BEFORE YOU...
IT WILL PROVIDE... THE PROPER INCENTIVE.

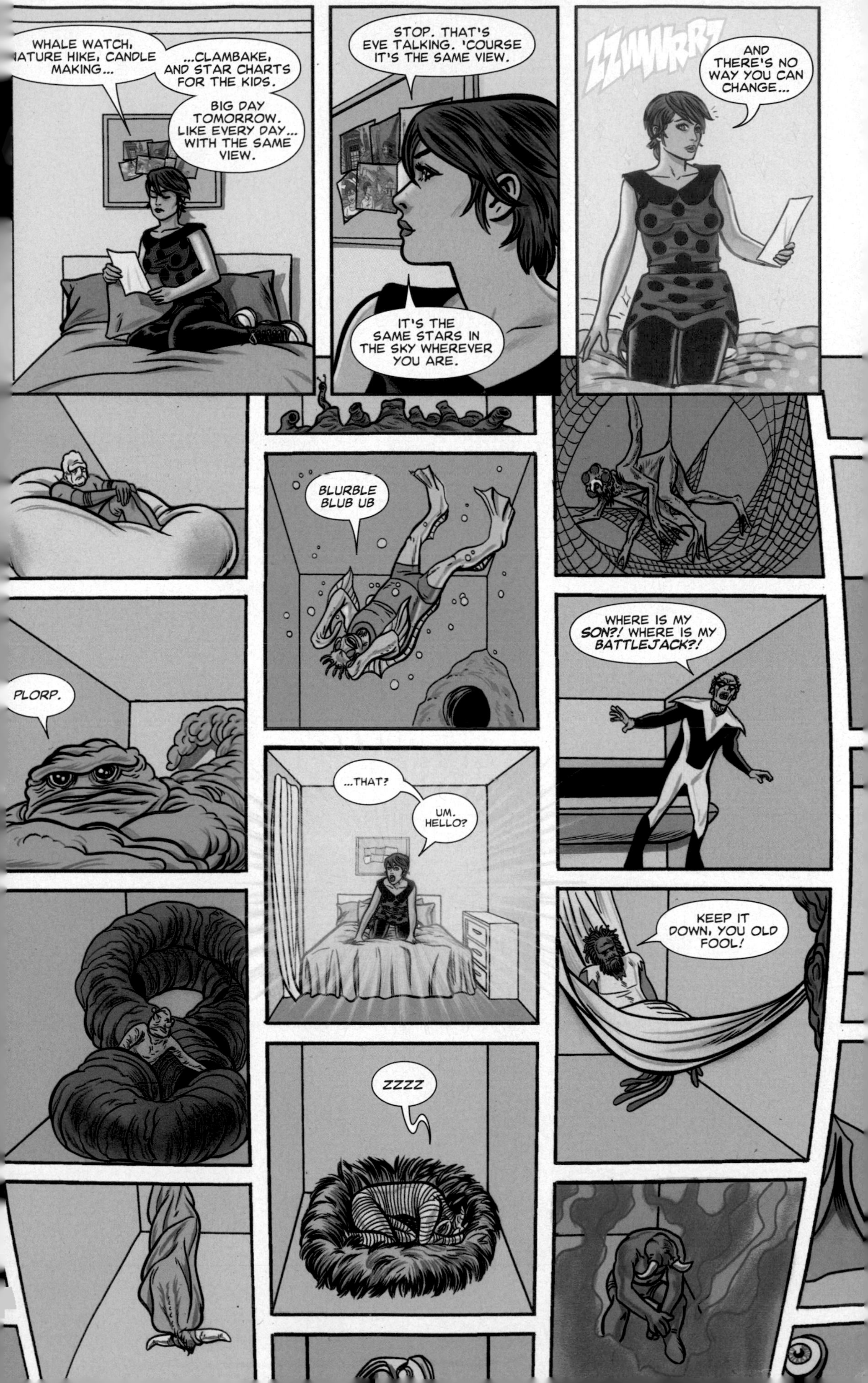

WHALE WATCH, NATURE HIKE, CANDLE MAKING...
...CLAMBAKE, AND STAR CHARTS FOR THE KIDS.
BIG DAY TOMORROW. LIKE EVERY DAY... WITH THE SAME VIEW.
STOP. THAT'S EVE TALKING. 'COURSE IT'S THE SAME VIEW.
IT'S THE SAME STARS IN THE SKY WHEREVER YOU ARE.
ZZWWRRZ
AND THERE'S NO WAY YOU CAN CHANGE...
BLURBLE BLUB UB
PLORP.
WHERE IS MY SON?! WHERE IS MY BATTLEJACK?!
...THAT?
UM. HELLO?
KEEP IT DOWN, YOU OLD FOOL!
ZZZZ

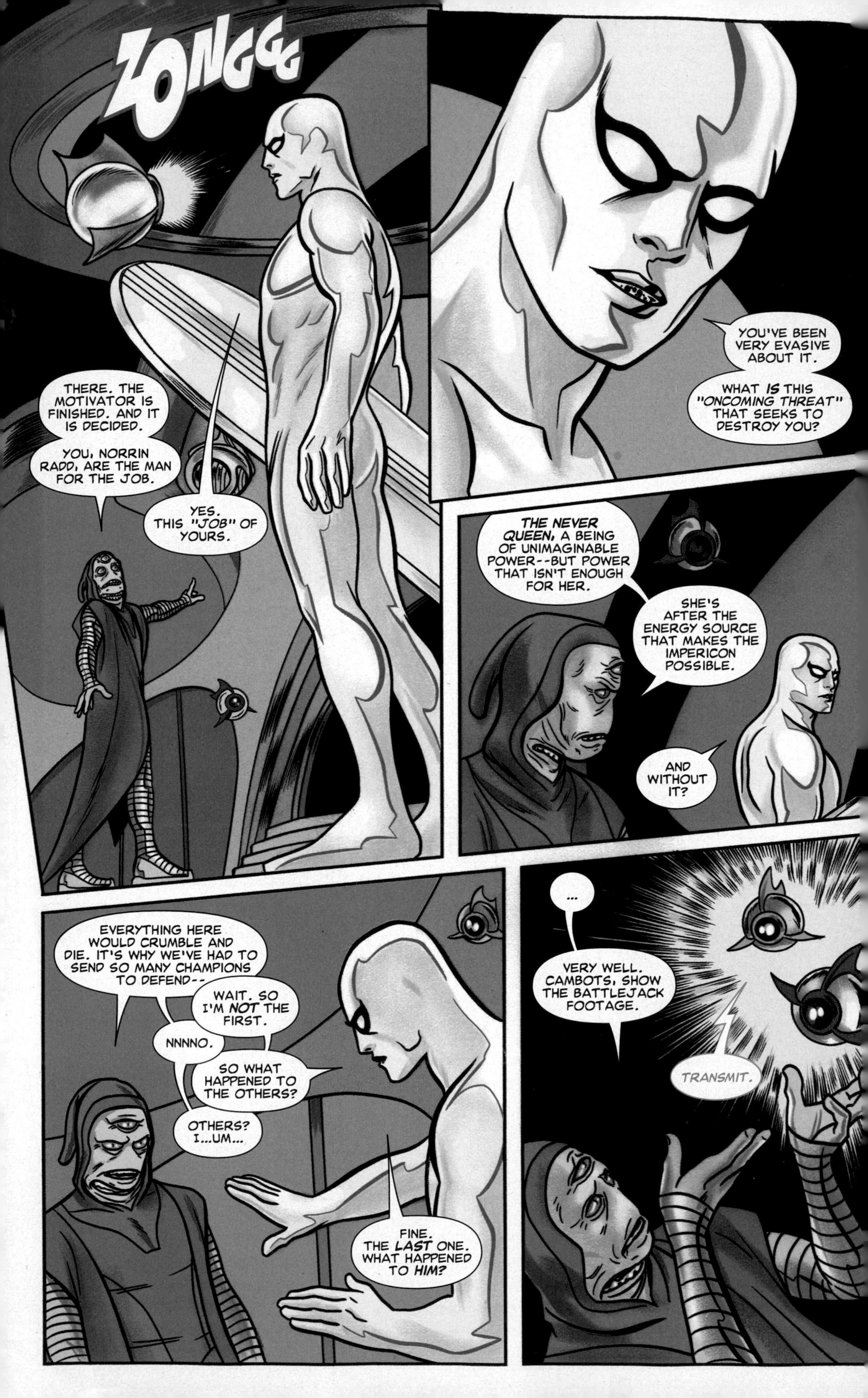
ZONGGG
THERE. THE MOTIVATOR IS FINISHED. AND IT IS DECIDED.
YOU, NORRIN RADD, ARE THE MAN FOR THE JOB.
YES. THIS "JOB" OF YOURS.
YOU'VE BEEN VERY EVASIVE ABOUT IT.
WHAT IS THIS "ONCOMING THREAT" THAT SEEKS TO DESTROY YOU?
THE NEVER QUEEN, A BEING OF UNIMAGINABLE POWER--BUT POWER THAT ISN'T ENOUGH FOR HER.
SHE'S AFTER THE ENERGY SOURCE THAT MAKES THE IMPERICON POSSIBLE.
AND WITHOUT IT?
EVERYTHING HERE WOULD CRUMBLE AND DIE. IT'S WHY WE'VE HAD TO SEND SO MANY CHAMPIONS TO DEFEND--
WAIT. SO I'M NOT THE FIRST.
NNNNO.
SO WHAT HAPPENED TO THE OTHERS?
OTHERS? I...UM...
FINE. THE LAST ONE. WHAT HAPPENED TO HIM?
...
VERY WELL. CAMBOTS, SHOW THE BATTLEJACK FOOTAGE.
TRANSMIT.

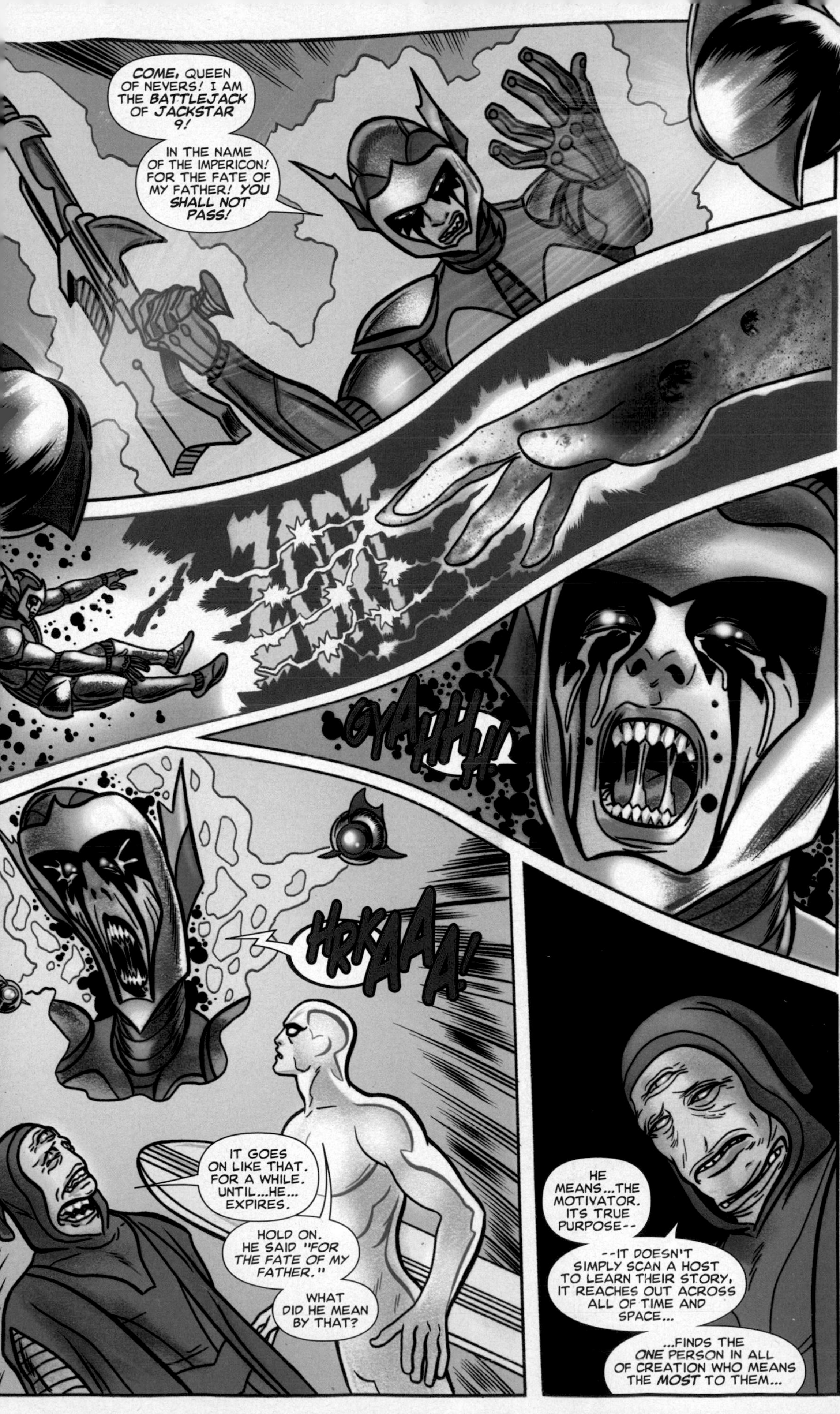
COME, QUEEN OF NEVERS! I AM THE BATTLEJACK OF JACKSTAR 9!
IN THE NAME OF THE IMPERICON! FOR THE FATE OF MY FATHER! YOU SHALL NOT PASS!
GYAHHHH!
HRKAAAA!
IT GOES ON LIKE THAT. FOR A WHILE. UNTIL...HE... EXPIRES.
HOLD ON. HE SAID "FOR THE FATE OF MY FATHER."
WHAT DID HE MEAN BY THAT?
HE MEANS...THE MOTIVATOR. ITS TRUE PURPOSE--
--IT DOESN'T SIMPLY SCAN A HOST TO LEARN THEIR STORY, IT REACHES OUT ACROSS ALL OF TIME AND SPACE...
...FINDS THE ONE PERSON IN ALL OF CREATION WHO MEANS THE MOST TO THEM...

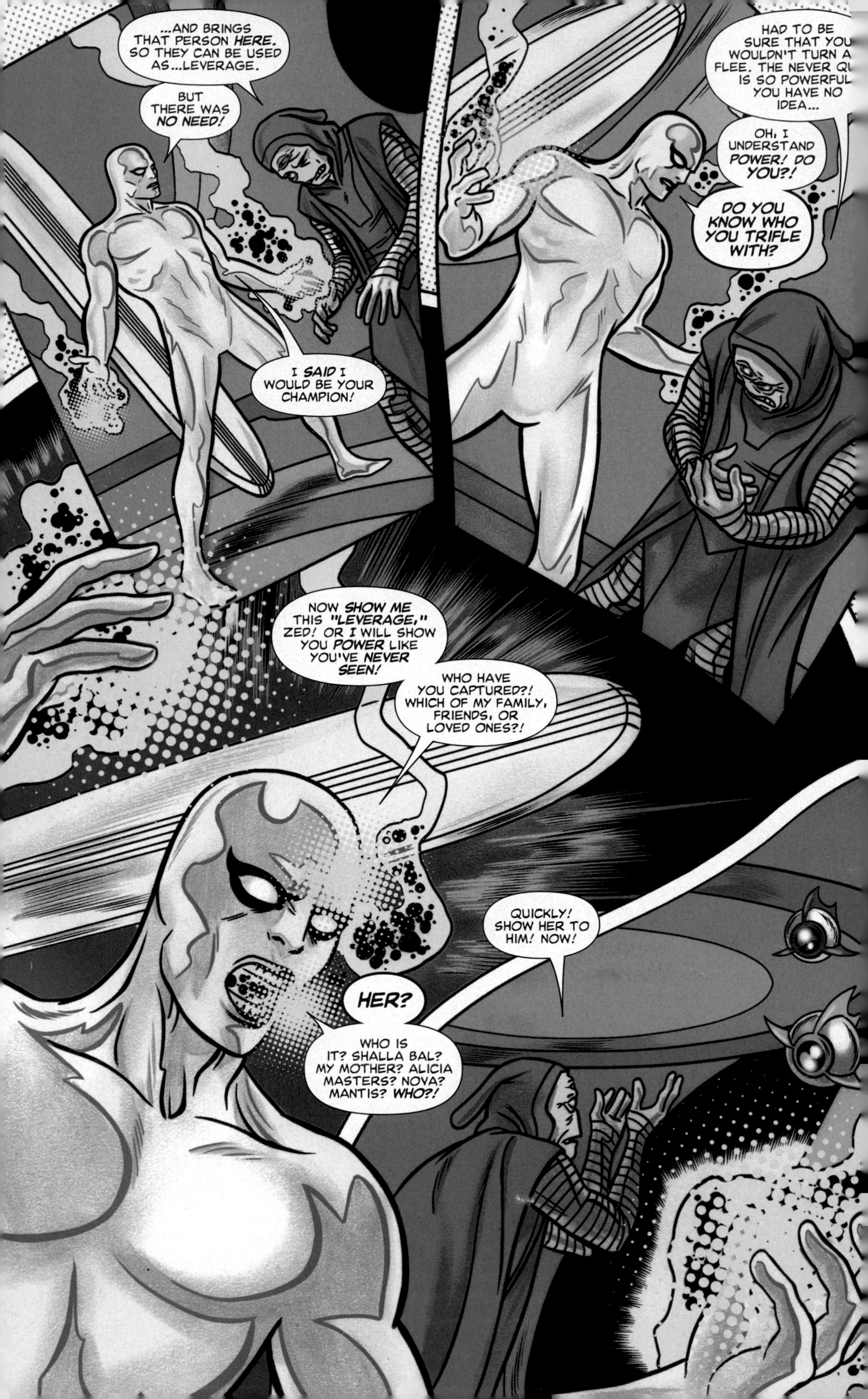
...AND BRINGS THAT PERSON HERE. SO THEY CAN BE USED AS...LEVERAGE.
BUT THERE WAS NO NEED!
I SAID I WOULD BE YOUR CHAMPION!
HAD TO BE SURE THAT YOU WOULDN'T TURN A FLEE. THE NEVER QU IS SO POWERFUL YOU HAVE NO IDEA...
OH, I UNDERSTAND POWER! DO YOU?!
DO YOU KNOW WHO YOU TRIFLE WITH?
NOW SHOW ME THIS "LEVERAGE," ZED! OR I WILL SHOW YOU POWER LIKE YOU'VE NEVER SEEN!
WHO HAVE YOU CAPTURED?! WHICH OF MY FAMILY, FRIENDS, OR LOVED ONES?!
QUICKLY! SHOW HER TO HIM! NOW!
HER?
WHO IS IT? SHALLA BAL? MY MOTHER? ALICIA MASTERS? NOVA? MANTIS? WHO?!

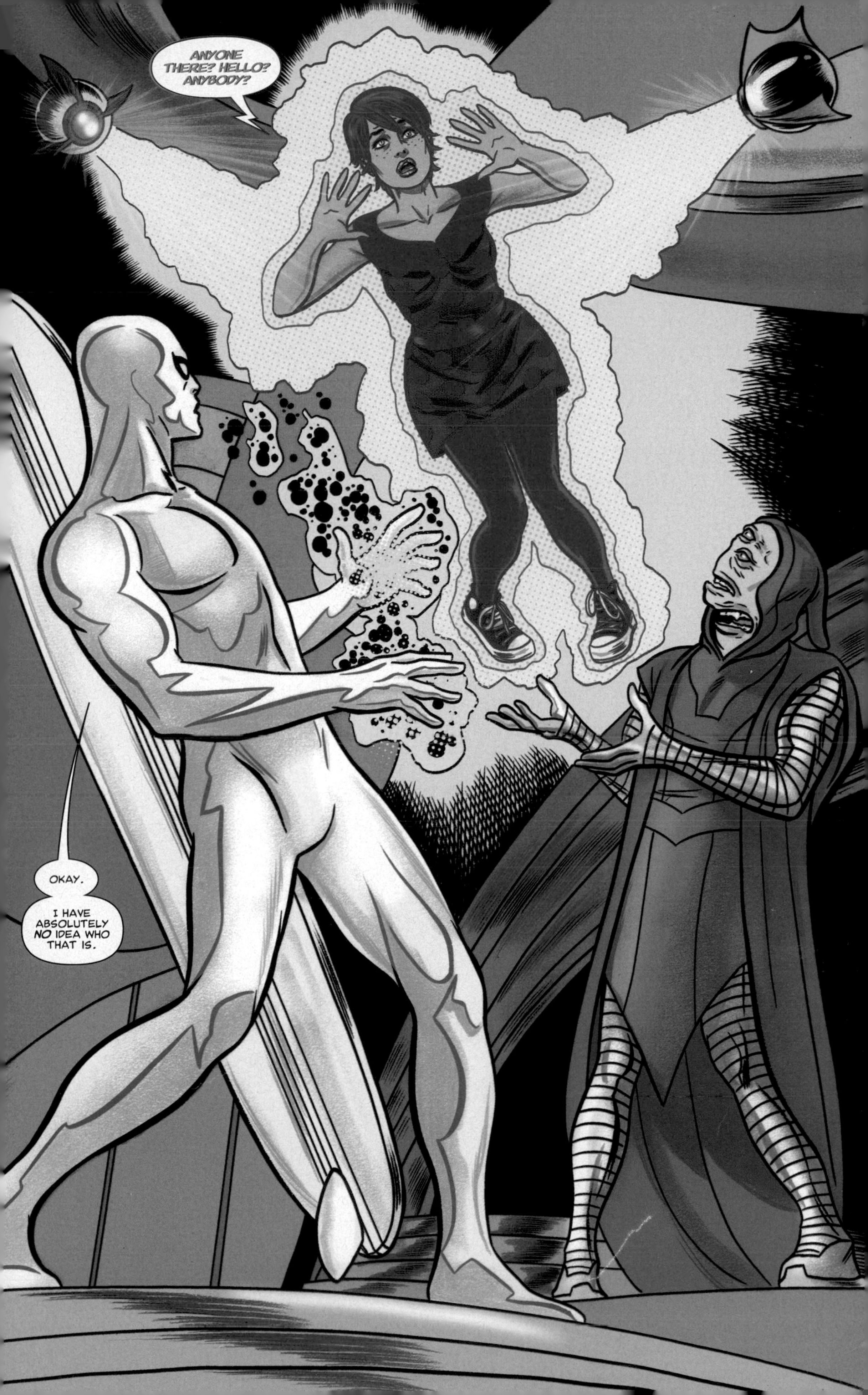
ANYONE THERE? HELLO? ANYBODY?
OKAY.
I HAVE ABSOLUTELY NO IDEA WHO THAT IS.

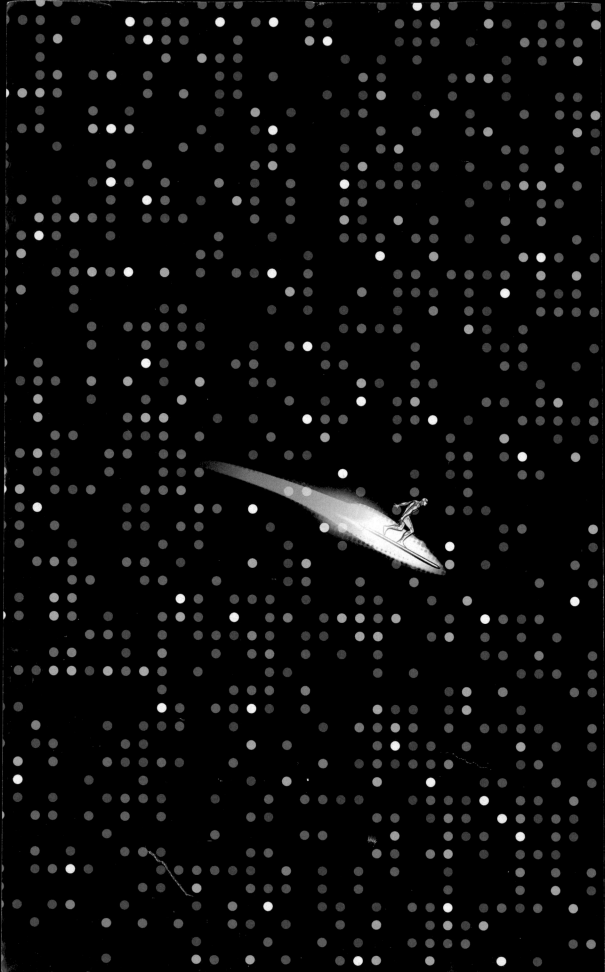

2

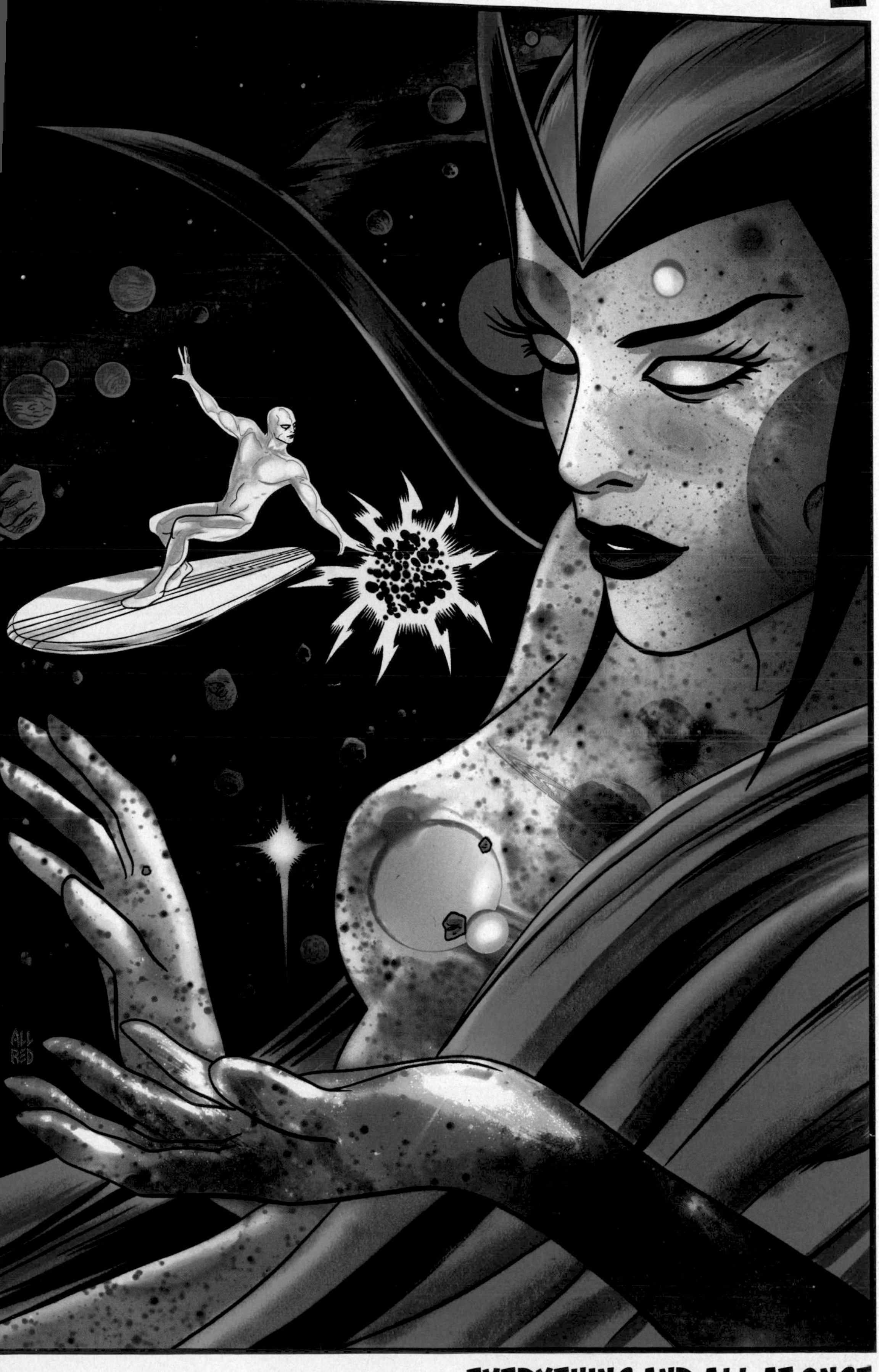

EVERYTHING AND ALL AT ONCE

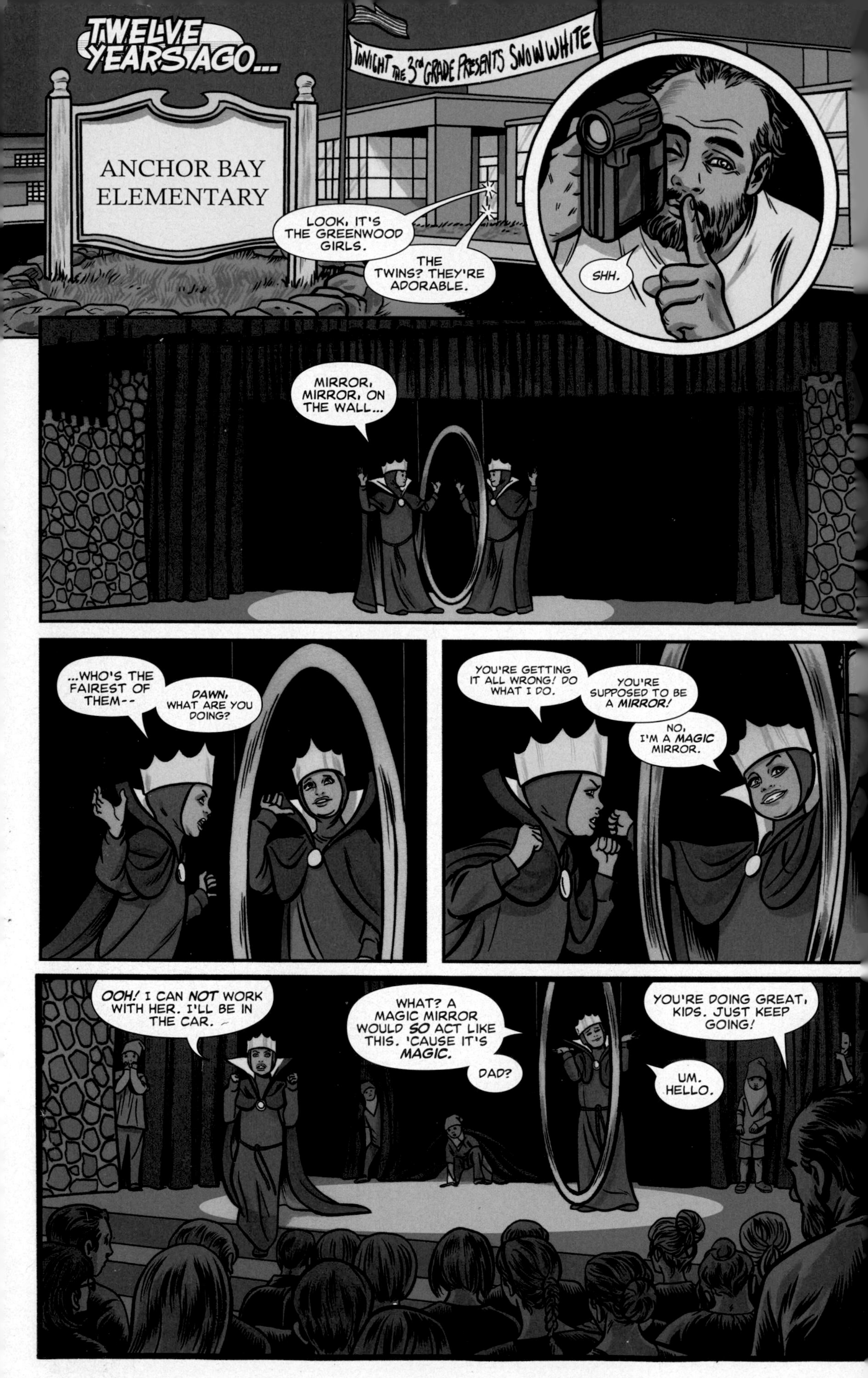
TWELVE YEARS AGO...
TONIGHT THE 3RD GRADE PRESENTS SNOW WHITE
ANCHOR BAY ELEMENTARY
LOOK, IT'S THE GREENWOOD GIRLS.
THE TWINS? THEY'RE ADORABLE.
SHH.
MIRROR, MIRROR, ON THE WALL...
...WHO'S THE FAIREST OF THEM--
DAWN, WHAT ARE YOU DOING?
YOU'RE GETTING IT ALL WRONG! DO WHAT I DO.
YOU'RE SUPPOSED TO BE A MIRROR!
NO, I'M A MAGIC MIRROR.
OOH! I CAN NOT WORK WITH HER. I'LL BE IN THE CAR.
WHAT? A MAGIC MIRROR WOULD SO ACT LIKE THIS. 'CAUSE IT'S MAGIC.
DAD?
YOU'RE DOING GREAT, KIDS. JUST KEEP GOING!
UM. HELLO.

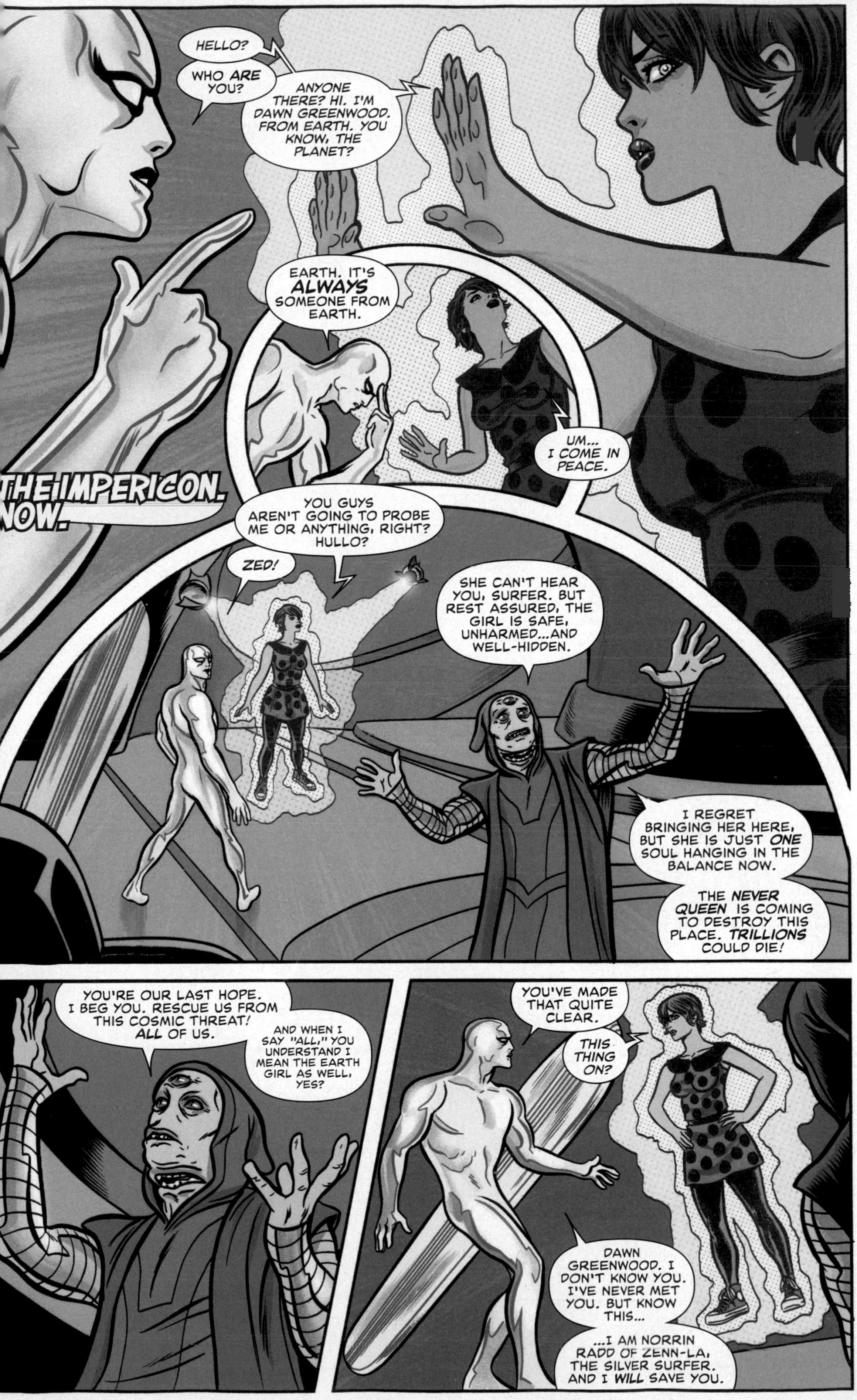
HELLO?
WHO ARE YOU?
ANYONE THERE? HI. I'M DAWN GREENWOOD. FROM EARTH. YOU KNOW, THE PLANET?
EARTH. IT'S ALWAYS SOMEONE FROM EARTH.
UM... I COME IN PEACE.
THE IMPERICON. NOW.
YOU GUYS AREN'T GOING TO PROBE ME OR ANYTHING, RIGHT? HULLO?
ZED!
SHE CAN'T HEAR YOU, SURFER. BUT REST ASSURED, THE GIRL IS SAFE, UNHARMED...AND WELL-HIDDEN.
I REGRET BRINGING HER HERE, BUT SHE IS JUST ONE SOUL HANGING IN THE BALANCE NOW.
THE NEVER QUEEN IS COMING TO DESTROY THIS PLACE. TRILLIONS COULD DIE!
YOU'RE OUR LAST HOPE. I BEG YOU. RESCUE US FROM THIS COSMIC THREAT! ALL OF US.
AND WHEN I SAY "ALL," YOU UNDERSTAND I MEAN THE EARTH GIRL AS WELL, YES?
YOU'VE MADE THAT QUITE CLEAR.
THIS THING ON?
DAWN GREENWOOD. I DON'T KNOW YOU. I'VE NEVER MET YOU. BUT KNOW THIS...
...I AM NORRIN RADD OF ZENN-LA, THE SILVER SURFER. AND I WILL SAVE YOU.

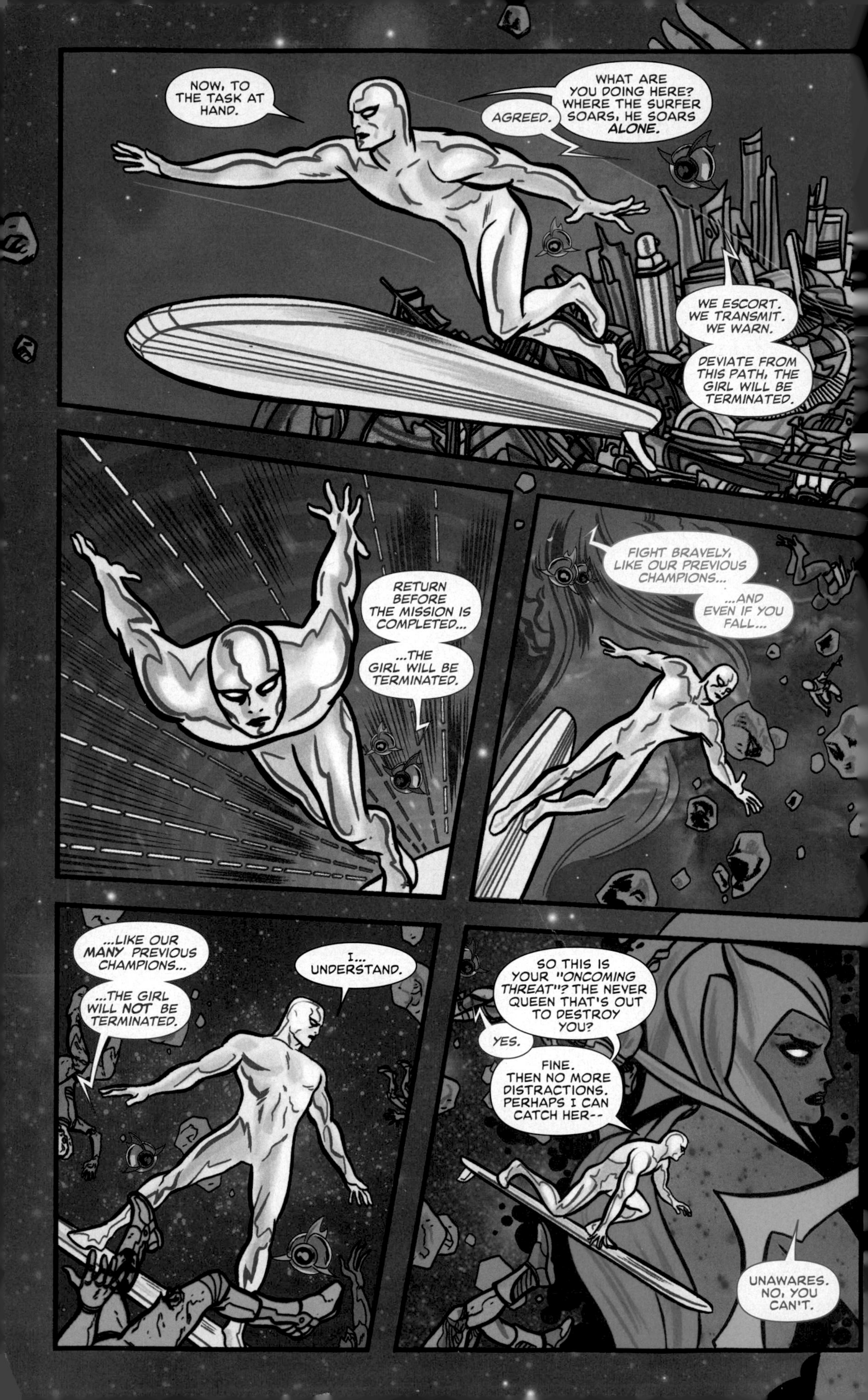
NOW, TO THE TASK AT HAND.
WHAT ARE YOU DOING HERE? WHERE THE SURFER SOARS, HE SOARS ALONE.
AGREED.
WE ESCORT. WE TRANSMIT. WE WARN.
DEVIATE FROM THIS PATH, THE GIRL WILL BE TERMINATED.
RETURN BEFORE THE MISSION IS COMPLETED...
...THE GIRL WILL BE TERMINATED.
FIGHT BRAVELY, LIKE OUR PREVIOUS CHAMPIONS...
...AND EVEN IF YOU FALL...
...LIKE OUR MANY PREVIOUS CHAMPIONS...
...THE GIRL WILL NOT BE TERMINATED.
I... UNDERSTAND.
SO THIS IS YOUR "ONCOMING THREAT"? THE NEVER QUEEN THAT'S OUT TO DESTROY YOU?
YES.
FINE. THEN NO MORE DISTRACTIONS. PERHAPS I CAN CATCH HER--
UNAWARES. NO, YOU CAN'T.

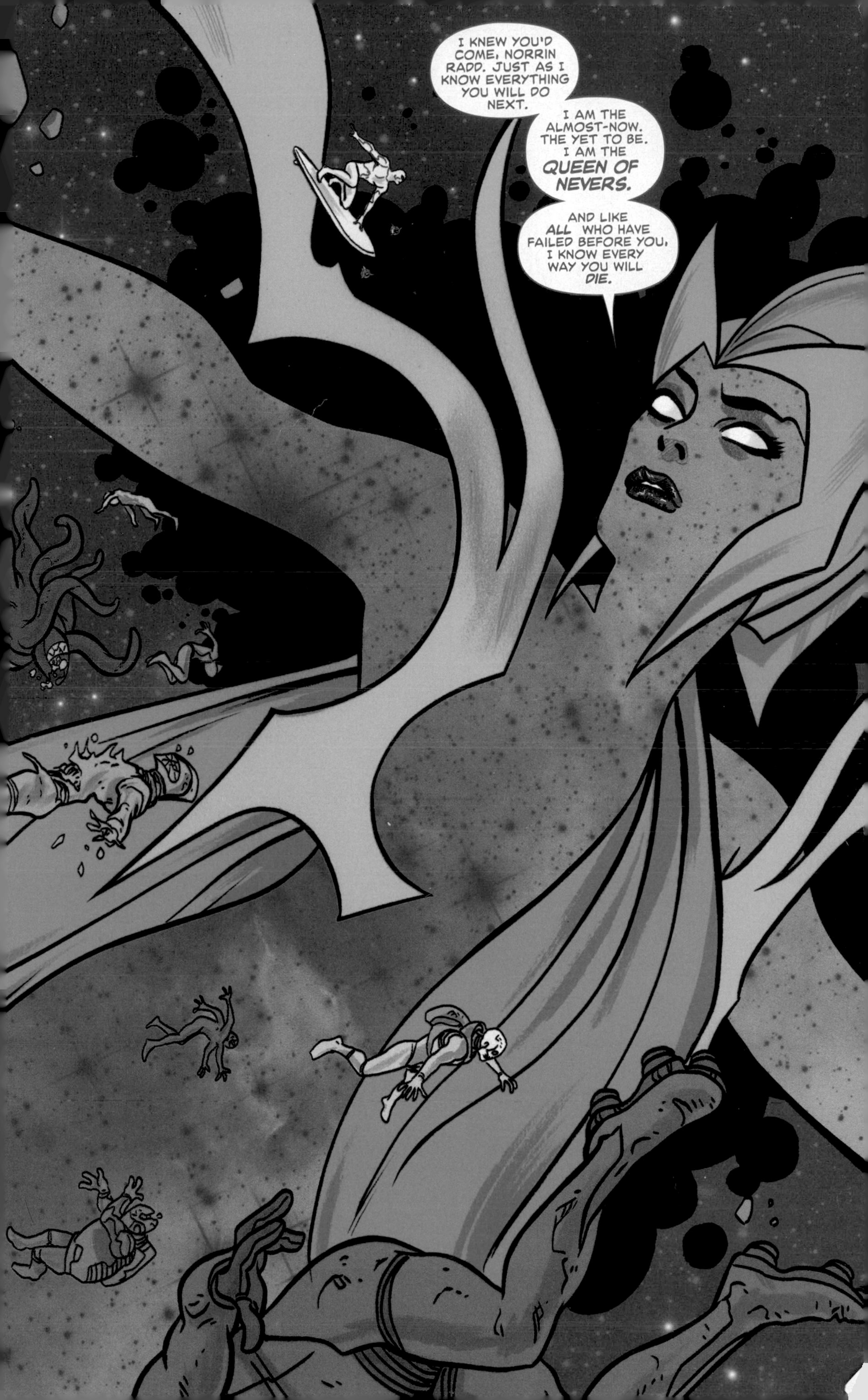
I KNEW YOU'D COME, NORRIN RADD. JUST AS I KNOW EVERYTHING YOU WILL DO NEXT.
I AM THE ALMOST-NOW. THE YET TO BE. I AM THE QUEEN OF NEVERS.
AND LIKE ALL WHO HAVE FAILED BEFORE YOU, I KNOW EVERY WAY YOU WILL DIE.

PLORP.

SO, MR. PLORP, YOU'RE SAYING I UNDERSTAND YOU BECAUSE OUR PRISON CELLS--WAIT, WHAT DID YOU CALL THEM?

PLORP.

RIGHT. BECAUSE OUR "MOTIVATOR CUBES" HAVE UNIVERSAL TRANSLATORS?

PLORP.

OH. YES. I'M DAWN. NICE TO MEET YOU, TOO.

HEADS UP! GATEKEEPERS COMIN'! WHY, IF THESE FLARKIN' FORCE-WALLS WEREN'T HERE, I'D SHOW 'EM--

THAT'S ENOUGH OUT OF YOU, OLD TIMER! MEAL TIME.

HMM. BOG-EGGS IN FLOP-JAM. NOT BAD.

BAH! KEEP YOUR SWILL! I AM BATTLE-LON, FATHER OF BATTLEJACK!

AND I WILL ONLY EAT AS A FREE MAN!

WHAK

YEAH! ME TOO! I CAN'T EAT THAT!

SMAK

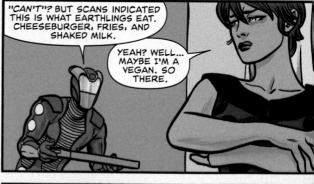

"CAN'T"? BUT SCANS INDICATED THIS IS WHAT EARTHLINGS EAT. CHEESEBURGER, FRIES, AND SHAKED MILK.

YEAH? WELL... MAYBE I'M A VEGAN. SO THERE.

HM. MUST BE A FAULTY SCANNER.

BE RIGHT BACK...

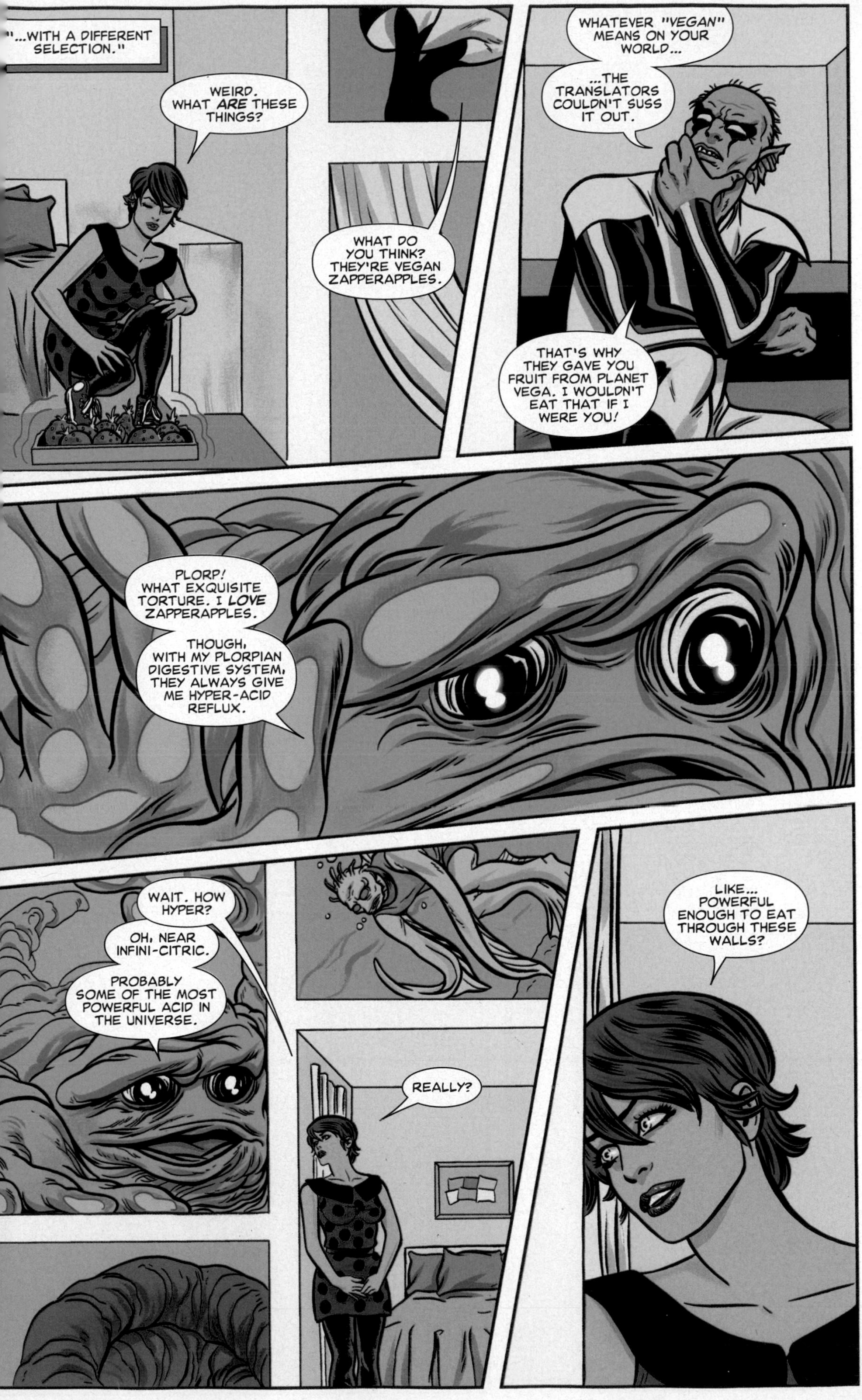
"...WITH A DIFFERENT SELECTION."
WEIRD. WHAT ARE THESE THINGS?
WHAT DO YOU THINK? THEY'RE VEGAN ZAPPERAPPLES.
WHATEVER "VEGAN" MEANS ON YOUR WORLD...
...THE TRANSLATORS COULDN'T SUSS IT OUT.
THAT'S WHY THEY GAVE YOU FRUIT FROM PLANET VEGA. I WOULDN'T EAT THAT IF I WERE YOU!
PLORP! WHAT EXQUISITE TORTURE. I LOVE ZAPPERAPPLES.
THOUGH, WITH MY PLORPIAN DIGESTIVE SYSTEM, THEY ALWAYS GIVE ME HYPER-ACID REFLUX.
WAIT. HOW HYPER?
OH, NEAR INFINI-CITRIC.
PROBABLY SOME OF THE MOST POWERFUL ACID IN THE UNIVERSE.
REALLY?
LIKE... POWERFUL ENOUGH TO EAT THROUGH THESE WALLS?

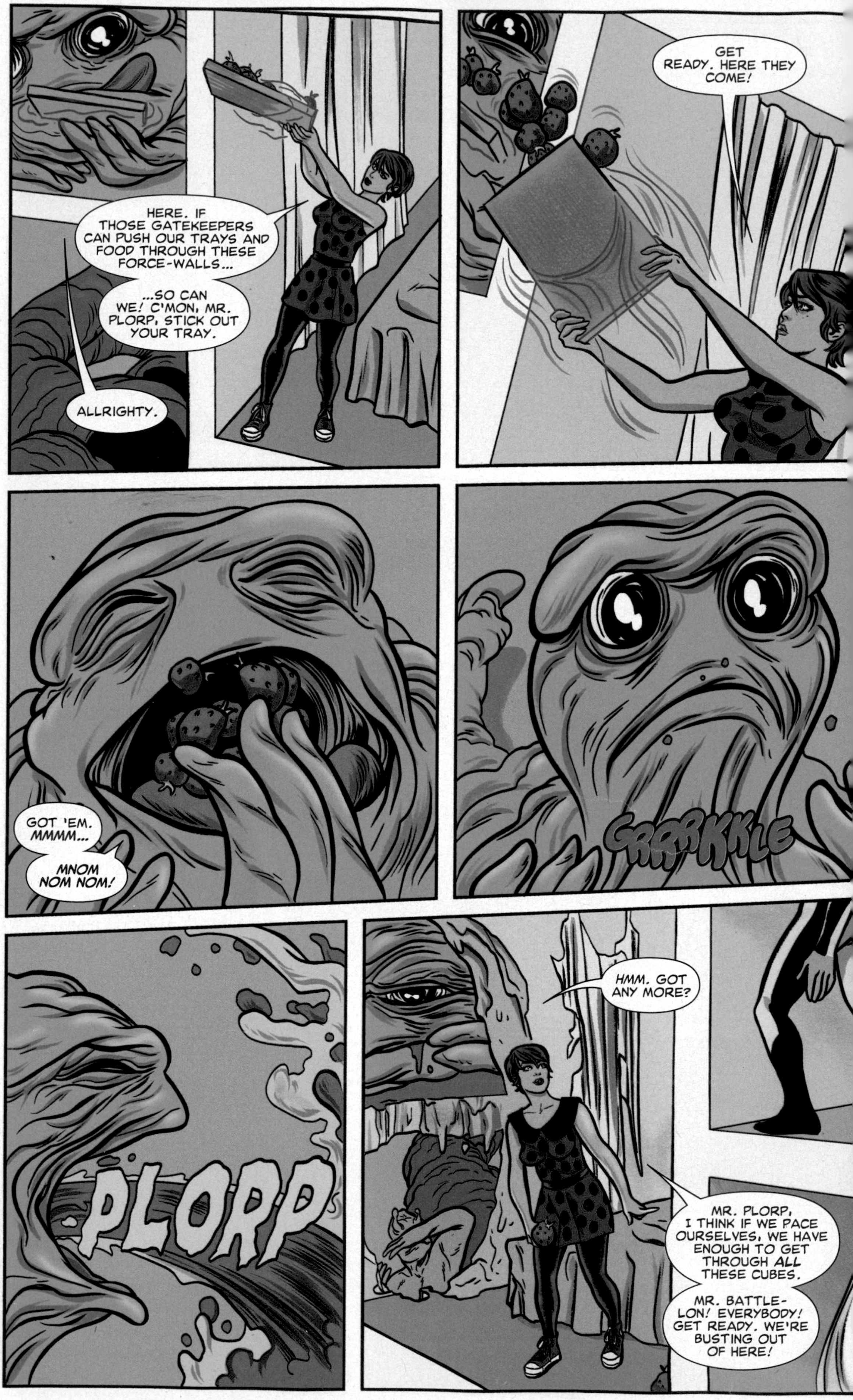
HERE. IF THOSE GATEKEEPERS CAN PUSH OUR TRAYS AND FOOD THROUGH THESE FORCE-WALLS...
...SO CAN WE! C'MON, MR. PLORP, STICK OUT YOUR TRAY.
ALLRIGHTY.
GET READY. HERE THEY COME!
GOT 'EM. MMMM...
MNOM NOM NOM!
GRRRKKLE
PLORP
HMM. GOT ANY MORE?
MR. PLORP, I THINK IF WE PACE OURSELVES, WE HAVE ENOUGH TO GET THROUGH ALL THESE CUBES.
MR. BATTLE-LON! EVERYBODY! GET READY. WE'RE BUSTING OUT OF HERE!

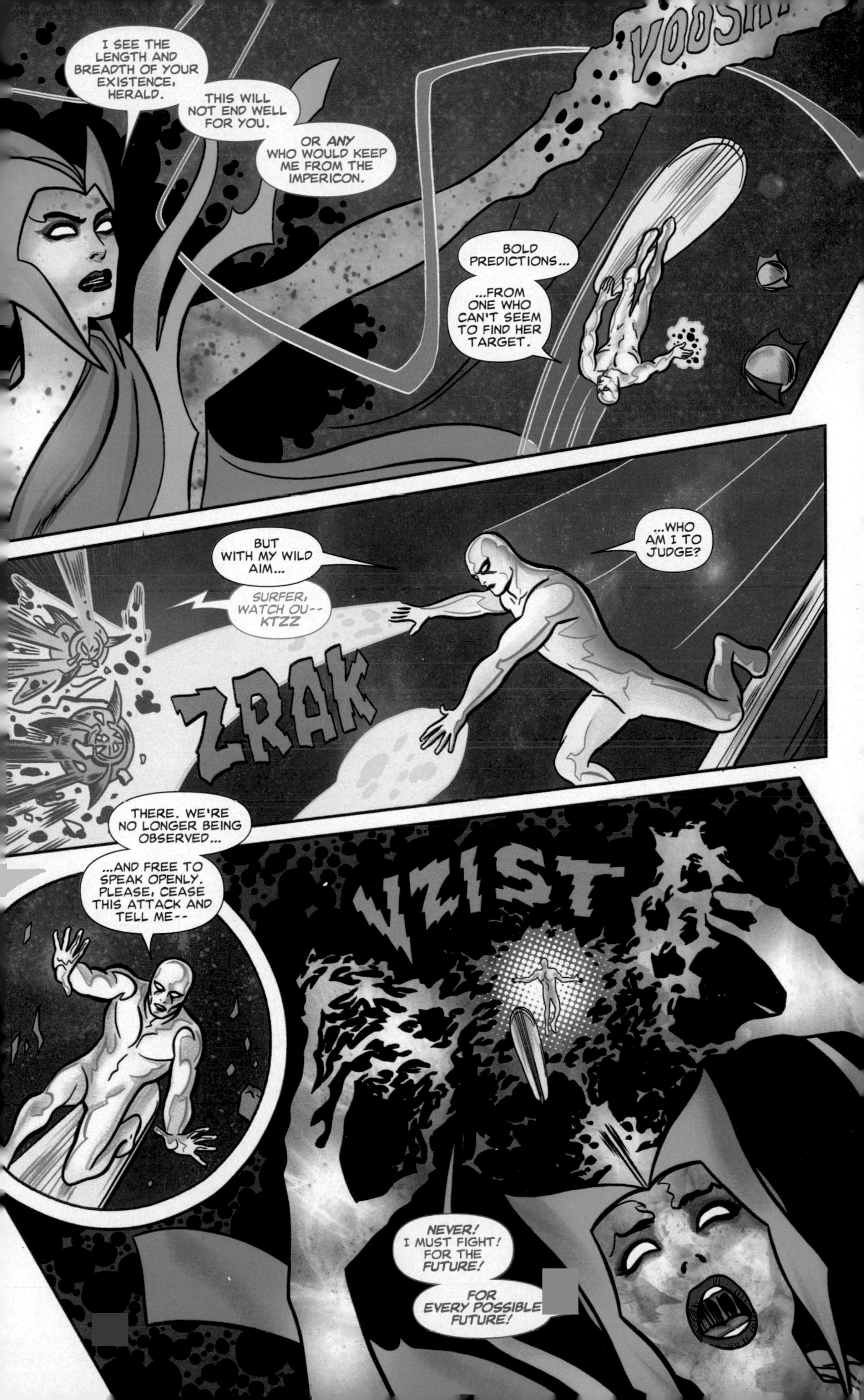
VOOSH!
I SEE THE LENGTH AND BREADTH OF YOUR EXISTENCE, HERALD.
THIS WILL NOT END WELL FOR YOU.
OR ANY WHO WOULD KEEP ME FROM THE IMPERICON.
BOLD PREDICTIONS...
...FROM ONE WHO CAN'T SEEM TO FIND HER TARGET.
BUT WITH MY WILD AIM...
...WHO AM I TO JUDGE?
SURFER, WATCH OU-- KTZZ
ZRAK
THERE. WE'RE NO LONGER BEING OBSERVED...
...AND FREE TO SPEAK OPENLY. PLEASE, CEASE THIS ATTACK AND TELL ME--
VZIST
NEVER! I MUST FIGHT! FOR THE FUTURE!
FOR EVERY POSSIBLE FUTURE!

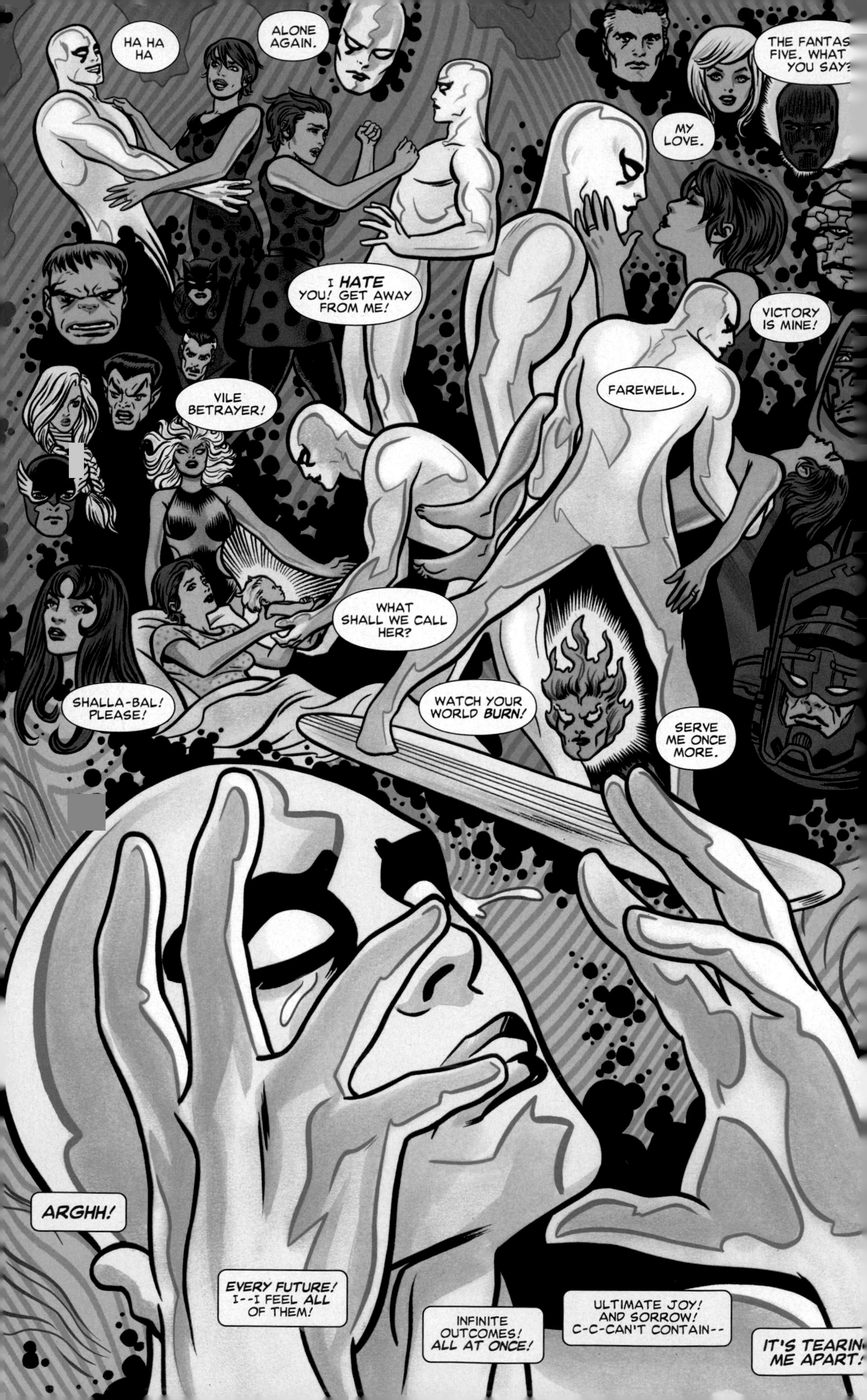
HA HA HA
ALONE AGAIN.
THE FANTAS FIVE. WHAT YOU SAY?
MY LOVE.
I HATE YOU! GET AWAY FROM ME!
VICTORY IS MINE!
FAREWELL.
VILE BETRAYER!
WHAT SHALL WE CALL HER?
SHALLA-BAL! PLEASE!
WATCH YOUR WORLD BURN!
SERVE ME ONCE MORE.
ARGHH!
EVERY FUTURE! I--I FEEL ALL OF THEM!
INFINITE OUTCOMES! ALL AT ONCE!
ULTIMATE JOY! AND SORROW! C-C-CAN'T CONTAIN--
IT'S TEARIN ME APART!

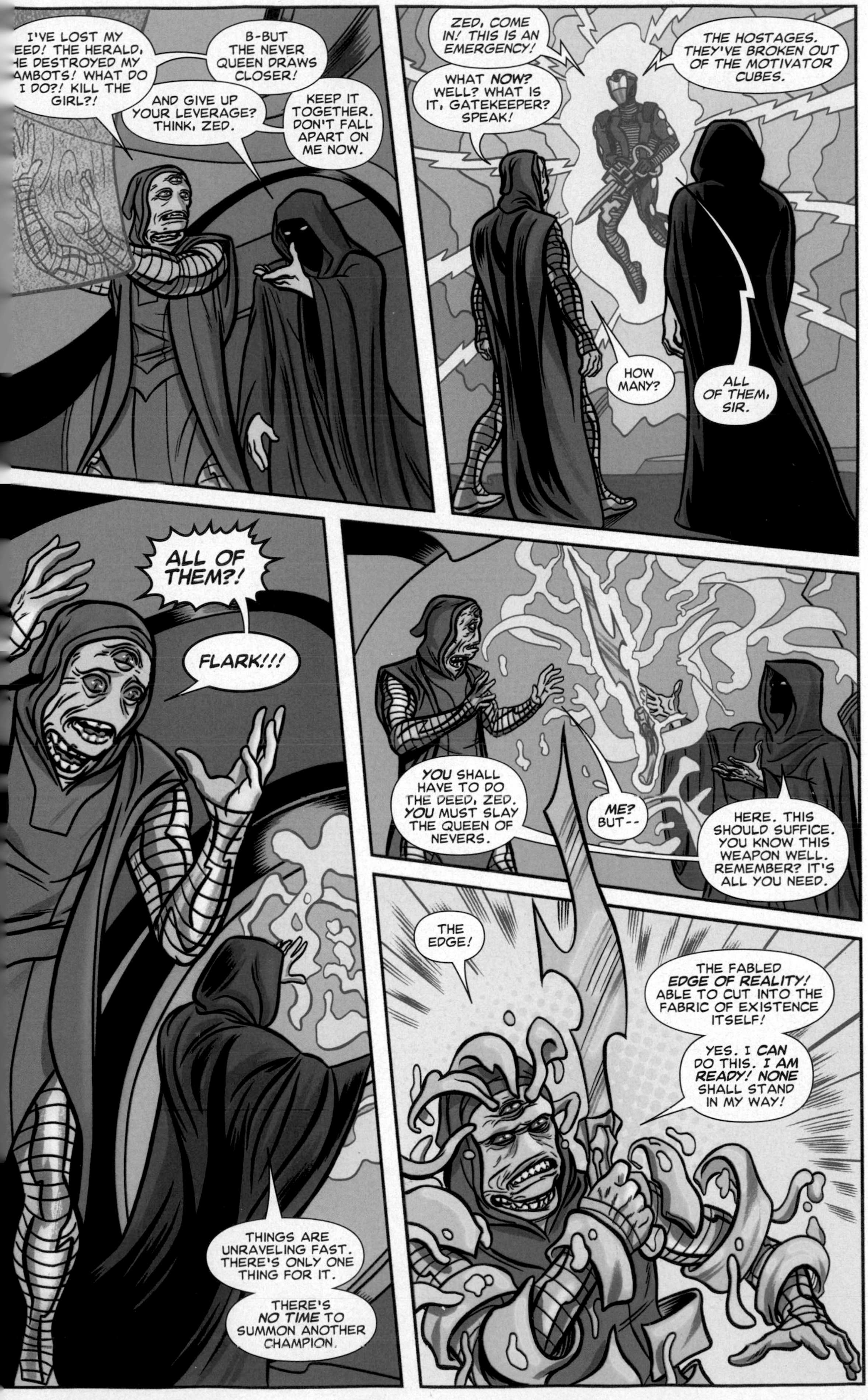

I'VE LOST MY
EED! THE HERALD,
HE DESTROYED MY
AMBOTS! WHAT DO
I DO?! KILL THE
GIRL?!
B-BUT
THE NEVER
QUEEN DRAWS
CLOSER!
AND GIVE UP
YOUR LEVERAGE?
THINK, ZED.
KEEP IT
TOGETHER.
DON'T FALL
APART ON
ME NOW.
ZED, COME IN! THIS IS AN EMERGENCY!
WHAT NOW? WELL? WHAT IS IT, GATEKEEPER? SPEAK!
THE HOSTAGES. THEY'VE BROKEN OUT OF THE MOTIVATOR CUBES.
HOW MANY?
ALL OF THEM, SIR.
ALL OF THEM?!
FLARK!!!
THINGS ARE UNRAVELING FAST. THERE'S ONLY ONE THING FOR IT.
THERE'S NO TIME TO SUMMON ANOTHER CHAMPION.
YOU SHALL HAVE TO DO THE DEED, ZED. YOU MUST SLAY THE QUEEN OF NEVERS.
ME? BUT--
HERE. THIS SHOULD SUFFICE. YOU KNOW THIS WEAPON WELL. REMEMBER? IT'S ALL YOU NEED.
THE EDGE!
THE FABLED EDGE OF REALITY! ABLE TO CUT INTO THE FABRIC OF EXISTENCE ITSELF!
YES. I CAN DO THIS. I AM READY! NONE SHALL STAND IN MY WAY!

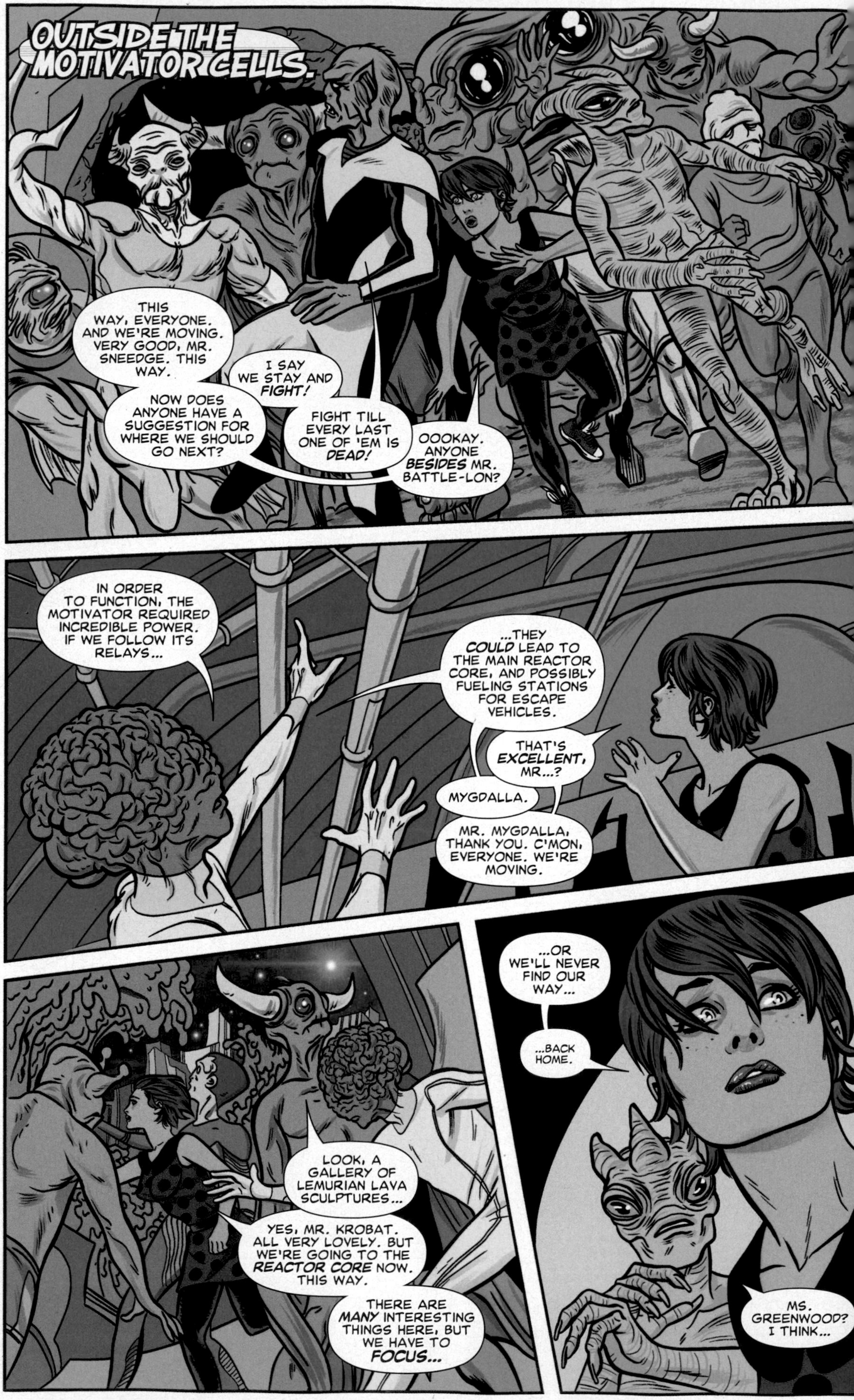
OUTSIDE THE MOTIVATOR CELLS.
THIS WAY, EVERYONE. AND WE'RE MOVING. VERY GOOD, MR. SNEEDGE. THIS WAY.
NOW DOES ANYONE HAVE A SUGGESTION FOR WHERE WE SHOULD GO NEXT?
I SAY WE STAY AND FIGHT!
FIGHT TILL EVERY LAST ONE OF 'EM IS DEAD!
OOOKAY. ANYONE BESIDES MR. BATTLE-LON?
IN ORDER TO FUNCTION, THE MOTIVATOR REQUIRED INCREDIBLE POWER. IF WE FOLLOW ITS RELAYS...
...THEY COULD LEAD TO THE MAIN REACTOR CORE, AND POSSIBLY FUELING STATIONS FOR ESCAPE VEHICLES.
THAT'S EXCELLENT, MR...?
MYGDALLA.
MR. MYGDALLA, THANK YOU. C'MON, EVERYONE. WE'RE MOVING.
LOOK, A GALLERY OF LEMURIAN LAVA SCULPTURES...
YES, MR. KROBAT. ALL VERY LOVELY. BUT WE'RE GOING TO THE REACTOR CORE NOW. THIS WAY.
THERE ARE MANY INTERESTING THINGS HERE, BUT WE HAVE TO FOCUS...
...OR WE'LL NEVER FIND OUR WAY...
...BACK HOME.
MS. GREENWOOD? I THINK...

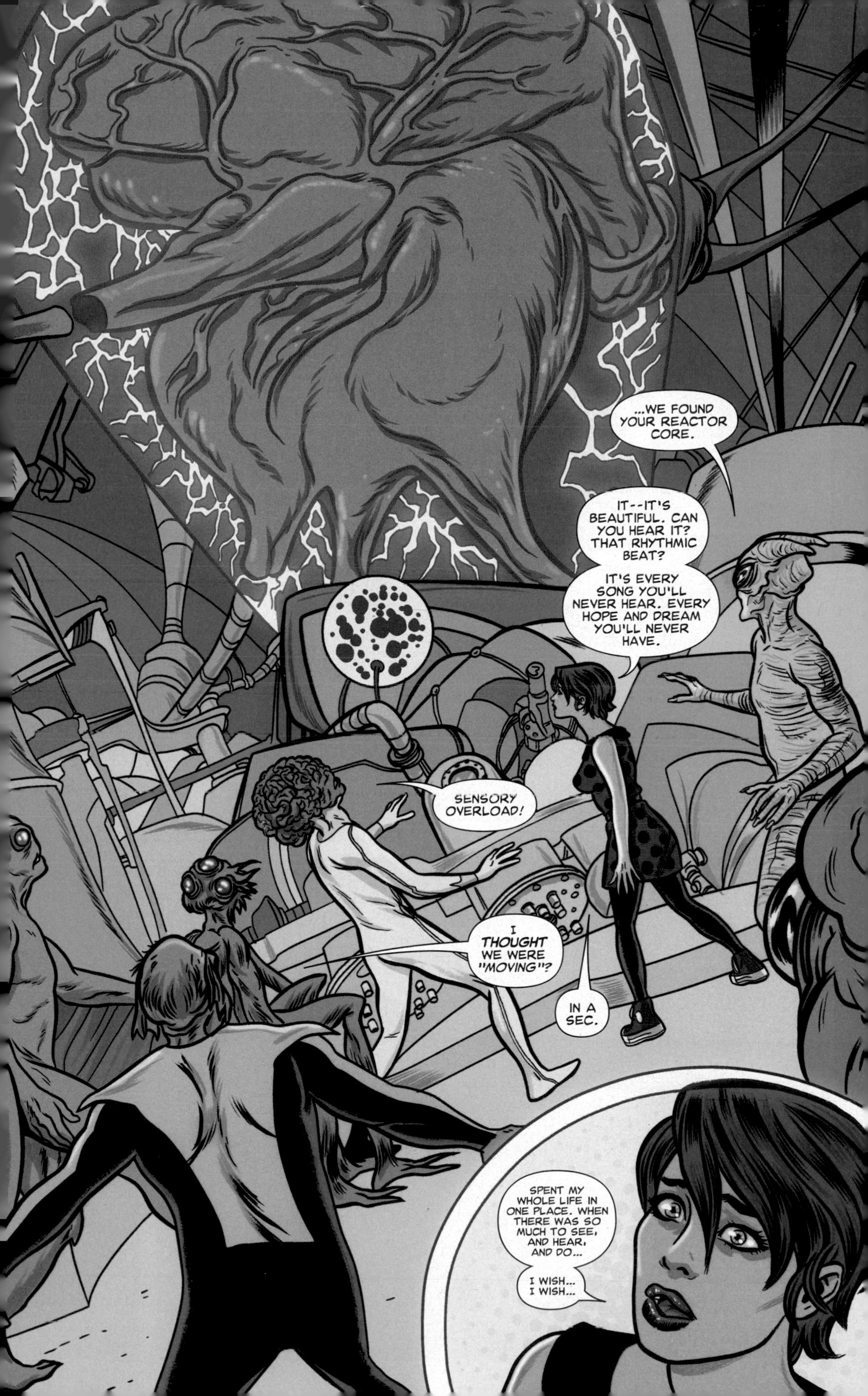
...WE FOUND YOUR REACTOR CORE.
IT--IT'S BEAUTIFUL. CAN YOU HEAR IT? THAT RHYTHMIC BEAT?
IT'S EVERY SONG YOU'LL NEVER HEAR. EVERY HOPE AND DREAM YOU'LL NEVER HAVE.
SENSORY OVERLOAD!
I *THOUGHT* WE WERE *"MOVING"*?
IN A SEC.
SPENT MY WHOLE LIFE IN ONE PLACE. WHEN THERE WAS SO MUCH TO SEE, AND HEAR, AND DO...
I WISH... I WISH...

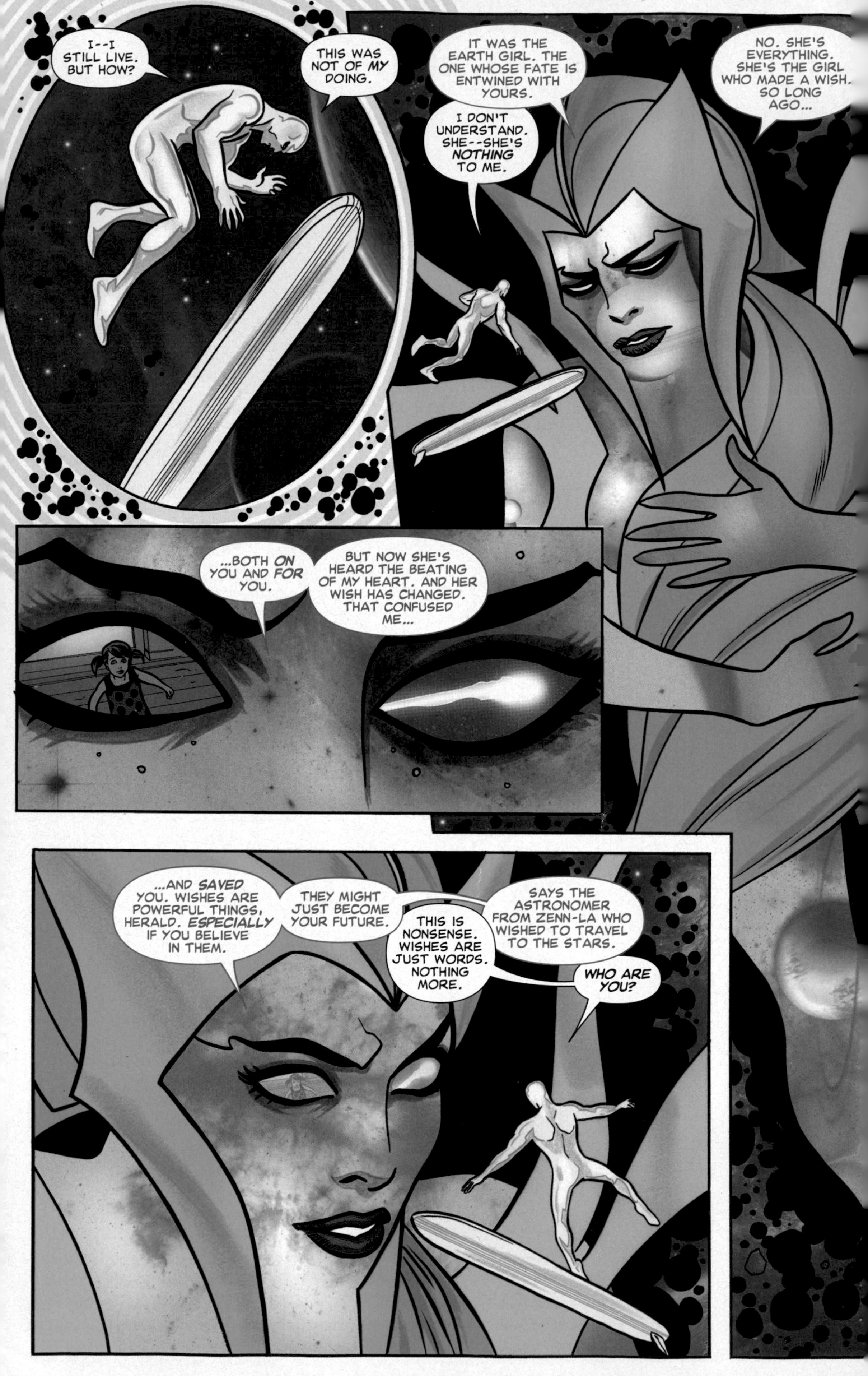
I--I STILL LIVE. BUT HOW?
THIS WAS NOT OF MY DOING.
IT WAS THE EARTH GIRL. THE ONE WHOSE FATE IS ENTWINED WITH YOURS.
I DON'T UNDERSTAND. SHE--SHE'S NOTHING TO ME.
NO. SHE'S EVERYTHING. SHE'S THE GIRL WHO MADE A WISH. SO LONG AGO...
...BOTH ON YOU AND FOR YOU.
BUT NOW SHE'S HEARD THE BEATING OF MY HEART. AND HER WISH HAS CHANGED. THAT CONFUSED ME...
...AND SAVED YOU. WISHES ARE POWERFUL THINGS, HERALD. ESPECIALLY IF YOU BELIEVE IN THEM.
THEY MIGHT JUST BECOME YOUR FUTURE.
THIS IS NONSENSE. WISHES ARE JUST WORDS. NOTHING MORE.
SAYS THE ASTRONOMER FROM ZENN-LA WHO WISHED TO TRAVEL TO THE STARS.
WHO ARE YOU?

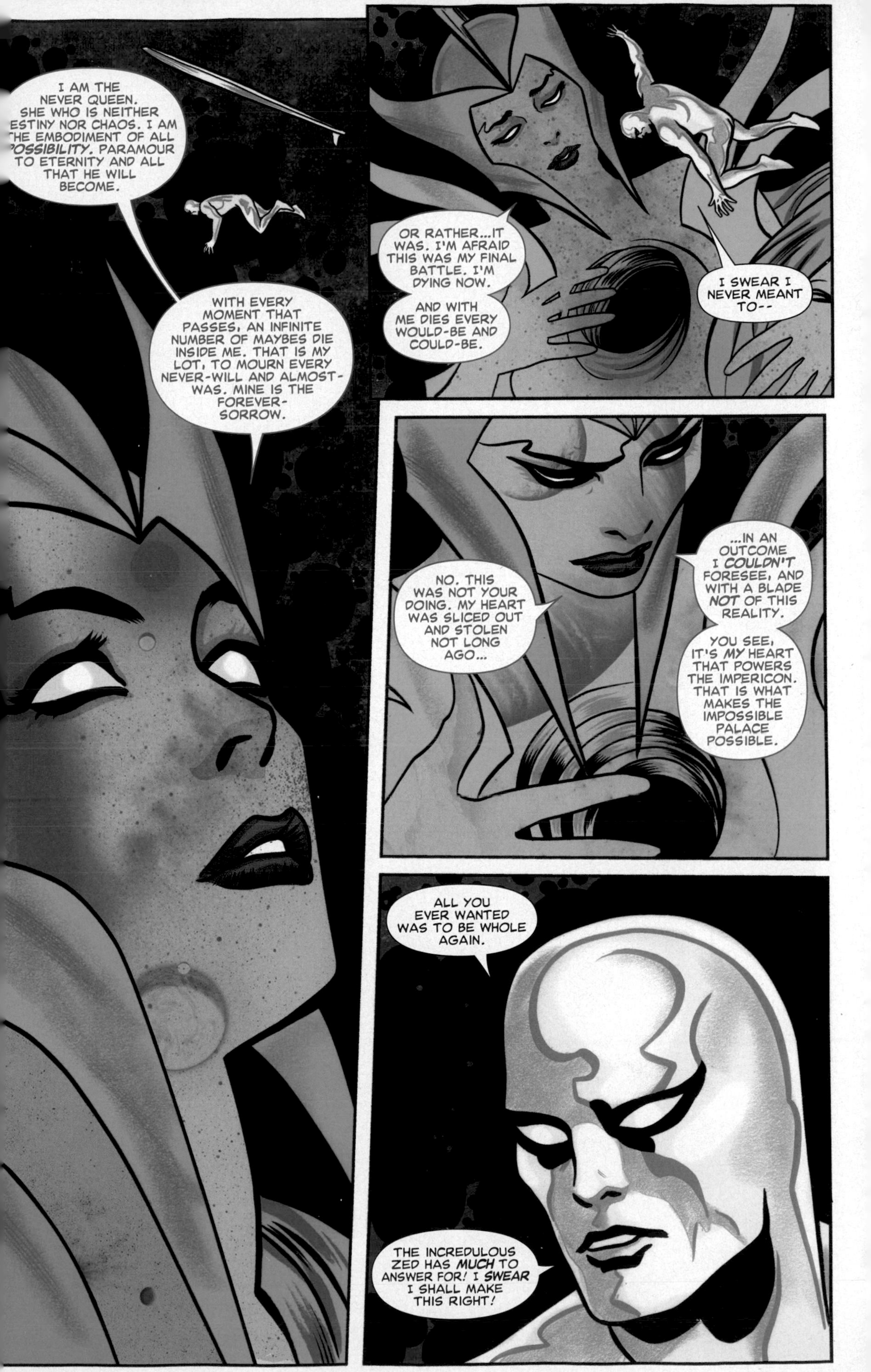
I AM THE NEVER QUEEN. SHE WHO IS NEITHER ESTINY NOR CHAOS. I AM THE EMBODIMENT OF ALL POSSIBILITY. PARAMOUR TO ETERNITY AND ALL THAT HE WILL BECOME.
WITH EVERY MOMENT THAT PASSES, AN INFINITE NUMBER OF MAYBES DIE INSIDE ME. THAT IS MY LOT, TO MOURN EVERY NEVER-WILL AND ALMOST-WAS. MINE IS THE FOREVER-SORROW.
OR RATHER...IT WAS. I'M AFRAID THIS WAS MY FINAL BATTLE. I'M DYING NOW.
AND WITH ME DIES EVERY WOULD-BE AND COULD-BE.
I SWEAR I NEVER MEANT TO--
NO. THIS WAS NOT YOUR DOING. MY HEART WAS SLICED OUT AND STOLEN NOT LONG AGO...
...IN AN OUTCOME I COULDN'T FORESEE, AND WITH A BLADE NOT OF THIS REALITY.
YOU SEE, IT'S MY HEART THAT POWERS THE IMPERICON. THAT IS WHAT MAKES THE IMPOSSIBLE PALACE POSSIBLE.
ALL YOU EVER WANTED WAS TO BE WHOLE AGAIN.
THE INCREDULOUS ZED HAS MUCH TO ANSWER FOR! I SWEAR I SHALL MAKE THIS RIGHT!

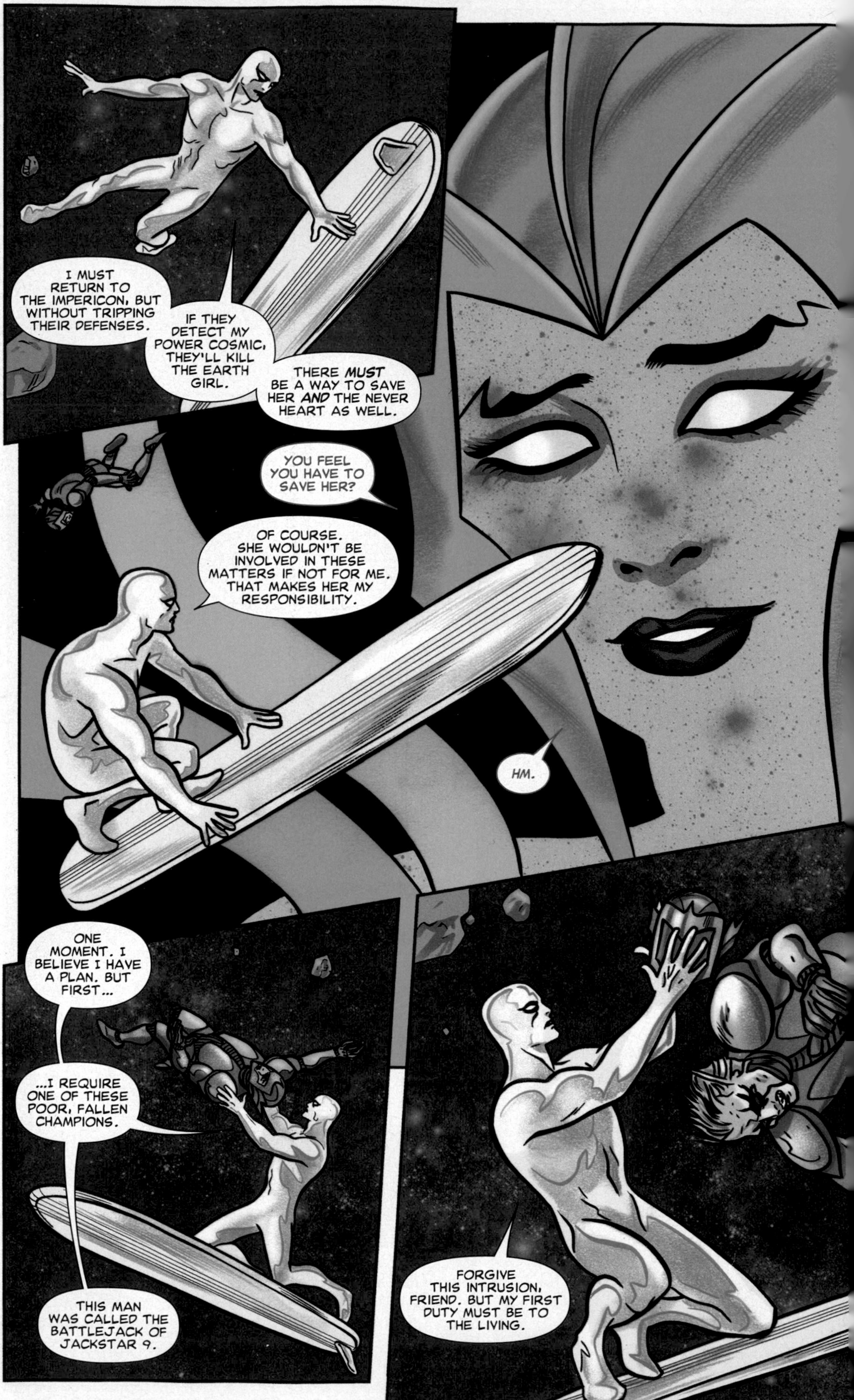

I MUST RETURN TO THE IMPERICON, BUT WITHOUT TRIPPING THEIR DEFENSES.
IF THEY DETECT MY POWER COSMIC, THEY'LL KILL THE EARTH GIRL.
THERE MUST BE A WAY TO SAVE HER AND THE NEVER HEART AS WELL.
YOU FEEL YOU HAVE TO SAVE HER?
OF COURSE. SHE WOULDN'T BE INVOLVED IN THESE MATTERS IF NOT FOR ME. THAT MAKES HER MY RESPONSIBILITY.
HM.
ONE MOMENT. I BELIEVE I HAVE A PLAN. BUT FIRST...
...I REQUIRE ONE OF THESE POOR, FALLEN CHAMPIONS.
THIS MAN WAS CALLED THE BATTLEJACK OF JACKSTAR 9.
FORGIVE THIS INTRUSION, FRIEND. BUT MY FIRST DUTY MUST BE TO THE LIVING.

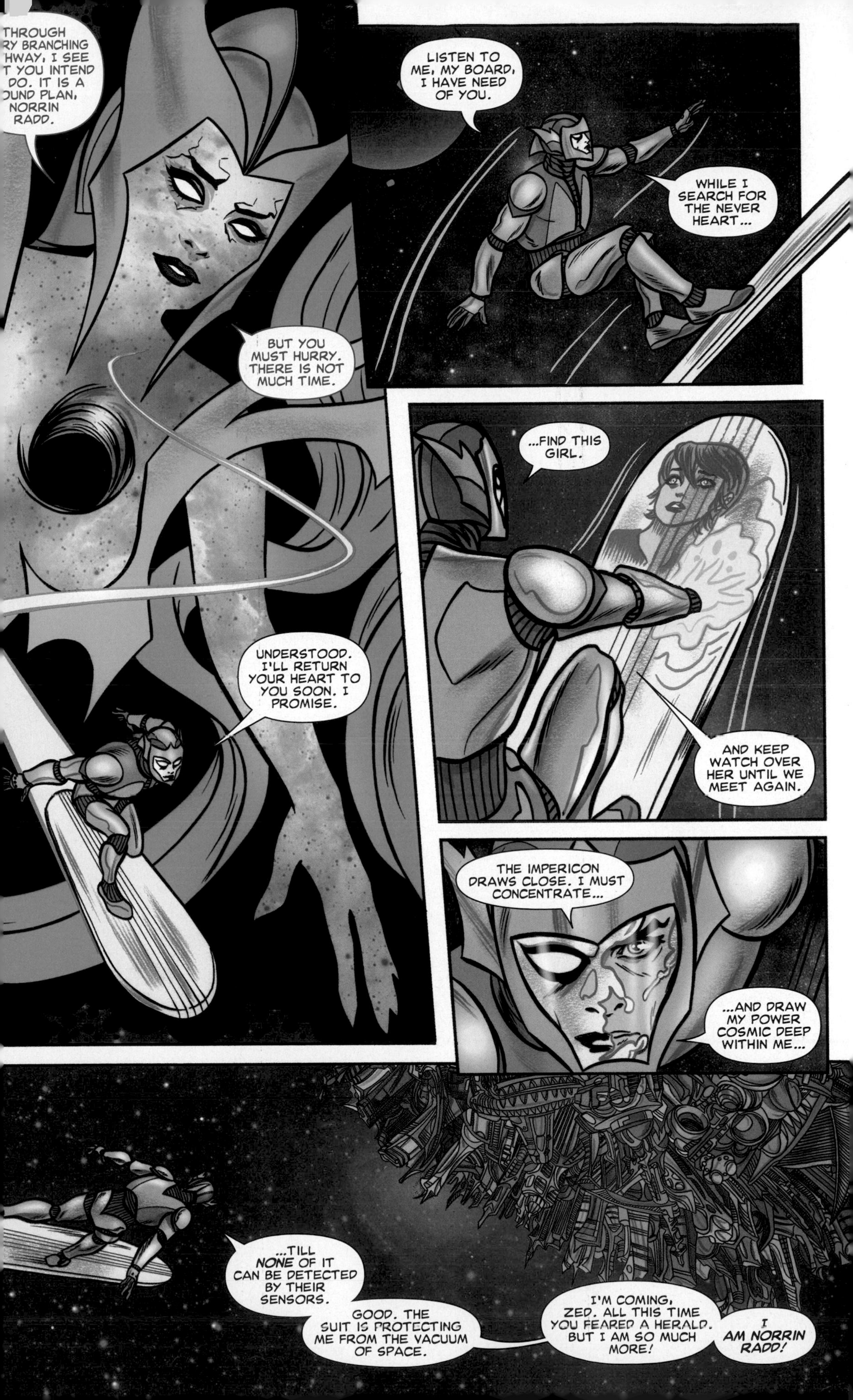
THROUGH
RY BRANCHING
HWAY, I SEE
T YOU INTEND
DO. IT IS A
OUND PLAN,
NORRIN
RADD.
LISTEN TO
ME, MY BOARD,
I HAVE NEED
OF YOU.
WHILE I
SEARCH FOR
THE NEVER
HEART...
BUT YOU
MUST HURRY.
THERE IS NOT
MUCH TIME.
...FIND THIS
GIRL.
AND KEEP
WATCH OVER
HER UNTIL WE
MEET AGAIN.
UNDERSTOOD.
I'LL RETURN
YOUR HEART TO
YOU SOON. I
PROMISE.
THE IMPERICON
DRAWS CLOSE. I MUST
CONCENTRATE...
...AND DRAW
MY POWER
COSMIC DEEP
WITHIN ME...
...TILL
NONE OF IT
CAN BE DETECTED
BY THEIR
SENSORS.
GOOD. THE
SUIT IS PROTECTING
ME FROM THE VACUUM
OF SPACE.
I'M COMING,
ZED. ALL THIS TIME
YOU FEARED A HERALD.
BUT I AM SO MUCH
MORE!
I
*AM NORRIN
RADD!*

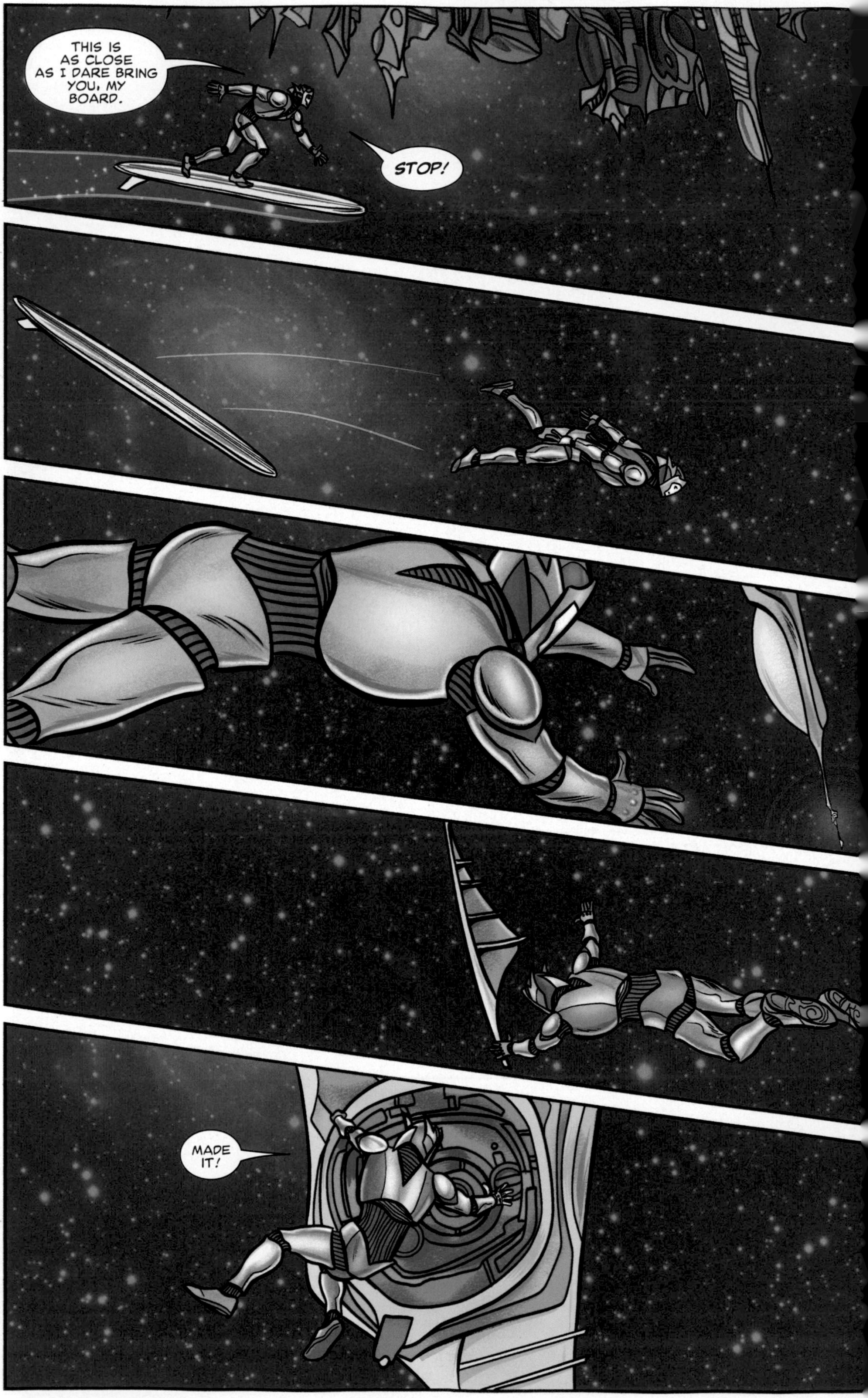
THIS IS AS CLOSE AS I DARE BRING YOU, MY BOARD.
STOP!
MADE IT!

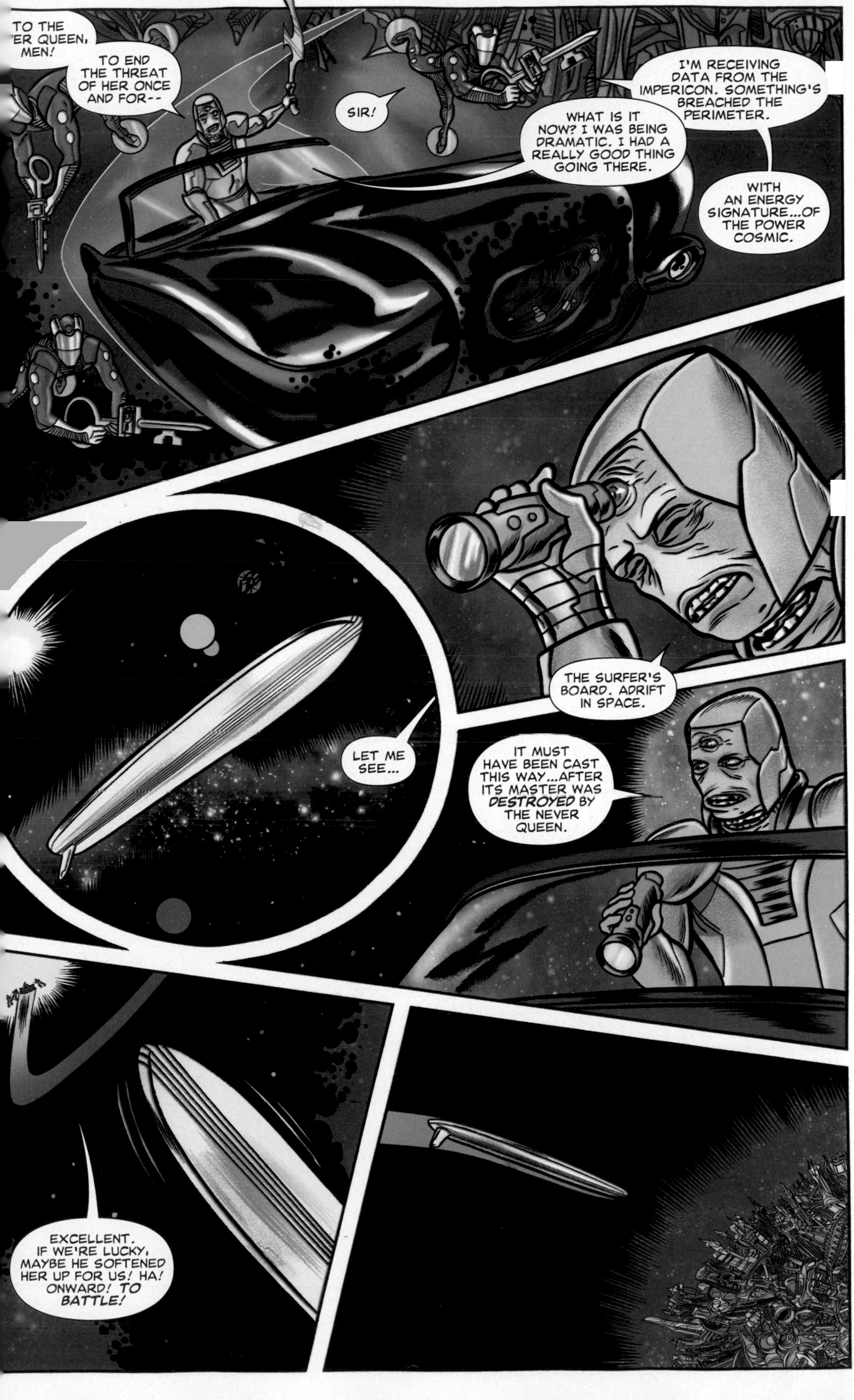

TO THE
ER QUEEN,
MEN!
TO END THE THREAT OF HER ONCE AND FOR--
SIR!
WHAT IS IT NOW? I WAS BEING DRAMATIC. I HAD A REALLY GOOD THING GOING THERE.
I'M RECEIVING DATA FROM THE IMPERICON. SOMETHING'S BREACHED THE PERIMETER.
WITH AN ENERGY SIGNATURE...OF THE POWER COSMIC.
LET ME SEE...
THE SURFER'S BOARD. ADRIFT IN SPACE.
IT MUST HAVE BEEN CAST THIS WAY...AFTER ITS MASTER WAS *DESTROYED* BY THE NEVER QUEEN.
EXCELLENT. IF WE'RE LUCKY, MAYBE HE SOFTENED HER UP FOR US! HA! ONWARD! *TO BATTLE!*

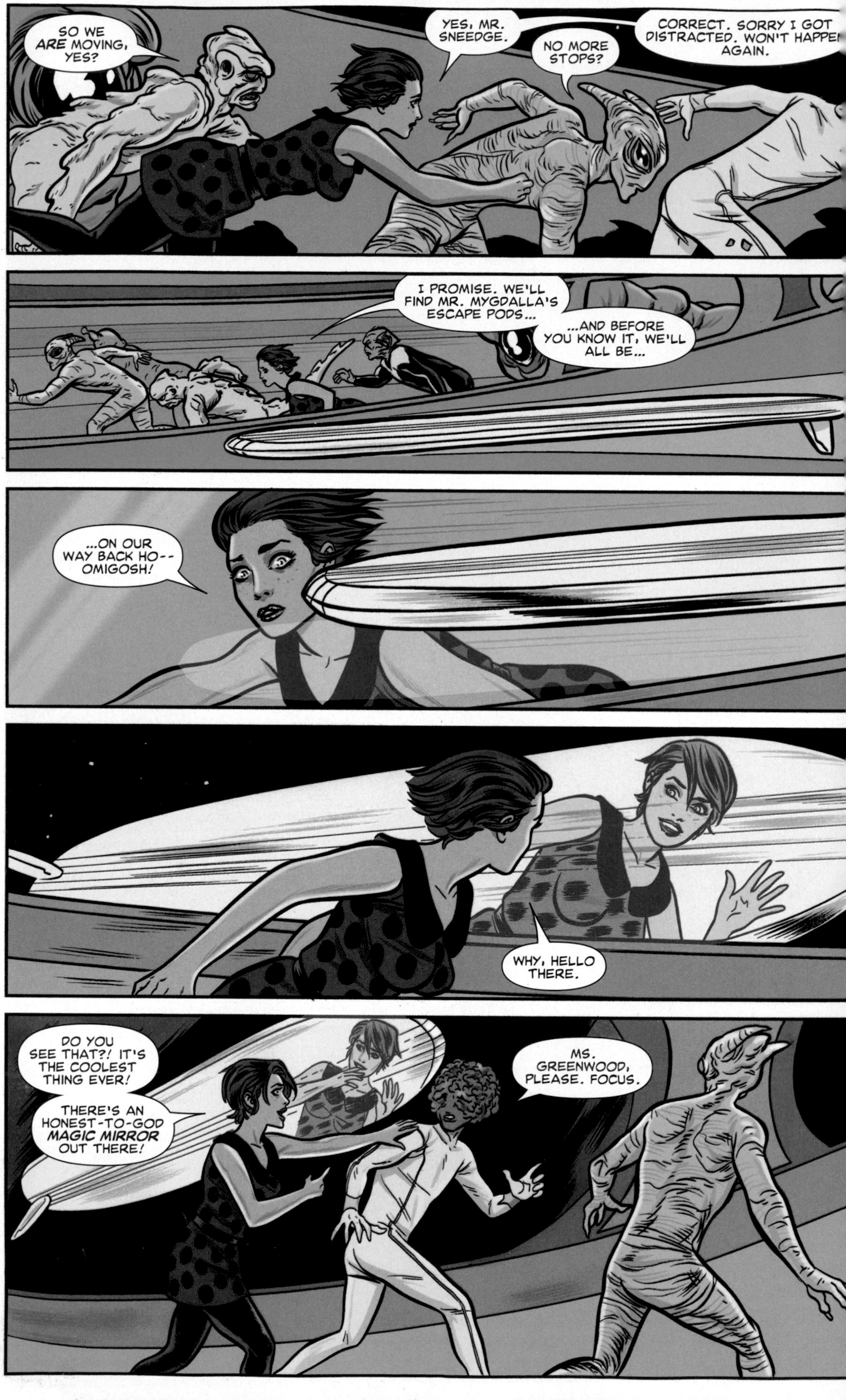

SO WE *ARE* MOVING, YES?
YES, MR. SNEEDGE.
NO MORE STOPS?
CORRECT. SORRY I GOT DISTRACTED. WON'T HAPPEN AGAIN.
I PROMISE. WE'LL FIND MR. MYGDALLA'S ESCAPE PODS...
...AND BEFORE YOU KNOW IT, WE'LL ALL BE...
...ON OUR WAY BACK HO-- OMIGOSH!
WHY, HELLO THERE.
DO YOU SEE THAT?! IT'S THE COOLEST THING EVER!
THERE'S AN HONEST-TO-GOD *MAGIC MIRROR* OUT THERE!
MS. GREENWOOD, PLEASE. FOCUS.

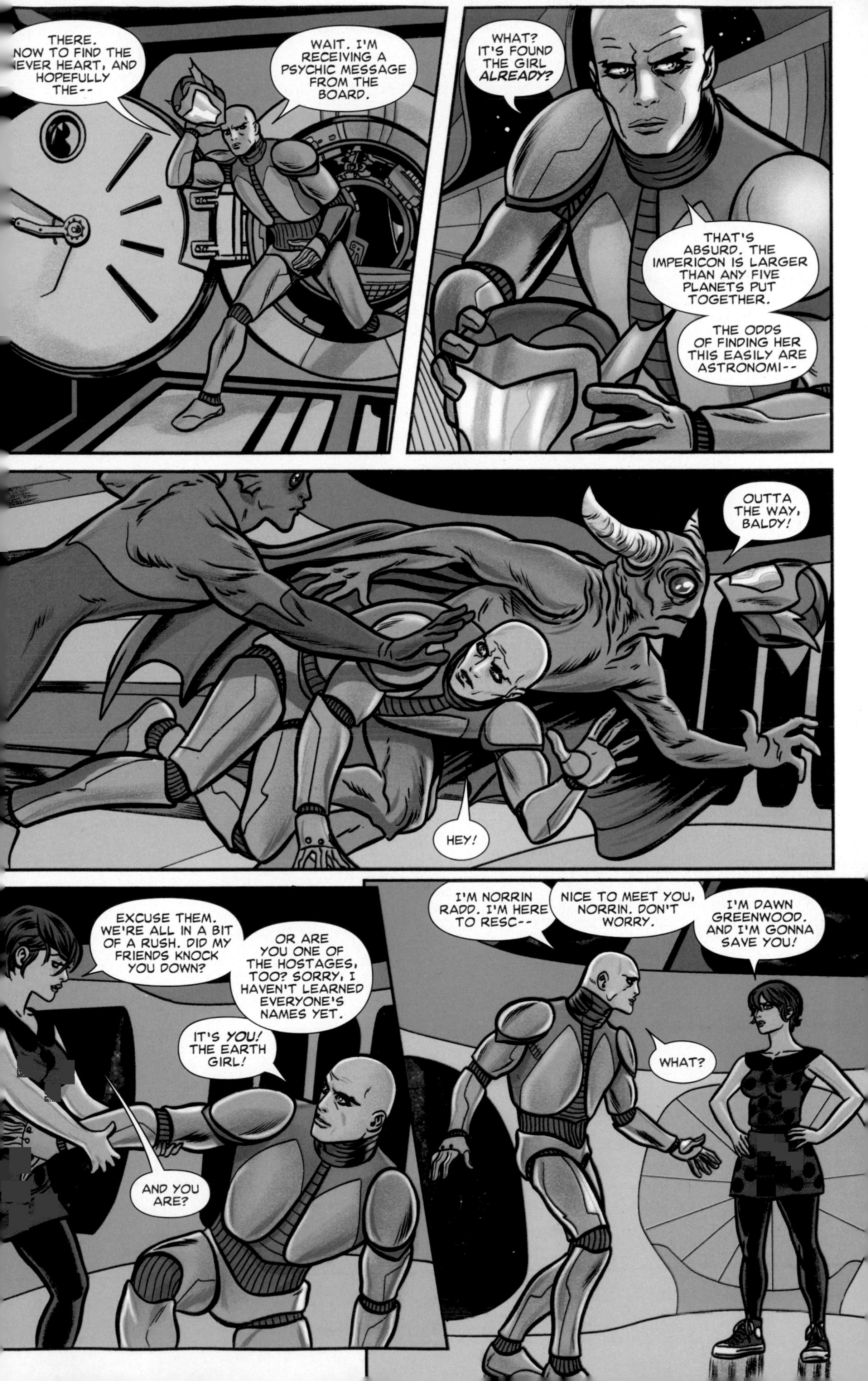

THERE. NOW TO FIND THE EVER HEART, AND HOPEFULLY THE--
WAIT. I'M RECEIVING A PSYCHIC MESSAGE FROM THE BOARD.
WHAT? IT'S FOUND THE GIRL *ALREADY?*
THAT'S ABSURD. THE IMPERICON IS LARGER THAN ANY FIVE PLANETS PUT TOGETHER.
THE ODDS OF FINDING HER THIS EASILY ARE ASTRONOMI--
OUTTA THE WAY, BALDY!
HEY!
EXCUSE THEM. WE'RE ALL IN A BIT OF A RUSH. DID MY FRIENDS KNOCK YOU DOWN?
OR ARE YOU ONE OF THE HOSTAGES, TOO? SORRY, I HAVEN'T LEARNED EVERYONE'S NAMES YET.
IT'S *YOU!* THE EARTH GIRL!
AND YOU ARE?
I'M NORRIN RADD. I'M HERE TO RESC--
NICE TO MEET YOU, NORRIN. DON'T WORRY.
I'M DAWN GREENWOOD. AND I'M GONNA SAVE YOU!
WHAT?

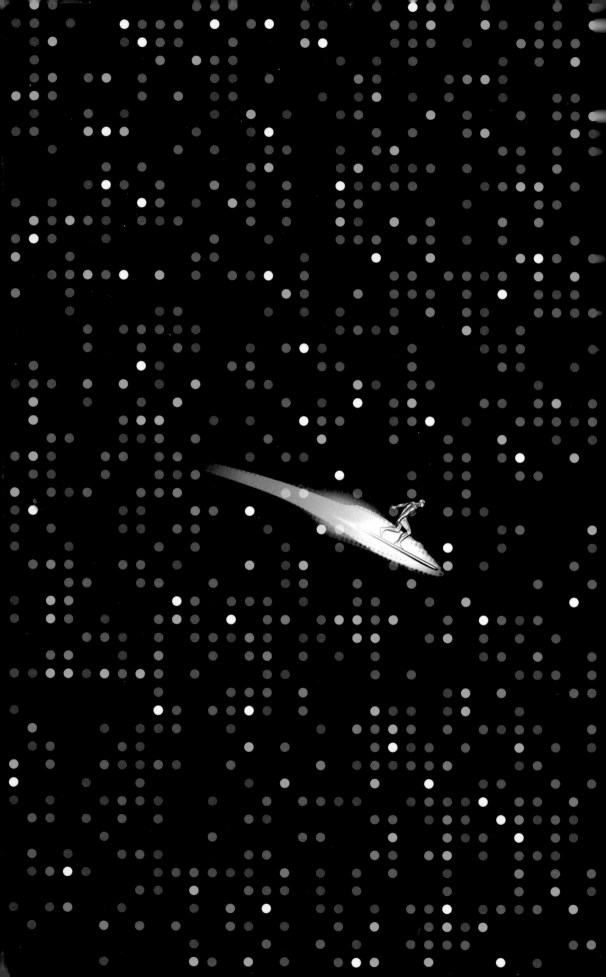

3

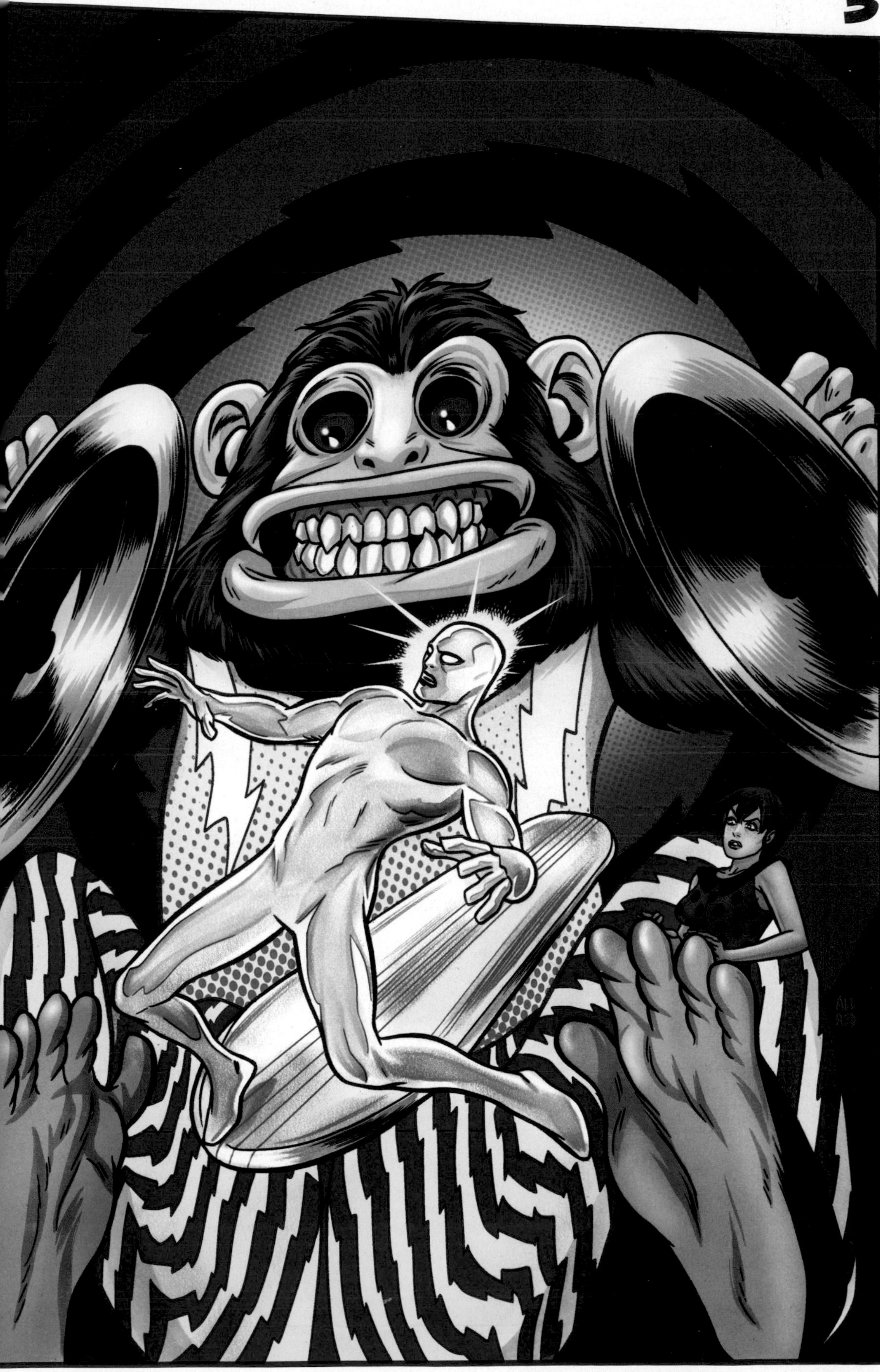

CHANGE OF HEART

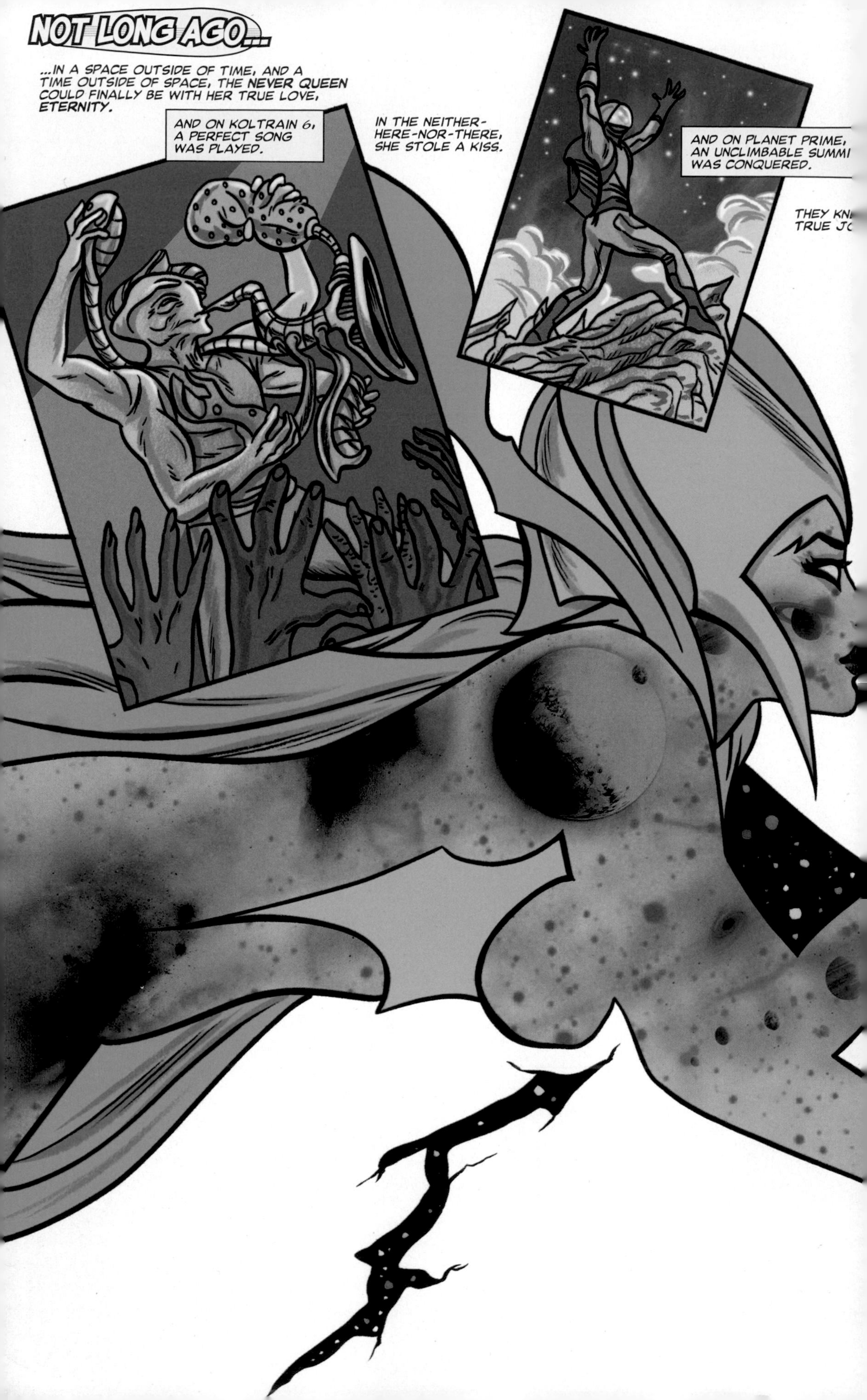
NOT LONG AGO...
...IN A SPACE OUTSIDE OF TIME, AND A TIME OUTSIDE OF SPACE, THE NEVER QUEEN COULD FINALLY BE WITH HER TRUE LOVE, ETERNITY.
AND ON KOLTRAIN 6, A PERFECT SONG WAS PLAYED.
IN THE NEITHER-HERE-NOR-THERE, SHE STOLE A KISS.
AND ON PLANET PRIME, AN UNCLIMBABLE SUMMI
WAS CONQUERED.
THEY KN
TRUE JO

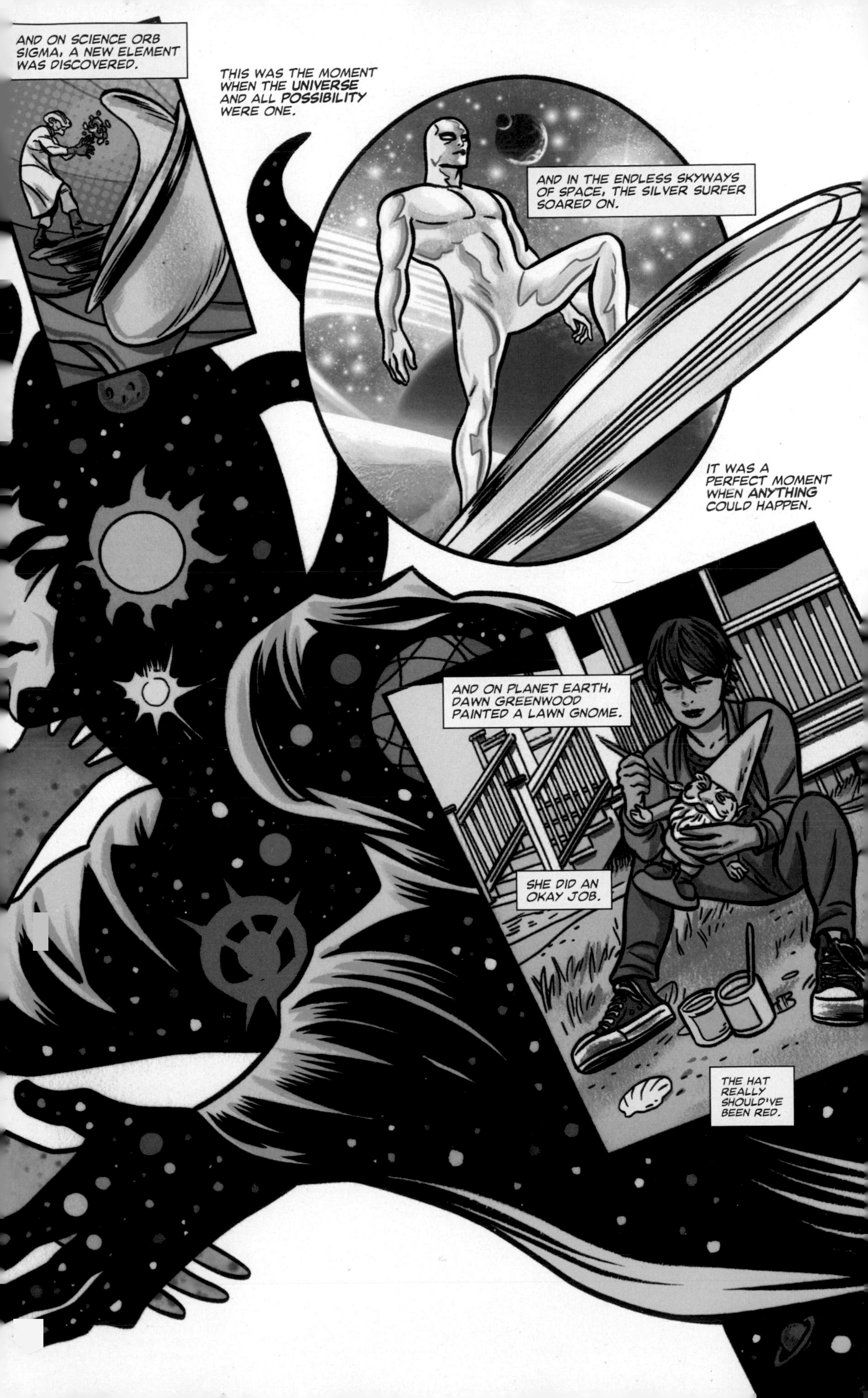
AND ON SCIENCE ORB SIGMA, A NEW ELEMENT WAS DISCOVERED.
THIS WAS THE MOMENT WHEN THE UNIVERSE AND ALL POSSIBILITY WERE ONE.
AND IN THE ENDLESS SKYWAYS OF SPACE, THE SILVER SURFER SOARED ON.
IT WAS A PERFECT MOMENT WHEN ANYTHING COULD HAPPEN.
AND ON PLANET EARTH, DAWN GREENWOOD PAINTED A LAWN GNOME.
SHE DID AN OKAY JOB.
THE HAT REALLY SHOULD'VE BEEN RED.

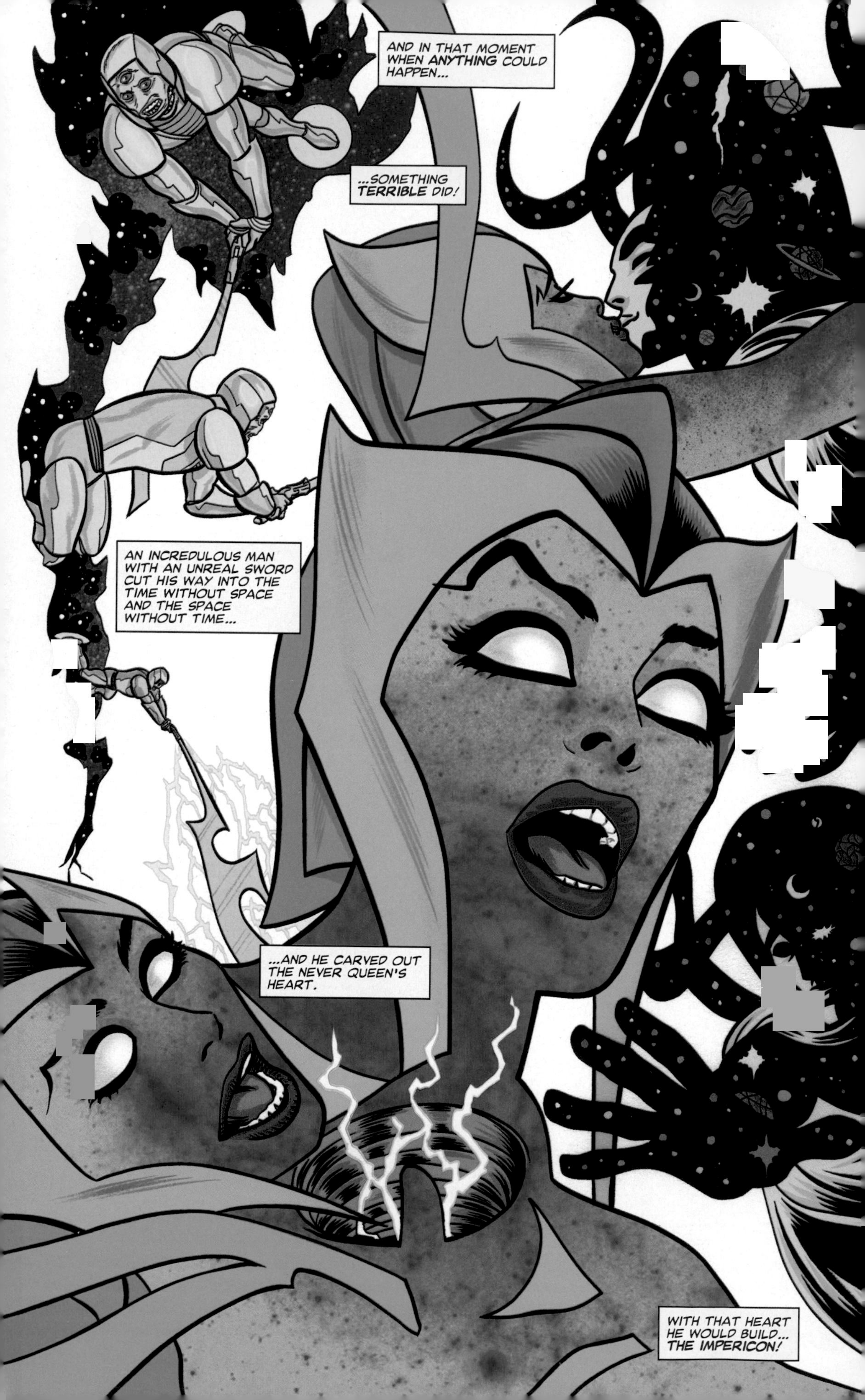
AND IN THAT MOMENT WHEN ANYTHING COULD HAPPEN...
...SOMETHING TERRIBLE DID!
AN INCREDULOUS MAN WITH AN UNREAL SWORD CUT HIS WAY INTO THE TIME WITHOUT SPACE AND THE SPACE WITHOUT TIME...
...AND HE CARVED OUT THE NEVER QUEEN'S HEART.
WITH THAT HEART HE WOULD BUILD... THE IMPERICON!

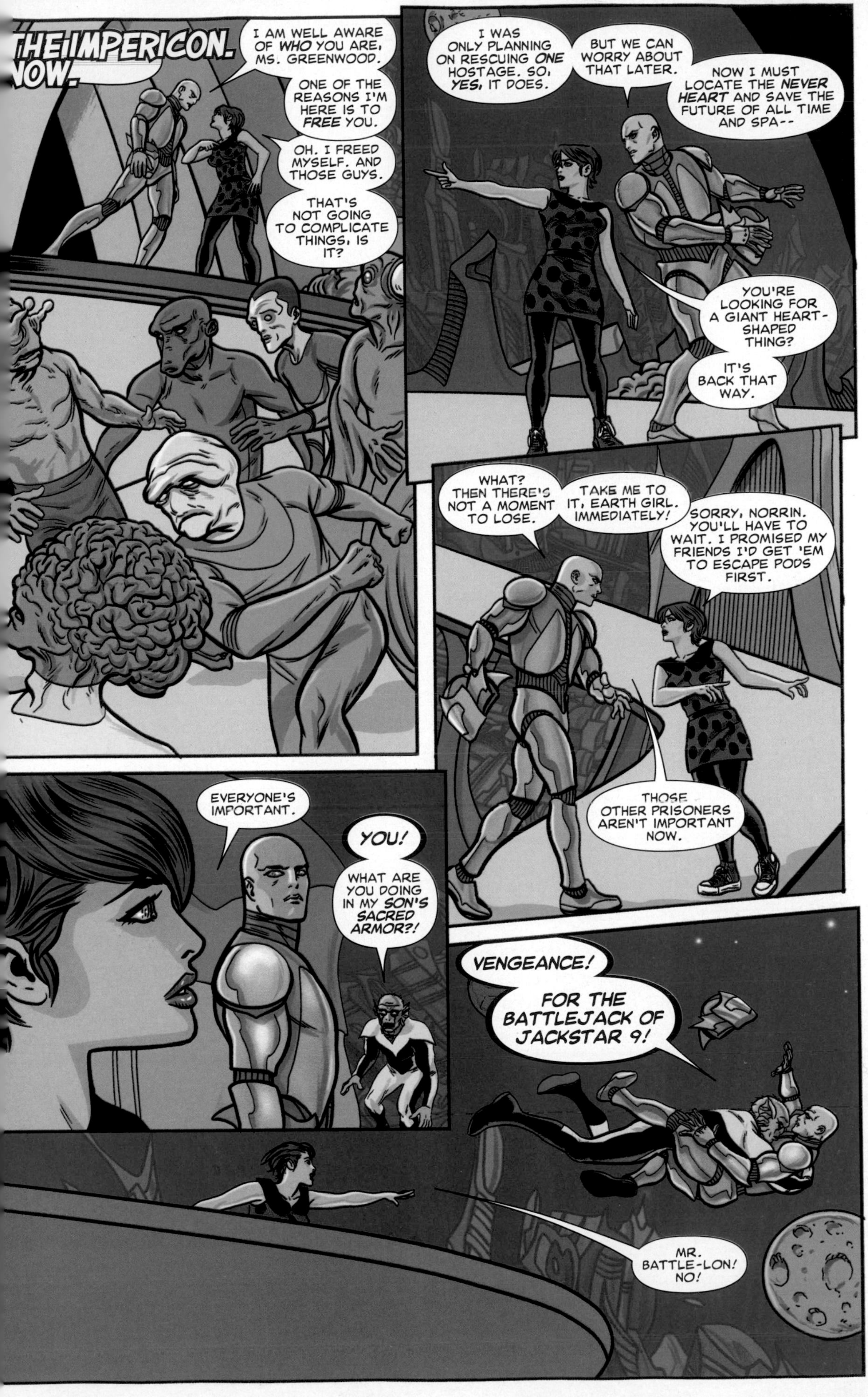
THE IMPERICON. NOW.
I AM WELL AWARE OF WHO YOU ARE, MS. GREENWOOD.
ONE OF THE REASONS I'M HERE IS TO FREE YOU.
OH. I FREED MYSELF. AND THOSE GUYS.
THAT'S NOT GOING TO COMPLICATE THINGS, IS IT?
I WAS ONLY PLANNING ON RESCUING ONE HOSTAGE. SO, YES, IT DOES.
BUT WE CAN WORRY ABOUT THAT LATER.
NOW I MUST LOCATE THE NEVER HEART AND SAVE THE FUTURE OF ALL TIME AND SPA--
YOU'RE LOOKING FOR A GIANT HEART-SHAPED THING?
IT'S BACK THAT WAY.
WHAT? THEN THERE'S NOT A MOMENT TO LOSE.
TAKE ME TO IT, EARTH GIRL. IMMEDIATELY!
SORRY, NORRIN. YOU'LL HAVE TO WAIT. I PROMISED MY FRIENDS I'D GET 'EM TO ESCAPE PODS FIRST.
THOSE OTHER PRISONERS AREN'T IMPORTANT NOW.
EVERYONE'S IMPORTANT.
YOU!
WHAT ARE YOU DOING IN MY SON'S SACRED ARMOR?!
VENGEANCE!
FOR THE BATTLEJACK OF JACKSTAR 9!
MR. BATTLE-LON! NO!

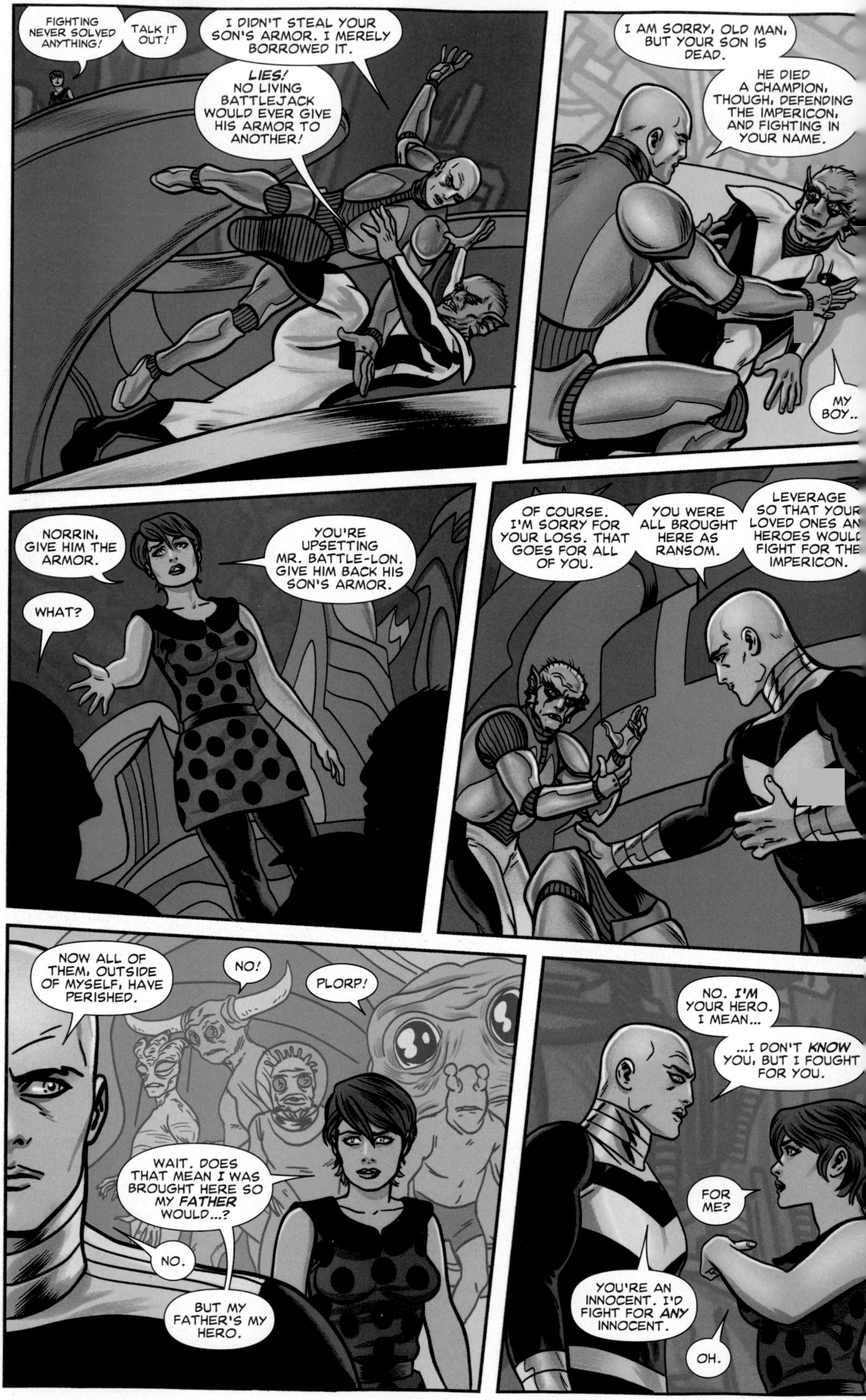
FIGHTING NEVER SOLVED ANYTHING!
TALK IT OUT!
I DIDN'T STEAL YOUR SON'S ARMOR. I MERELY BORROWED IT.
LIES! NO LIVING BATTLEJACK WOULD EVER GIVE HIS ARMOR TO ANOTHER!
I AM SORRY, OLD MAN, BUT YOUR SON IS DEAD.
HE DIED A CHAMPION, THOUGH, DEFENDING THE IMPERICON, AND FIGHTING IN YOUR NAME.
MY BOY...
NORRIN, GIVE HIM THE ARMOR.
WHAT?
YOU'RE UPSETTING MR. BATTLE-LON. GIVE HIM BACK HIS SON'S ARMOR.
OF COURSE. I'M SORRY FOR YOUR LOSS. THAT GOES FOR ALL OF YOU.
YOU WERE ALL BROUGHT HERE AS RANSOM.
LEVERAGE SO THAT YOUR LOVED ONES AN HEROES WOULD FIGHT FOR THE IMPERICON.
NOW ALL OF THEM, OUTSIDE OF MYSELF, HAVE PERISHED.
NO!
PLORP!
WAIT. DOES THAT MEAN I WAS BROUGHT HERE SO MY FATHER WOULD...?
NO.
BUT MY FATHER'S MY HERO.
NO. I'M YOUR HERO. I MEAN...
...I DON'T KNOW YOU, BUT I FOUGHT FOR YOU.
FOR ME?
YOU'RE AN INNOCENT. I'D FIGHT FOR ANY INNOCENT.
OH.

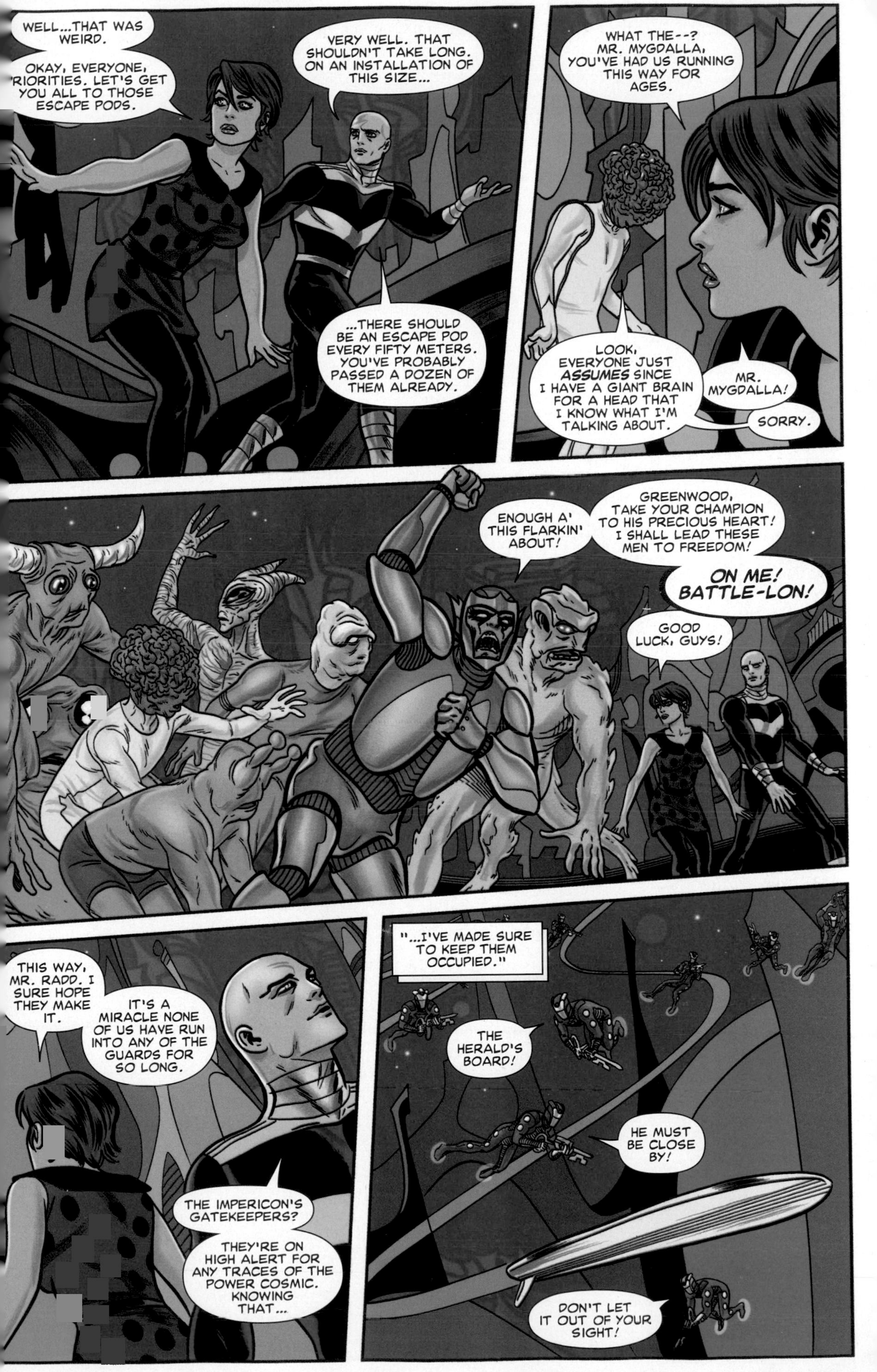
WELL...THAT WAS WEIRD.
OKAY, EVERYONE, PRIORITIES. LET'S GET YOU ALL TO THOSE ESCAPE PODS.
VERY WELL. THAT SHOULDN'T TAKE LONG. ON AN INSTALLATION OF THIS SIZE...
...THERE SHOULD BE AN ESCAPE POD EVERY FIFTY METERS. YOU'VE PROBABLY PASSED A DOZEN OF THEM ALREADY.
WHAT THE--? MR. MYGDALLA, YOU'VE HAD US RUNNING THIS WAY FOR AGES.
LOOK, EVERYONE JUST ASSUMES SINCE I HAVE A GIANT BRAIN FOR A HEAD THAT I KNOW WHAT I'M TALKING ABOUT.
MR. MYGDALLA!
SORRY.
ENOUGH A' THIS FLARKIN' ABOUT!
GREENWOOD, TAKE YOUR CHAMPION TO HIS PRECIOUS HEART! I SHALL LEAD THESE MEN TO FREEDOM!
ON ME! BATTLE-LON!
GOOD LUCK, GUYS!
THIS WAY, MR. RADD. I SURE HOPE THEY MAKE IT.
IT'S A MIRACLE NONE OF US HAVE RUN INTO ANY OF THE GUARDS FOR SO LONG.
THE IMPERICON'S GATEKEEPERS?
THEY'RE ON HIGH ALERT FOR ANY TRACES OF THE POWER COSMIC. KNOWING THAT...
"...I'VE MADE SURE TO KEEP THEM OCCUPIED."
THE HERALD'S BOARD!
HE MUST BE CLOSE BY!
DON'T LET IT OUT OF YOUR SIGHT!

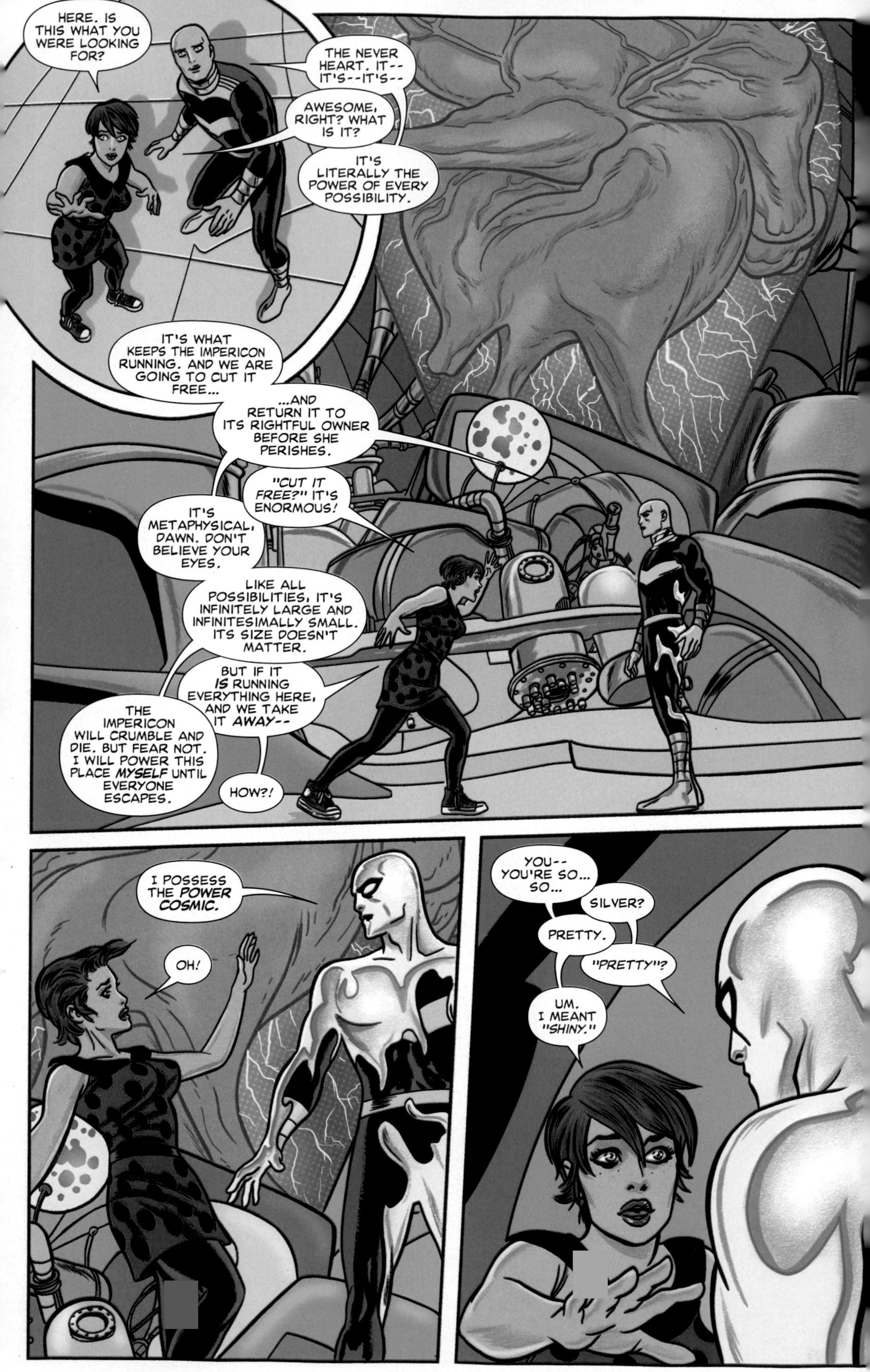
HERE. IS THIS WHAT YOU WERE LOOKING FOR?
THE NEVER HEART. IT-- IT'S--IT'S--
AWESOME, RIGHT? WHAT IS IT?
IT'S LITERALLY THE POWER OF EVERY POSSIBILITY.
IT'S WHAT KEEPS THE IMPERICON RUNNING. AND WE ARE GOING TO CUT IT FREE...
...AND RETURN IT TO ITS RIGHTFUL OWNER BEFORE SHE PERISHES.
"CUT IT FREE?" IT'S ENORMOUS!
IT'S METAPHYSICAL, DAWN. DON'T BELIEVE YOUR EYES.
LIKE ALL POSSIBILITIES, IT'S INFINITELY LARGE AND INFINITESIMALLY SMALL. ITS SIZE DOESN'T MATTER.
BUT IF IT IS RUNNING EVERYTHING HERE, AND WE TAKE IT AWAY--
THE IMPERICON WILL CRUMBLE AND DIE. BUT FEAR NOT. I WILL POWER THIS PLACE MYSELF UNTIL EVERYONE ESCAPES.
HOW?!
I POSSESS THE POWER COSMIC.
OH!
YOU-- YOU'RE SO... SO...
SILVER?
PRETTY.
"PRETTY"?
UM. I MEANT "SHINY."

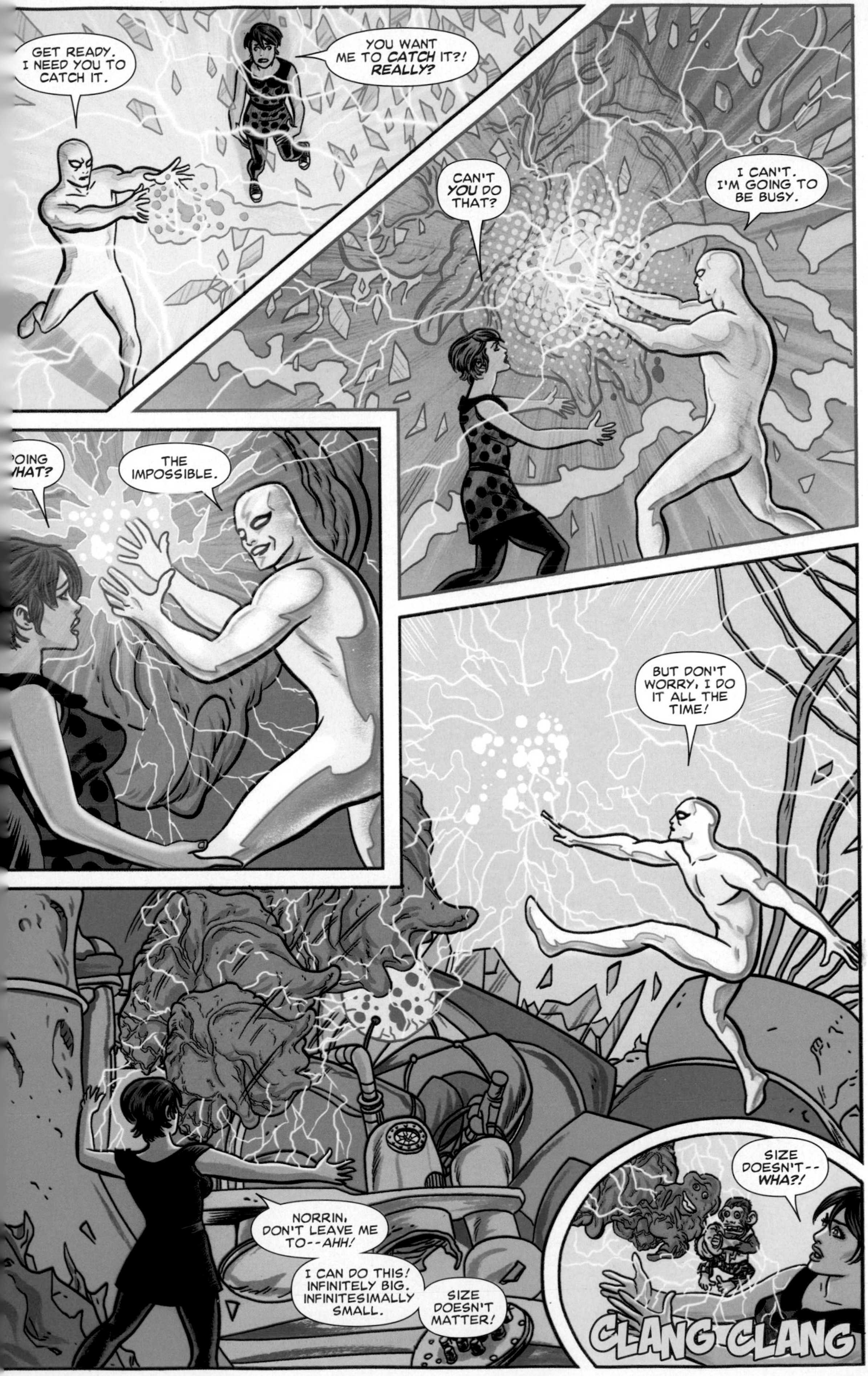
GET READY. I NEED YOU TO CATCH IT.
YOU WANT ME TO *CATCH* IT?! *REALLY?*
CAN'T *YOU* DO THAT?
I CAN'T. I'M GOING TO BE BUSY.
DOING WHAT?
THE IMPOSSIBLE.
BUT DON'T WORRY, I DO IT ALL THE TIME!
NORRIN, DON'T LEAVE ME TO--AHH!
I CAN DO THIS! INFINITELY BIG. INFINITESIMALLY SMALL.
SIZE DOESN'T MATTER!
SIZE DOESN'T-- *WHA?!*
CLANG CLANG

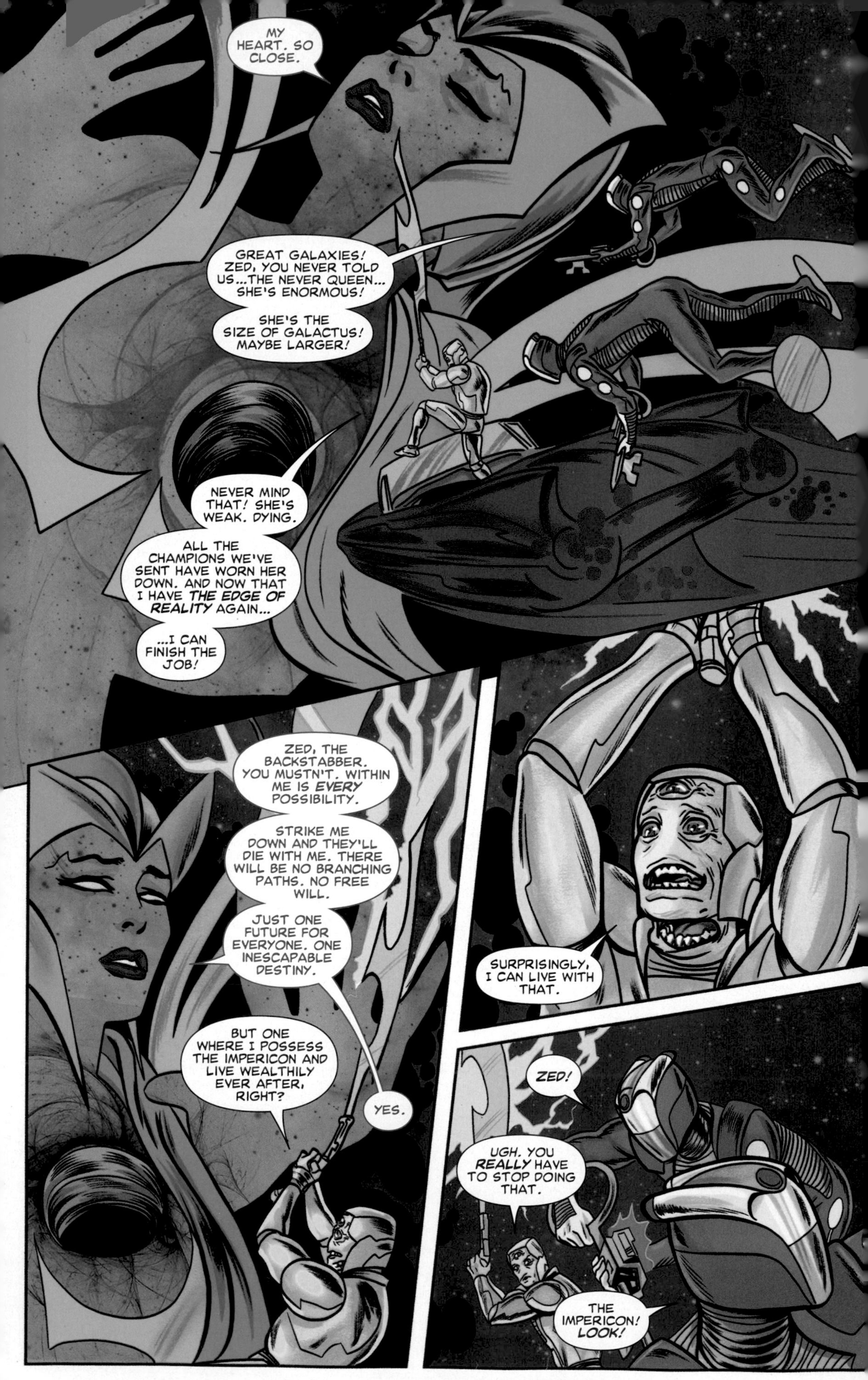
MY HEART. SO CLOSE.
GREAT GALAXIES! ZED, YOU NEVER TOLD US...THE NEVER QUEEN... SHE'S ENORMOUS!
SHE'S THE SIZE OF GALACTUS! MAYBE LARGER!
NEVER MIND THAT! SHE'S WEAK. DYING.
ALL THE CHAMPIONS WE'VE SENT HAVE WORN HER DOWN. AND NOW THAT I HAVE THE EDGE OF REALITY AGAIN...
...I CAN FINISH THE JOB!
ZED, THE BACKSTABBER. YOU MUSTN'T. WITHIN ME IS EVERY POSSIBILITY.
STRIKE ME DOWN AND THEY'LL DIE WITH ME. THERE WILL BE NO BRANCHING PATHS. NO FREE WILL.
JUST ONE FUTURE FOR EVERYONE. ONE INESCAPABLE DESTINY.
BUT ONE WHERE I POSSESS THE IMPERICON AND LIVE WEALTHILY EVER AFTER, RIGHT?
YES.
SURPRISINGLY, I CAN LIVE WITH THAT.
ZED!
UGH. YOU REALLY HAVE TO STOP DOING THAT.
THE IMPERICON! LOOK!

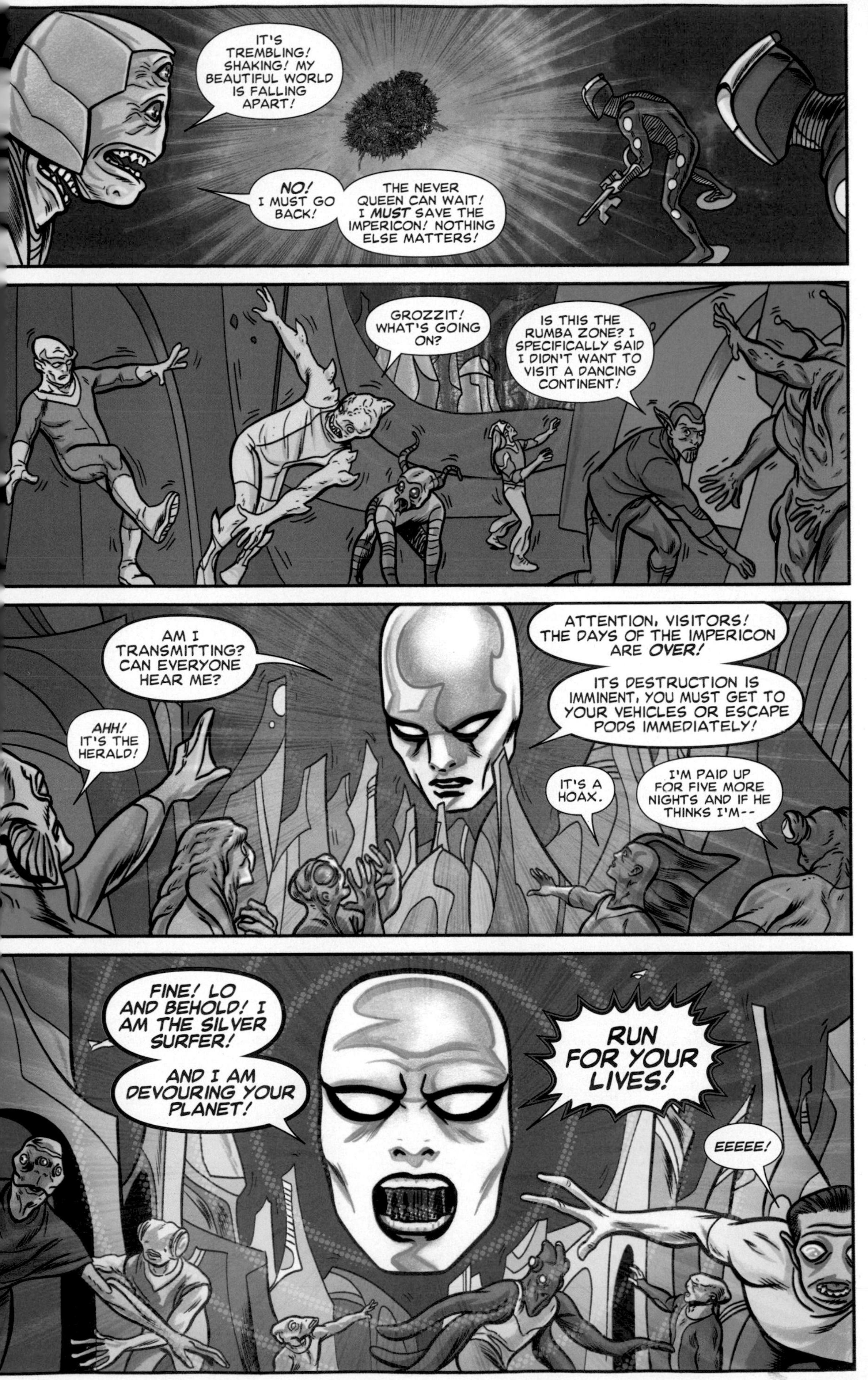
IT'S TREMBLING! SHAKING! MY BEAUTIFUL WORLD IS FALLING APART!
NO! I MUST GO BACK!
THE NEVER QUEEN CAN WAIT! I MUST SAVE THE IMPERICON! NOTHING ELSE MATTERS!
GROZZIT! WHAT'S GOING ON?
IS THIS THE RUMBA ZONE? I SPECIFICALLY SAID I DIDN'T WANT TO VISIT A DANCING CONTINENT!
AM I TRANSMITTING? CAN EVERYONE HEAR ME?
ATTENTION, VISITORS! THE DAYS OF THE IMPERICON ARE OVER!
ITS DESTRUCTION IS IMMINENT, YOU MUST GET TO YOUR VEHICLES OR ESCAPE PODS IMMEDIATELY!
AHH! IT'S THE HERALD!
IT'S A HOAX.
I'M PAID UP FOR FIVE MORE NIGHTS AND IF HE THINKS I'M--
FINE! LO AND BEHOLD! I AM THE SILVER SURFER!
AND I AM DEVOURING YOUR PLANET!
RUN FOR YOUR LIVES!
EEEEE!

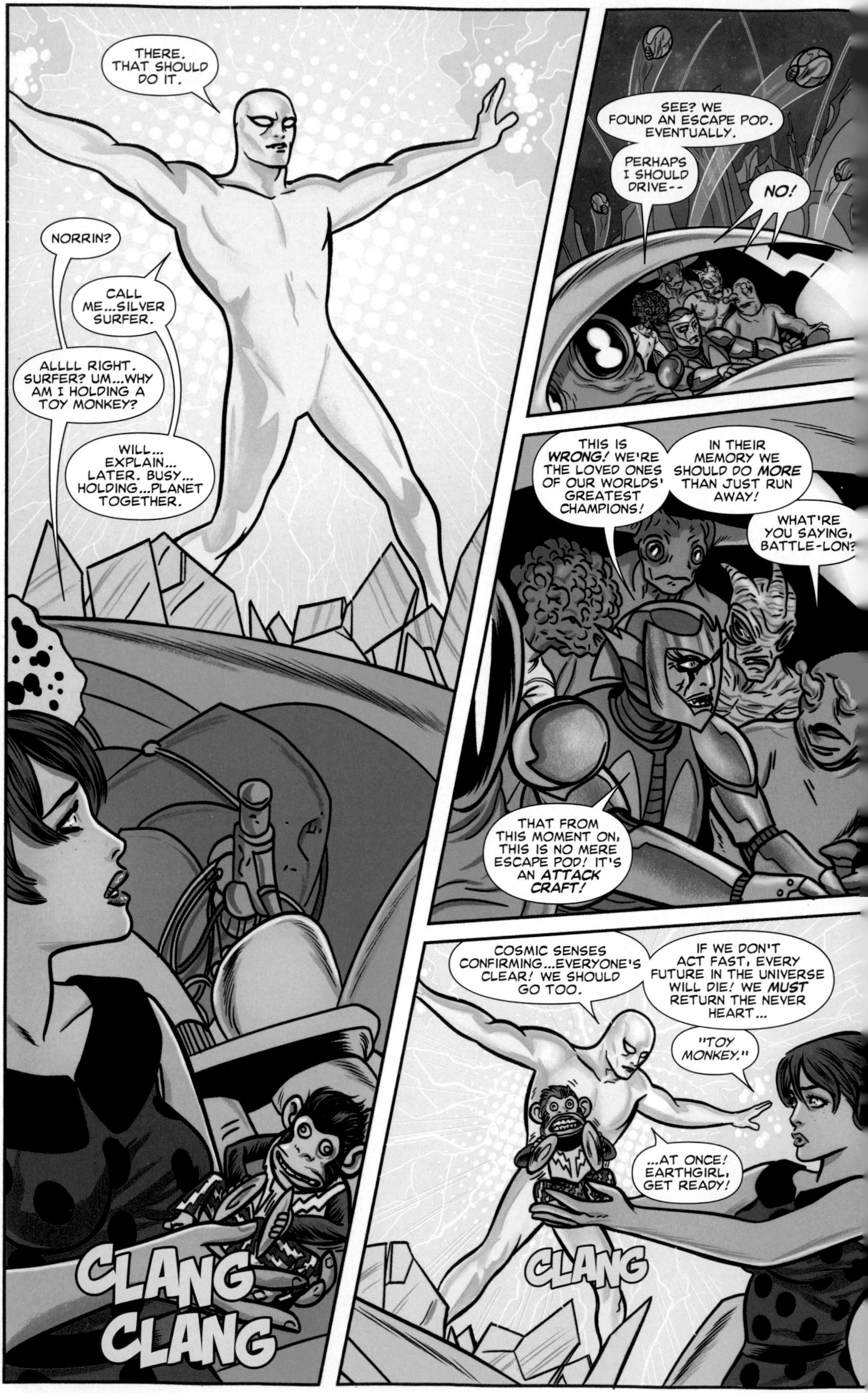
THERE. THAT SHOULD DO IT.
NORRIN?
CALL ME...SILVER SURFER.
ALLLL RIGHT. SURFER? UM...WHY AM I HOLDING A TOY MONKEY?
WILL... EXPLAIN... LATER. BUSY... HOLDING...PLANET TOGETHER.
CLANG CLANG
SEE? WE FOUND AN ESCAPE POD. EVENTUALLY.
PERHAPS I SHOULD DRIVE--
NO!
THIS IS WRONG! WE'RE THE LOVED ONES OF OUR WORLDS' GREATEST CHAMPIONS!
IN THEIR MEMORY WE SHOULD DO MORE THAN JUST RUN AWAY!
WHAT'RE YOU SAYING, BATTLE-LON?
THAT FROM THIS MOMENT ON, THIS IS NO MERE ESCAPE POD! IT'S AN ATTACK CRAFT!
COSMIC SENSES CONFIRMING...EVERYONE'S CLEAR! WE SHOULD GO TOO.
IF WE DON'T ACT FAST, EVERY FUTURE IN THE UNIVERSE WILL DIE! WE MUST RETURN THE NEVER HEART...
"TOY MONKEY."
...AT ONCE! EARTHGIRL, GET READY!
CLANG

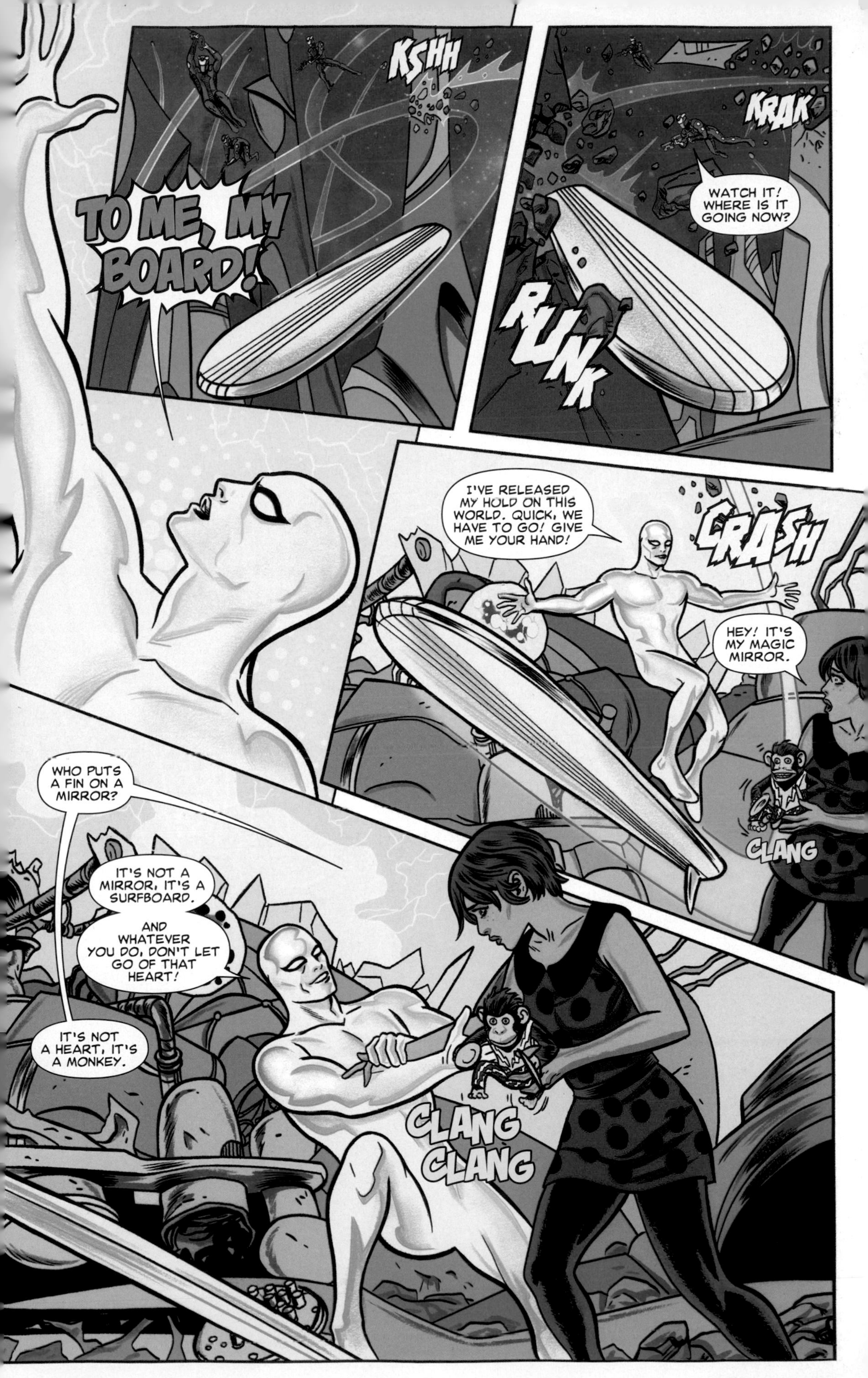
KSHH
TO ME, MY BOARD!
KRAK
WATCH IT! WHERE IS IT GOING NOW?
RUNK
I'VE RELEASED MY HOLD ON THIS WORLD. QUICK, WE HAVE TO GO! GIVE ME YOUR HAND!
CRASH
HEY! IT'S MY MAGIC MIRROR.
CLANG
WHO PUTS A FIN ON A MIRROR?
IT'S NOT A MIRROR, IT'S A SURFBOARD.
AND WHATEVER YOU DO, DON'T LET GO OF THAT HEART!
IT'S NOT A HEART, IT'S A MONKEY.
CLANG CLANG

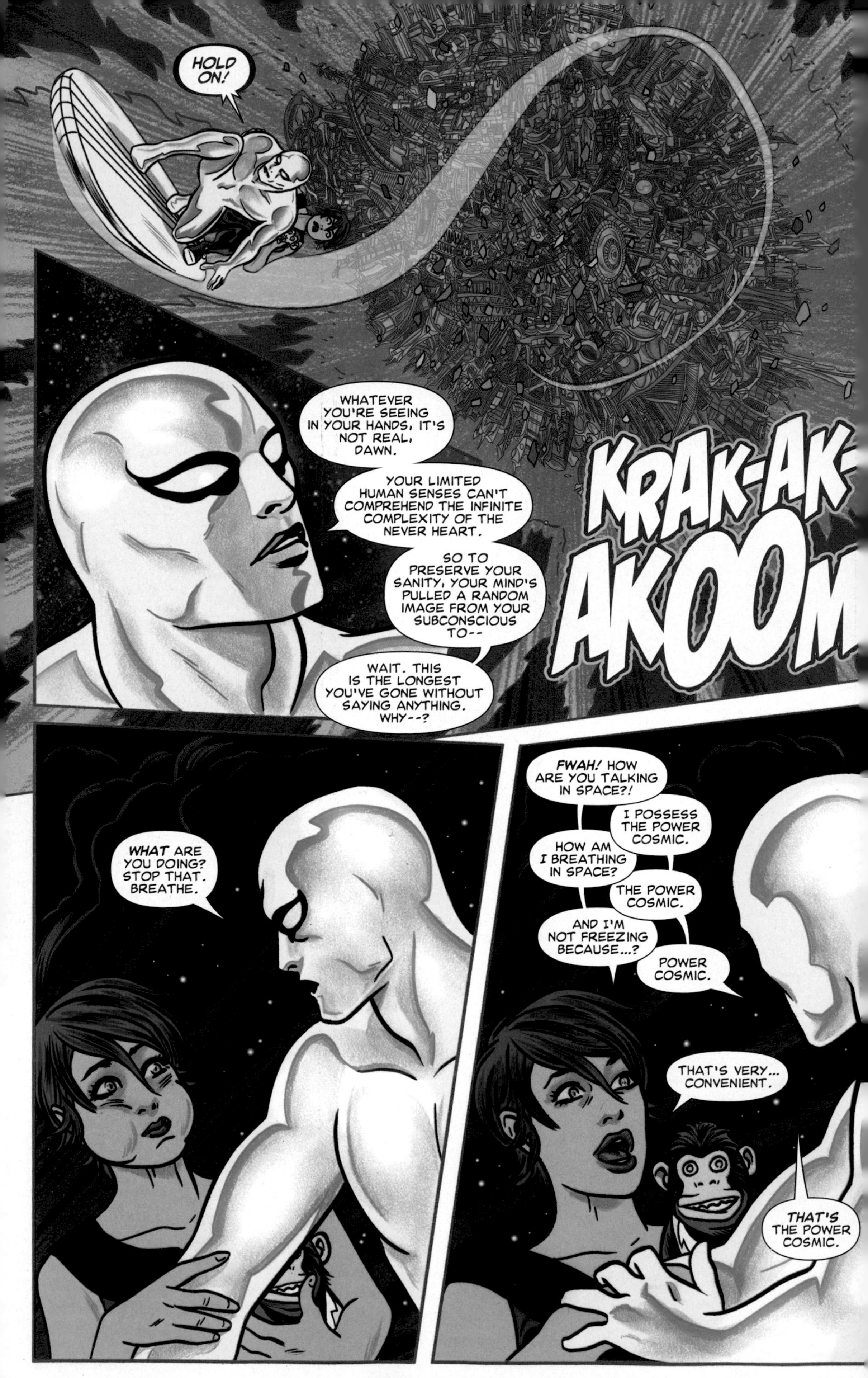
HOLD ON!
WHATEVER YOU'RE SEEING IN YOUR HANDS, IT'S NOT REAL, DAWN.
YOUR LIMITED HUMAN SENSES CAN'T COMPREHEND THE INFINITE COMPLEXITY OF THE NEVER HEART.
SO TO PRESERVE YOUR SANITY, YOUR MIND'S PULLED A RANDOM IMAGE FROM YOUR SUBCONSCIOUS TO--
KRAK-AK-AKOOM
WAIT. THIS IS THE LONGEST YOU'VE GONE WITHOUT SAYING ANYTHING. WHY--?
WHAT ARE YOU DOING? STOP THAT. BREATHE.
FWAH! HOW ARE YOU TALKING IN SPACE?!
I POSSESS THE POWER COSMIC.
HOW AM I BREATHING IN SPACE?
THE POWER COSMIC.
AND I'M NOT FREEZING BECAUSE...?
POWER COSMIC.
THAT'S VERY... CONVENIENT.
THAT'S THE POWER COSMIC.

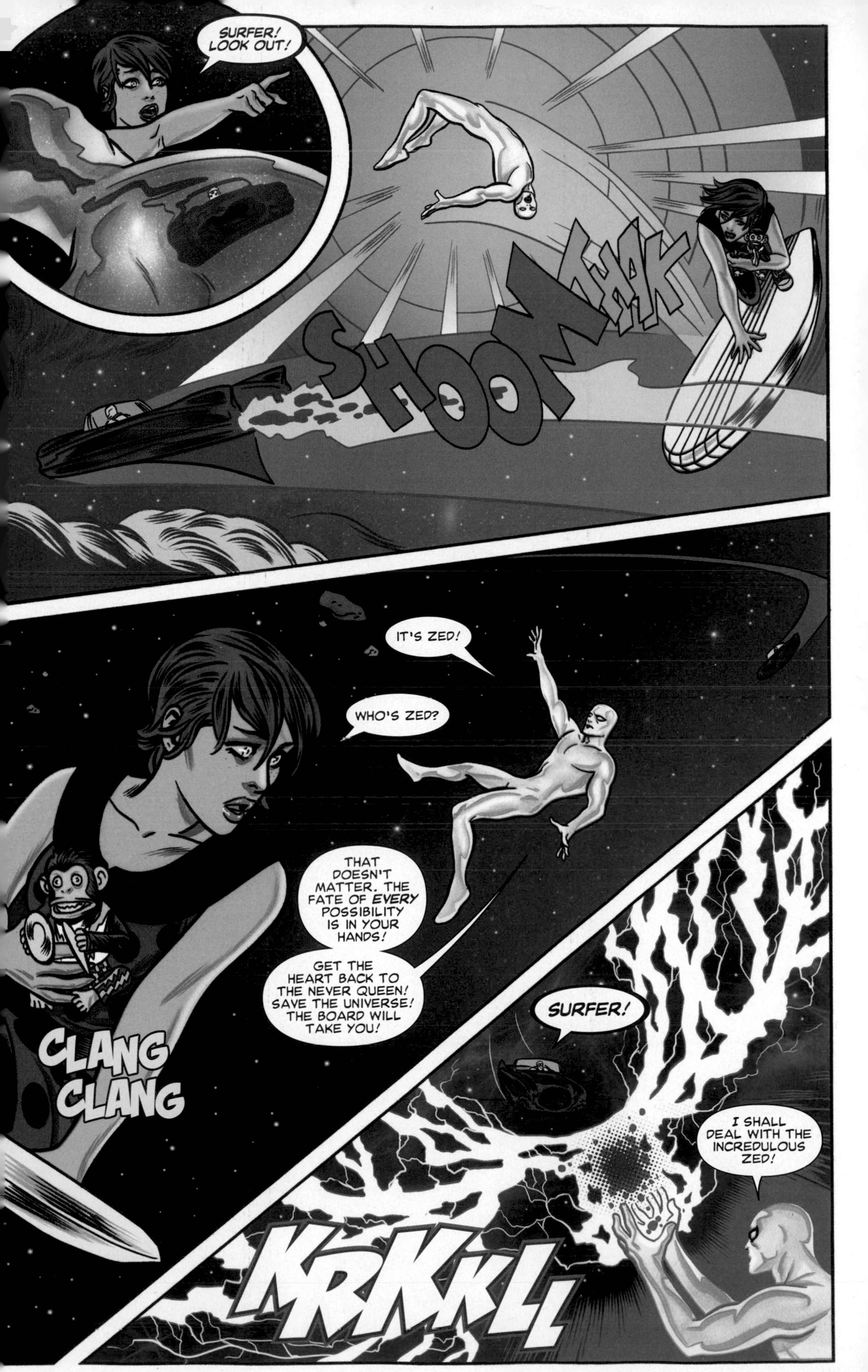
SURFER! LOOK OUT!
SHOOM
THAK
IT'S ZED!
WHO'S ZED?
THAT DOESN'T MATTER. THE FATE OF EVERY POSSIBILITY IS IN YOUR HANDS!
GET THE HEART BACK TO THE NEVER QUEEN! SAVE THE UNIVERSE! THE BOARD WILL TAKE YOU!
CLANG CLANG
SURFER!
I SHALL DEAL WITH THE INCREDULOUS ZED!
KRKKLL

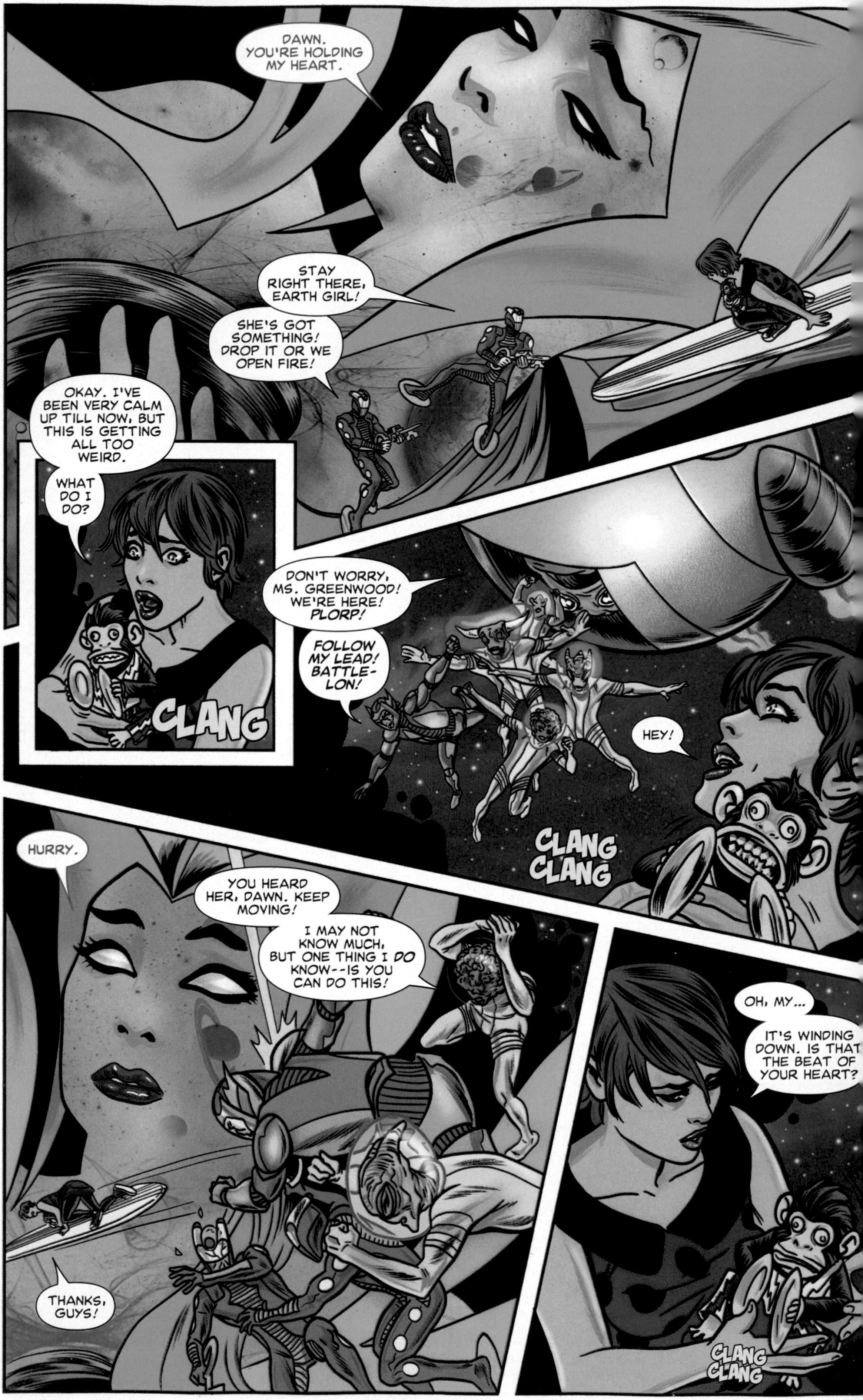
DAWN. YOU'RE HOLDING MY HEART.
STAY RIGHT THERE, EARTH GIRL!
SHE'S GOT SOMETHING! DROP IT OR WE OPEN FIRE!
OKAY. I'VE BEEN VERY CALM UP TILL NOW, BUT THIS IS GETTING ALL TOO WEIRD.
WHAT DO I DO?
CLANG
DON'T WORRY, MS. GREENWOOD! WE'RE HERE! PLORP!
FOLLOW MY LEAD! BATTLE-LON!
HEY!
CLANG CLANG
HURRY.
YOU HEARD HER, DAWN. KEEP MOVING!
I MAY NOT KNOW MUCH, BUT ONE THING I DO KNOW--IS YOU CAN DO THIS!
THANKS, GUYS!
OH, MY...
IT'S WINDING DOWN. IS THAT THE BEAT OF YOUR HEART?
CLANG CLANG

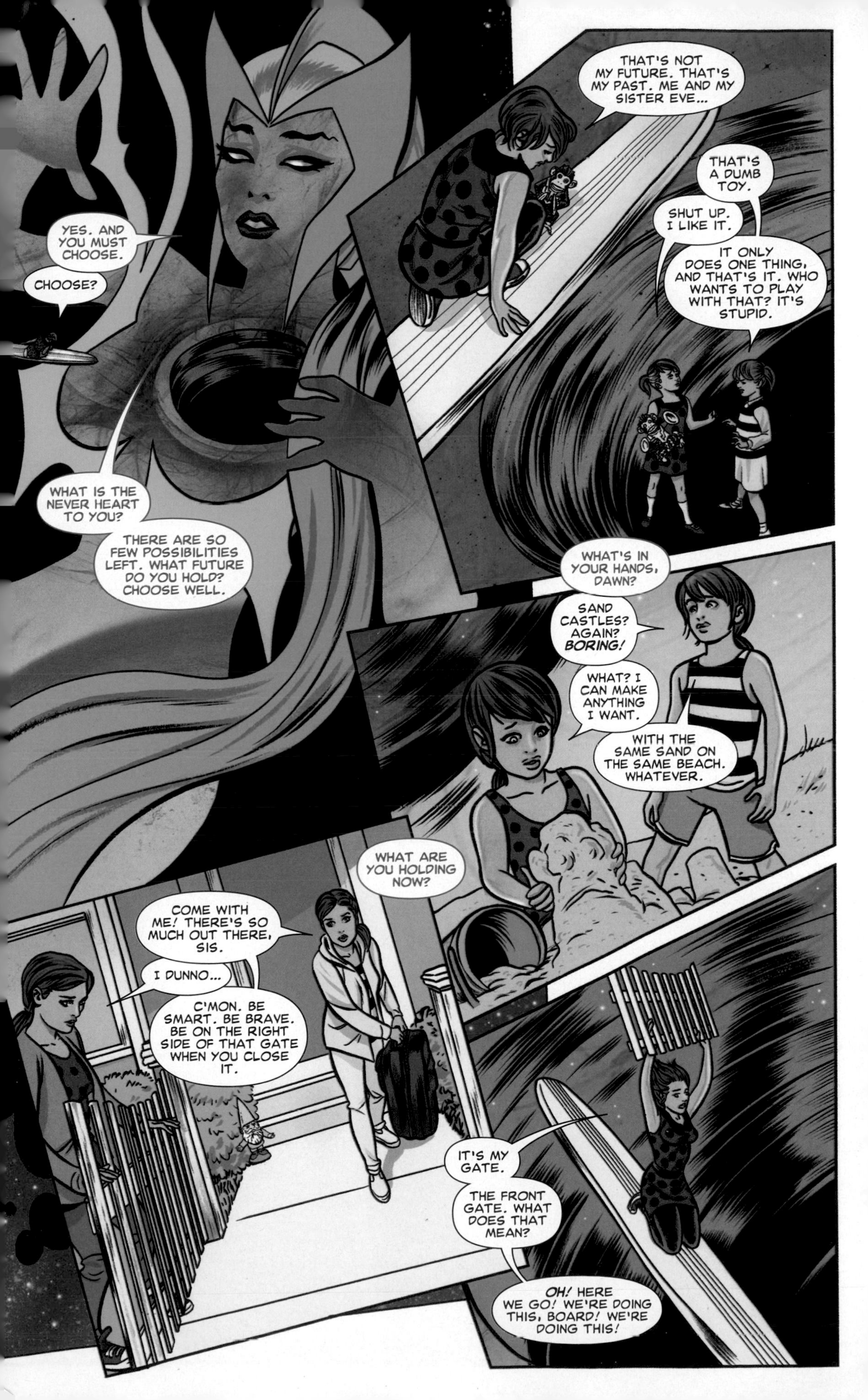
YES. AND YOU MUST CHOOSE.
CHOOSE?
WHAT IS THE NEVER HEART TO YOU?
THERE ARE SO FEW POSSIBILITIES LEFT. WHAT FUTURE DO YOU HOLD? CHOOSE WELL.
THAT'S NOT MY FUTURE. THAT'S MY PAST. ME AND MY SISTER EVE...
THAT'S A DUMB TOY.
SHUT UP. I LIKE IT.
IT ONLY DOES ONE THING, AND THAT'S IT. WHO WANTS TO PLAY WITH THAT? IT'S STUPID.
WHAT'S IN YOUR HANDS, DAWN?
SAND CASTLES? AGAIN? *BORING!*
WHAT? I CAN MAKE ANYTHING I WANT.
WITH THE SAME SAND ON THE SAME BEACH. WHATEVER.
WHAT ARE YOU HOLDING NOW?
COME WITH ME! THERE'S SO MUCH OUT THERE, SIS.
I DUNNO...
C'MON. BE SMART. BE BRAVE. BE ON THE RIGHT SIDE OF THAT GATE WHEN YOU CLOSE IT.
IT'S MY GATE.
THE FRONT GATE. WHAT DOES THAT MEAN?
OH! HERE WE GO! WE'RE DOING THIS, BOARD! WE'RE DOING THIS!

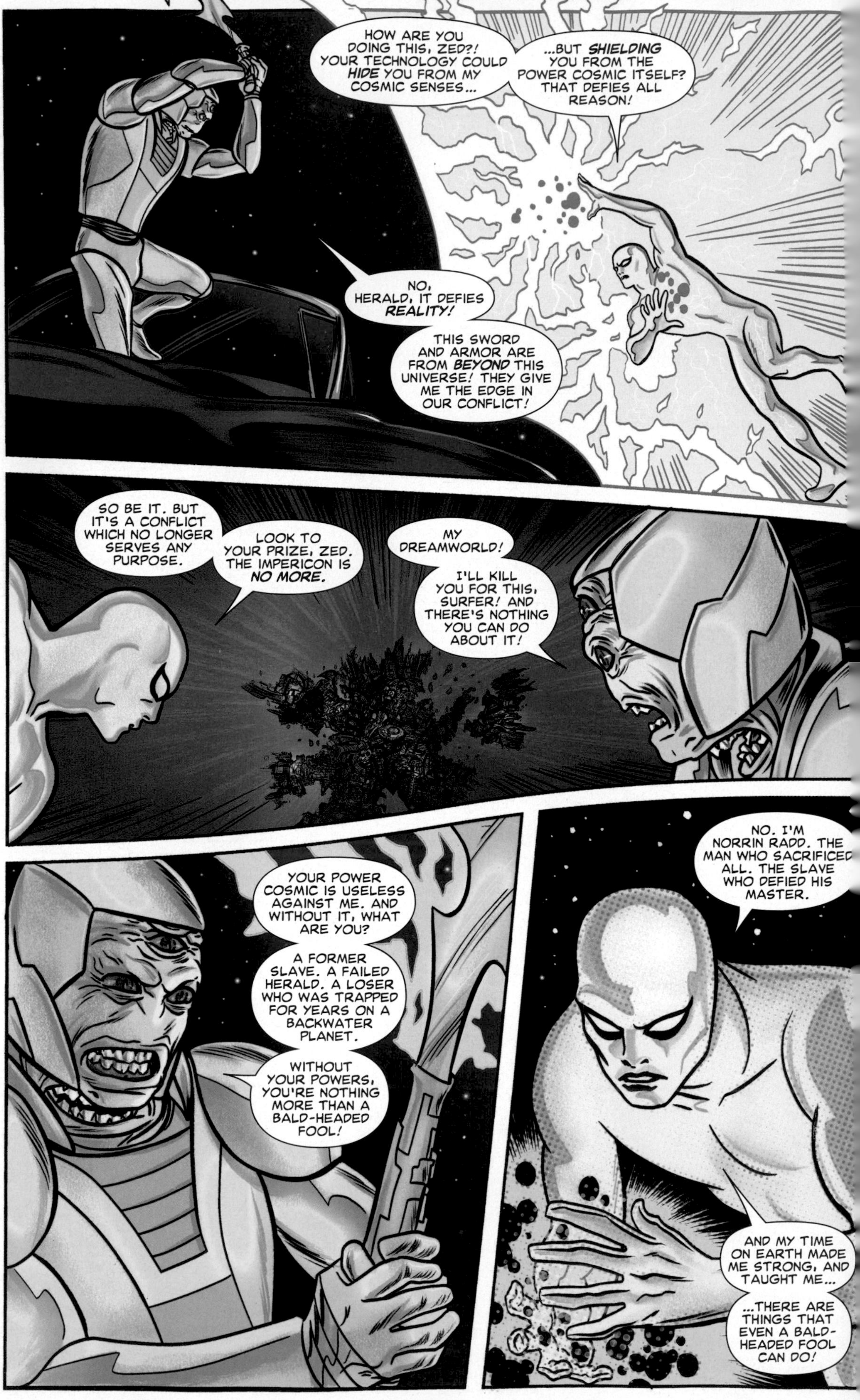
HOW ARE YOU DOING THIS, ZED?! YOUR TECHNOLOGY COULD *HIDE* YOU FROM MY COSMIC SENSES...
...BUT *SHIELDING* YOU FROM THE POWER COSMIC ITSELF? THAT DEFIES ALL REASON!
NO, HERALD, IT DEFIES *REALITY!*
THIS SWORD AND ARMOR ARE FROM *BEYOND* THIS UNIVERSE! THEY GIVE ME THE EDGE IN OUR CONFLICT!
SO BE IT. BUT IT'S A CONFLICT WHICH NO LONGER SERVES ANY PURPOSE.
LOOK TO YOUR PRIZE, ZED. THE IMPERICON IS *NO MORE.*
MY DREAMWORLD!
I'LL KILL YOU FOR THIS, SURFER! AND THERE'S NOTHING YOU CAN DO ABOUT IT!
YOUR POWER COSMIC IS USELESS AGAINST ME. AND WITHOUT IT, WHAT ARE YOU?
A FORMER SLAVE. A FAILED HERALD. A LOSER WHO WAS TRAPPED FOR YEARS ON A BACKWATER PLANET.
WITHOUT YOUR POWERS, YOU'RE NOTHING MORE THAN A BALD-HEADED FOOL!
NO. I'M NORRIN RADD. THE MAN WHO SACRIFICED ALL. THE SLAVE WHO DEFIED HIS MASTER.
AND MY TIME ON EARTH MADE ME STRONG, AND TAUGHT ME...
...THERE ARE THINGS THAT EVEN A BALD-HEADED FOOL CAN DO!

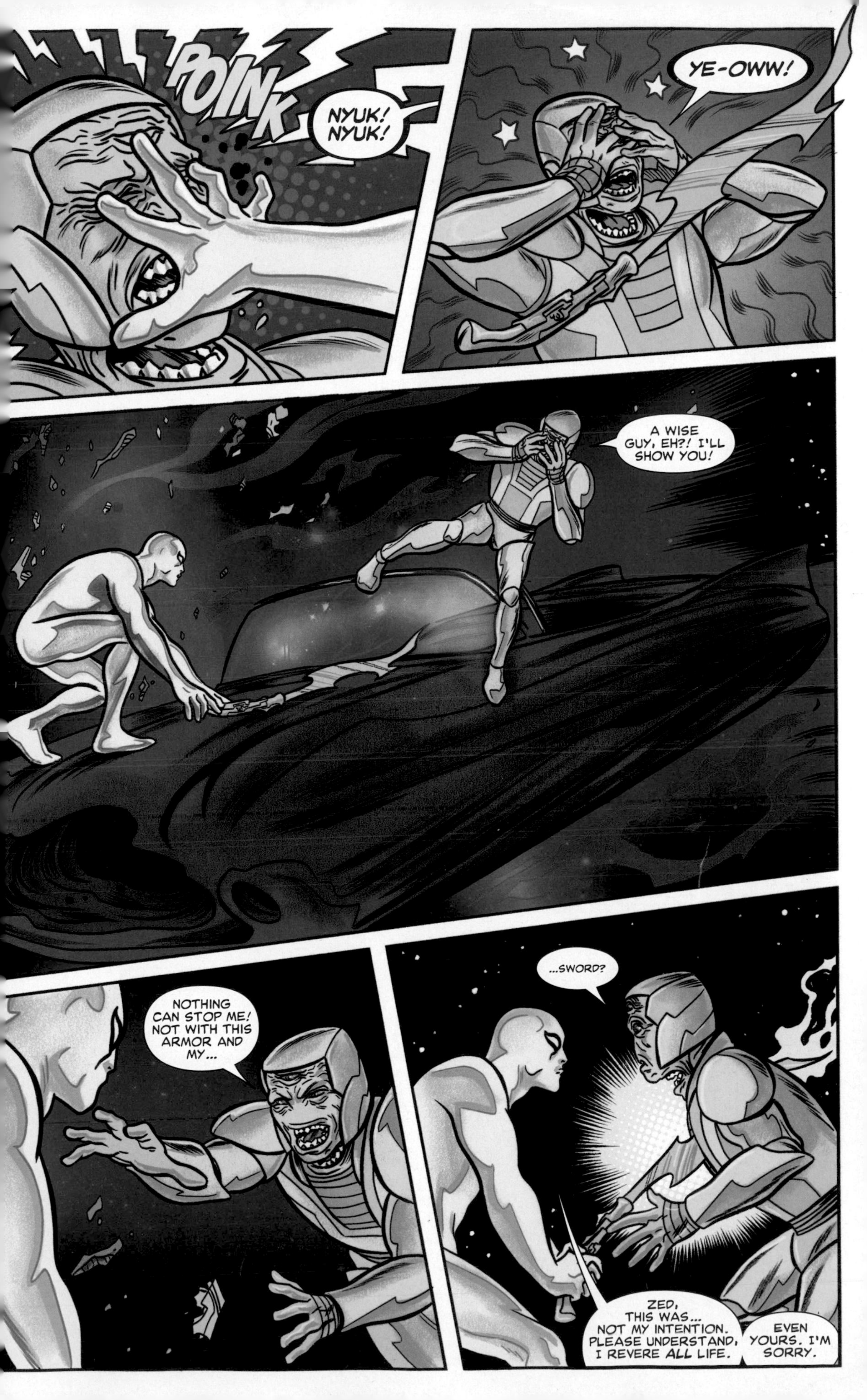
POINK
NYUK! NYUK!
YE-OWW!
A WISE GUY, EH?! I'LL SHOW YOU!
NOTHING CAN STOP ME! NOT WITH THIS ARMOR AND MY...
...SWORD?
ZED, THIS WAS... NOT MY INTENTION. PLEASE UNDERSTAND, I REVERE ALL LIFE.
EVEN YOURS. I'M SORRY.

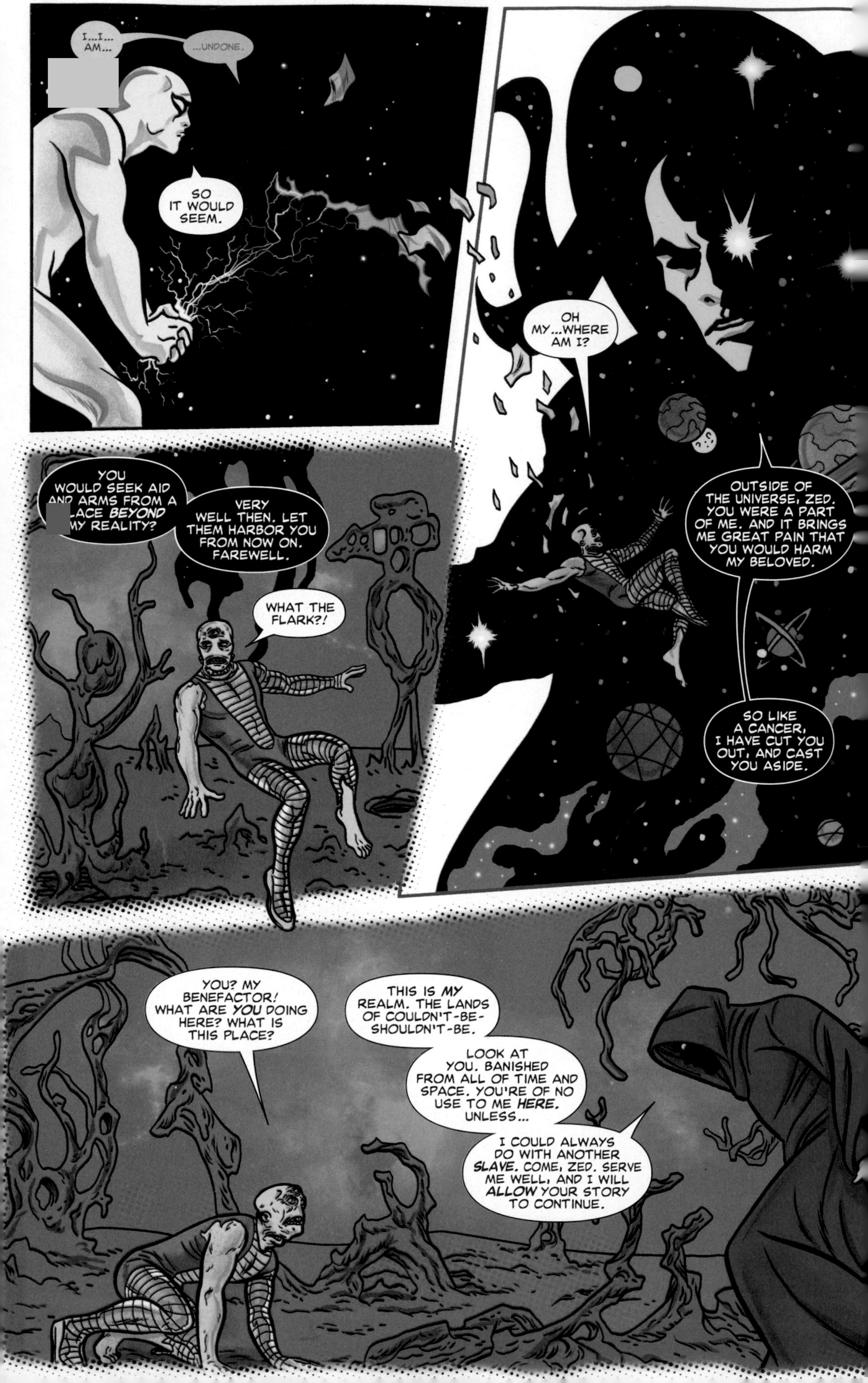

I...I... AM...
...UNDONE.
SO IT WOULD SEEM.
OH MY...WHERE AM I?
OUTSIDE OF THE UNIVERSE, ZED. YOU WERE A PART OF ME. AND IT BRINGS ME GREAT PAIN THAT YOU WOULD HARM MY BELOVED.
SO LIKE A CANCER, I HAVE CUT YOU OUT, AND CAST YOU ASIDE.
YOU WOULD SEEK AID AND ARMS FROM A LACE *BEYOND* MY REALITY?
VERY WELL THEN. LET THEM HARBOR YOU FROM NOW ON. FAREWELL.
WHAT THE FLARK?!
YOU? MY BENEFACTOR! WHAT ARE *YOU* DOING HERE? WHAT IS THIS PLACE?
THIS IS *MY* REALM. THE LANDS OF COULDN'T-BE-SHOULDN'T-BE.
LOOK AT YOU. BANISHED FROM ALL OF TIME AND SPACE. YOU'RE OF NO USE TO ME *HERE.* UNLESS...
I COULD ALWAYS DO WITH ANOTHER *SLAVE.* COME, ZED. SERVE ME WELL, AND I WILL *ALLOW* YOUR STORY TO CONTINUE.

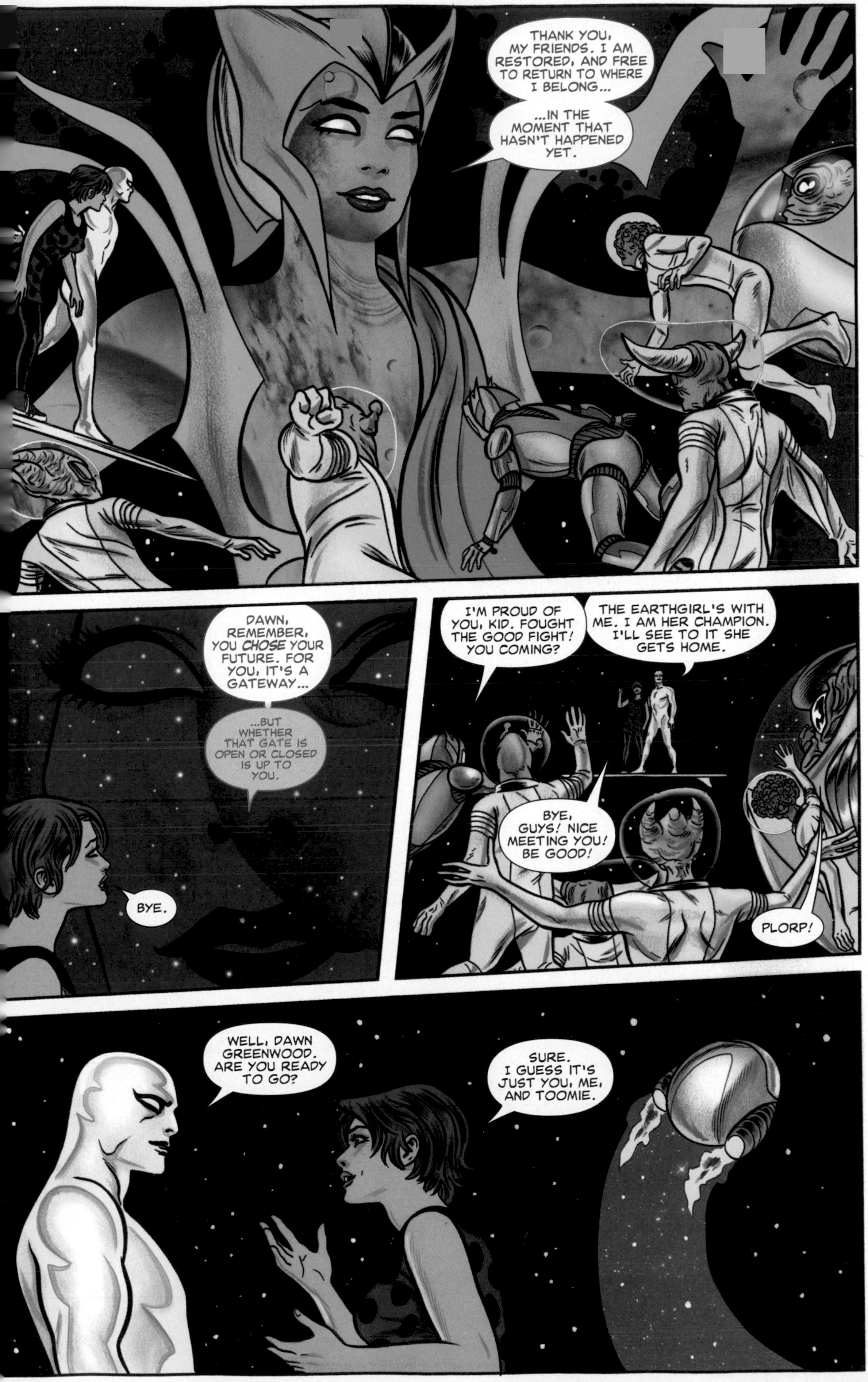
THANK YOU, MY FRIENDS. I AM RESTORED, AND FREE TO RETURN TO WHERE I BELONG...
...IN THE MOMENT THAT HASN'T HAPPENED YET.
DAWN, REMEMBER, YOU *CHOSE* YOUR FUTURE. FOR YOU, IT'S A GATEWAY...
...BUT WHETHER THAT GATE IS OPEN OR CLOSED IS UP TO YOU.
BYE.
I'M PROUD OF YOU, KID. FOUGHT THE GOOD FIGHT! YOU COMING?
THE EARTHGIRL'S WITH ME. I AM HER CHAMPION. I'LL SEE TO IT SHE GETS HOME.
BYE, GUYS! NICE MEETING YOU! BE GOOD!
PLORP!
WELL, DAWN GREENWOOD. ARE YOU READY TO GO?
SURE. I GUESS IT'S JUST YOU, ME, AND TOOMIE.

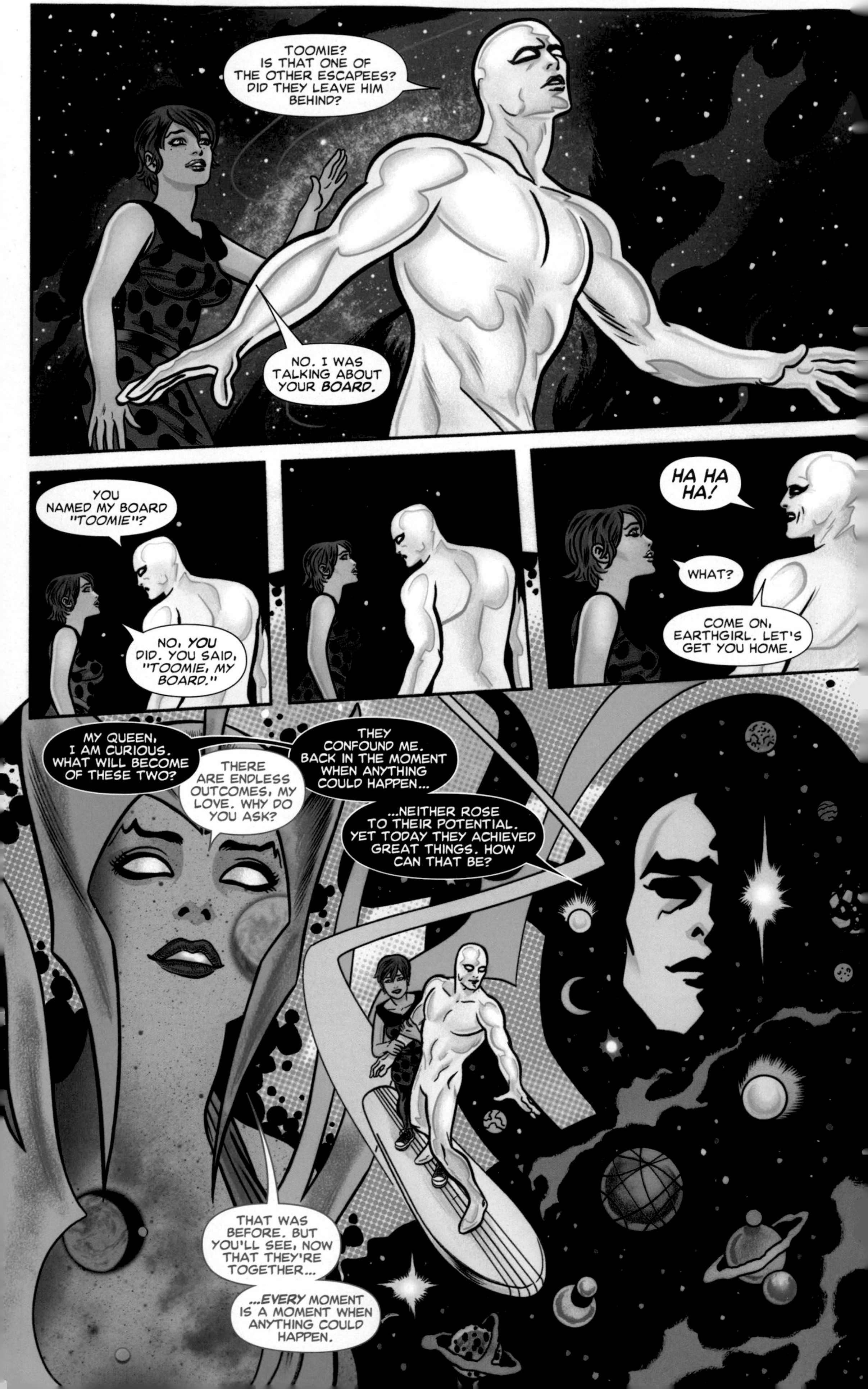
TOOMIE? IS THAT ONE OF THE OTHER ESCAPEES? DID THEY LEAVE HIM BEHIND?
NO. I WAS TALKING ABOUT YOUR BOARD.
YOU NAMED MY BOARD "TOOMIE"?
NO, YOU DID. YOU SAID, "TOOMIE, MY BOARD."
HA HA HA!
WHAT?
COME ON, EARTHGIRL. LET'S GET YOU HOME.
MY QUEEN, I AM CURIOUS. WHAT WILL BECOME OF THESE TWO?
THERE ARE ENDLESS OUTCOMES, MY LOVE. WHY DO YOU ASK?
THEY CONFOUND ME. BACK IN THE MOMENT WHEN ANYTHING COULD HAPPEN...
...NEITHER ROSE TO THEIR POTENTIAL. YET TODAY THEY ACHIEVED GREAT THINGS. HOW CAN THAT BE?
THAT WAS BEFORE. BUT YOU'LL SEE, NOW THAT THEY'RE TOGETHER...
...EVERY MOMENT IS A MOMENT WHEN ANYTHING COULD HAPPEN.

4

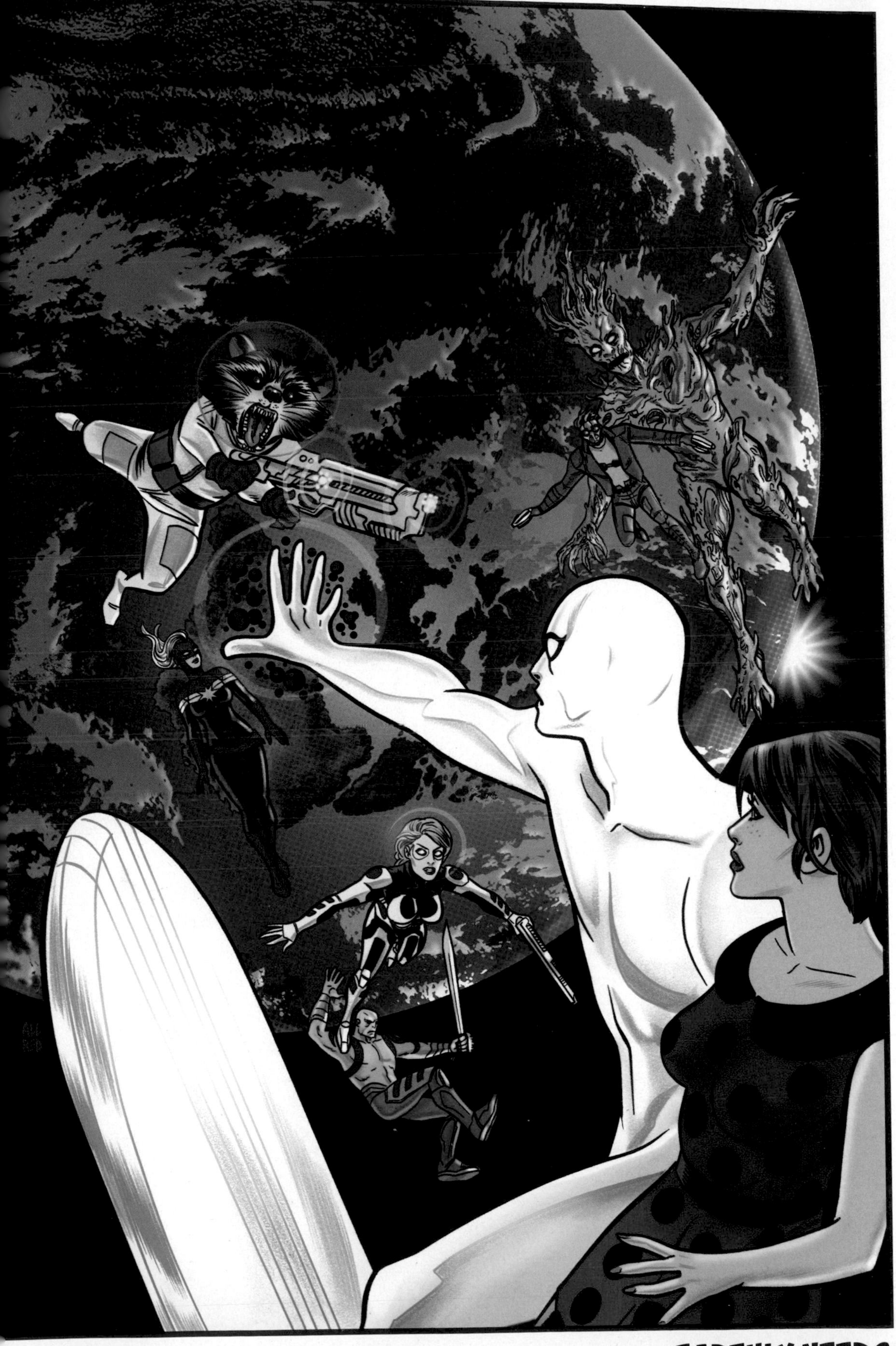

EARTHLY NEEDS

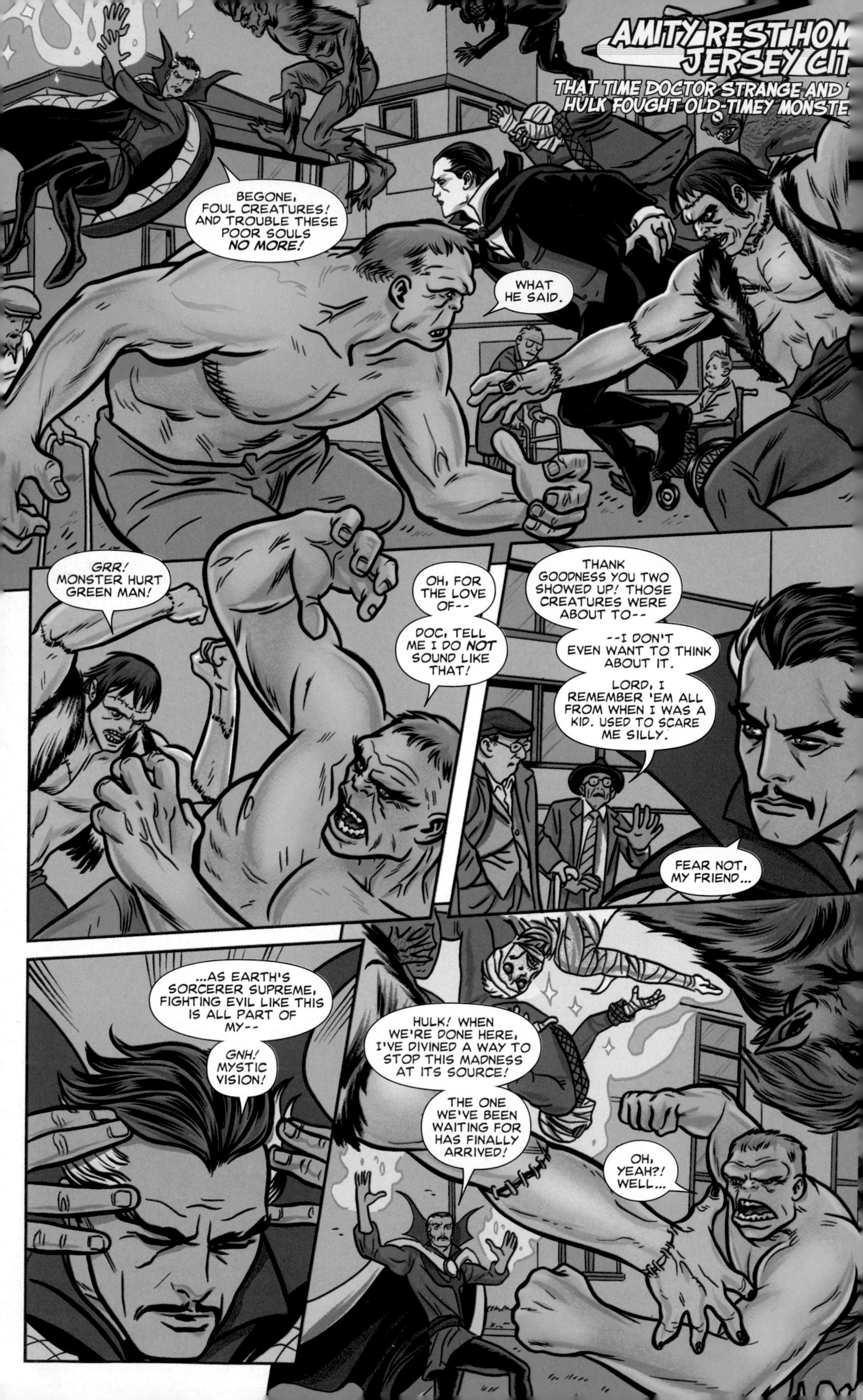
AMITY REST HOM
JERSEY CIT
THAT TIME DOCTOR STRANGE AND
HULK FOUGHT OLD-TIMEY MONSTE
BEGONE, FOUL CREATURES! AND TROUBLE THESE POOR SOULS NO MORE!
WHAT HE SAID.
GRR! MONSTER HURT GREEN MAN!
OH, FOR THE LOVE OF--
DOC, TELL ME I DO NOT SOUND LIKE THAT!
THANK GOODNESS YOU TWO SHOWED UP! THOSE CREATURES WERE ABOUT TO--
--I DON'T EVEN WANT TO THINK ABOUT IT.
LORD, I REMEMBER 'EM ALL FROM WHEN I WAS A KID. USED TO SCARE ME SILLY.
FEAR NOT, MY FRIEND...
...AS EARTH'S SORCERER SUPREME, FIGHTING EVIL LIKE THIS IS ALL PART OF MY--
GNH! MYSTIC VISION!
HULK! WHEN WE'RE DONE HERE, I'VE DIVINED A WAY TO STOP THIS MADNESS AT ITS SOURCE!
THE ONE WE'VE BEEN WAITING FOR HAS FINALLY ARRIVED!
OH, YEAH?! WELL...

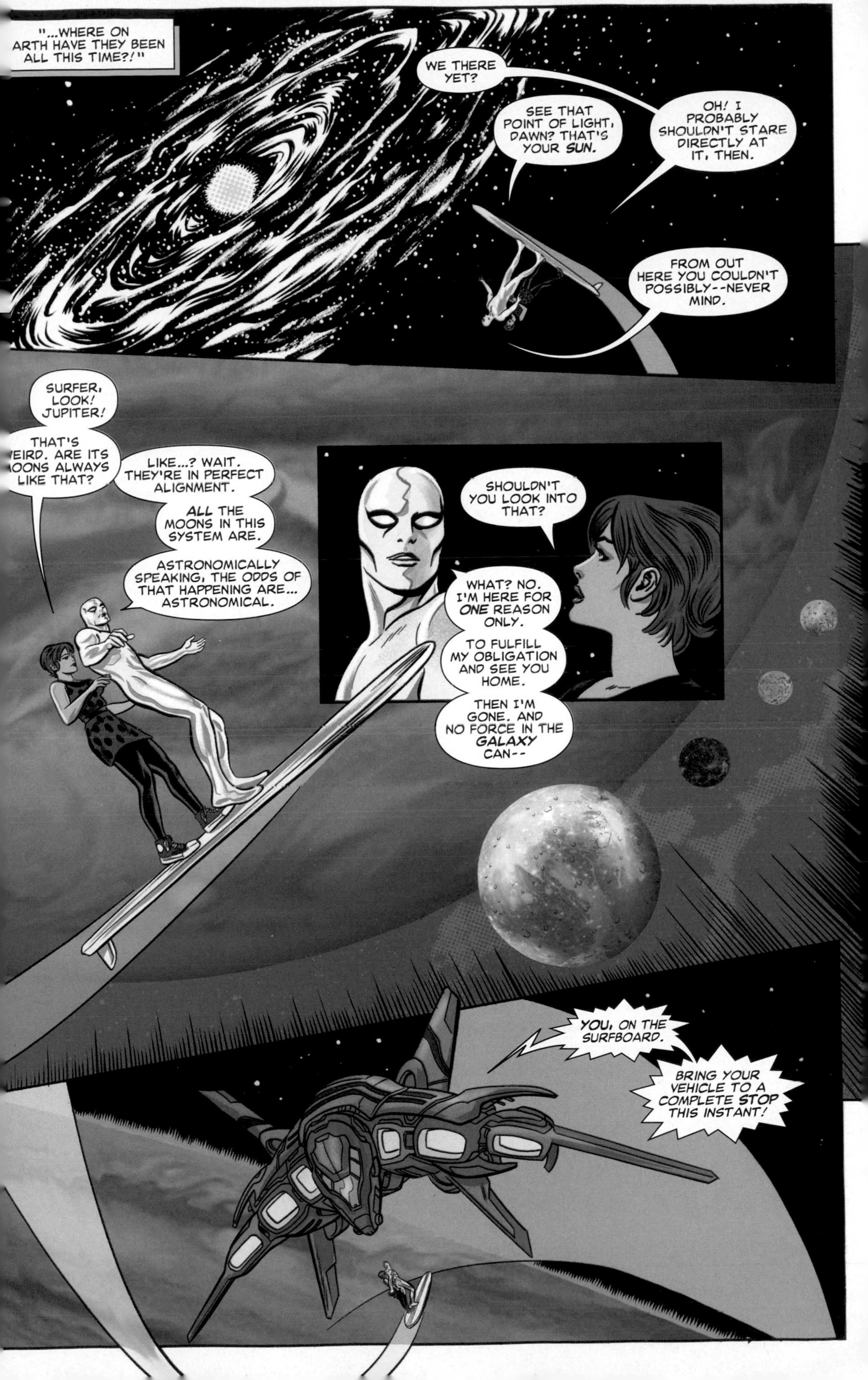
"...WHERE ON
ARTH HAVE THEY BEEN ALL THIS TIME?!"
WE THERE YET?
SEE THAT POINT OF LIGHT, DAWN? THAT'S YOUR SUN.
OH! I PROBABLY SHOULDN'T STARE DIRECTLY AT IT, THEN.
FROM OUT HERE YOU COULDN'T POSSIBLY--NEVER MIND.
SURFER, LOOK! JUPITER!
THAT'S EIRD. ARE ITS OONS ALWAYS LIKE THAT?
LIKE...? WAIT. THEY'RE IN PERFECT ALIGNMENT.
ALL THE MOONS IN THIS SYSTEM ARE.
ASTRONOMICALLY SPEAKING, THE ODDS OF THAT HAPPENING ARE... ASTRONOMICAL.
SHOULDN'T YOU LOOK INTO THAT?
WHAT? NO. I'M HERE FOR ONE REASON ONLY.
TO FULFILL MY OBLIGATION AND SEE YOU HOME.
THEN I'M GONE. AND NO FORCE IN THE GALAXY CAN--
YOU, ON THE SURFBOARD.
BRING YOUR VEHICLE TO A COMPLETE STOP THIS INSTANT!

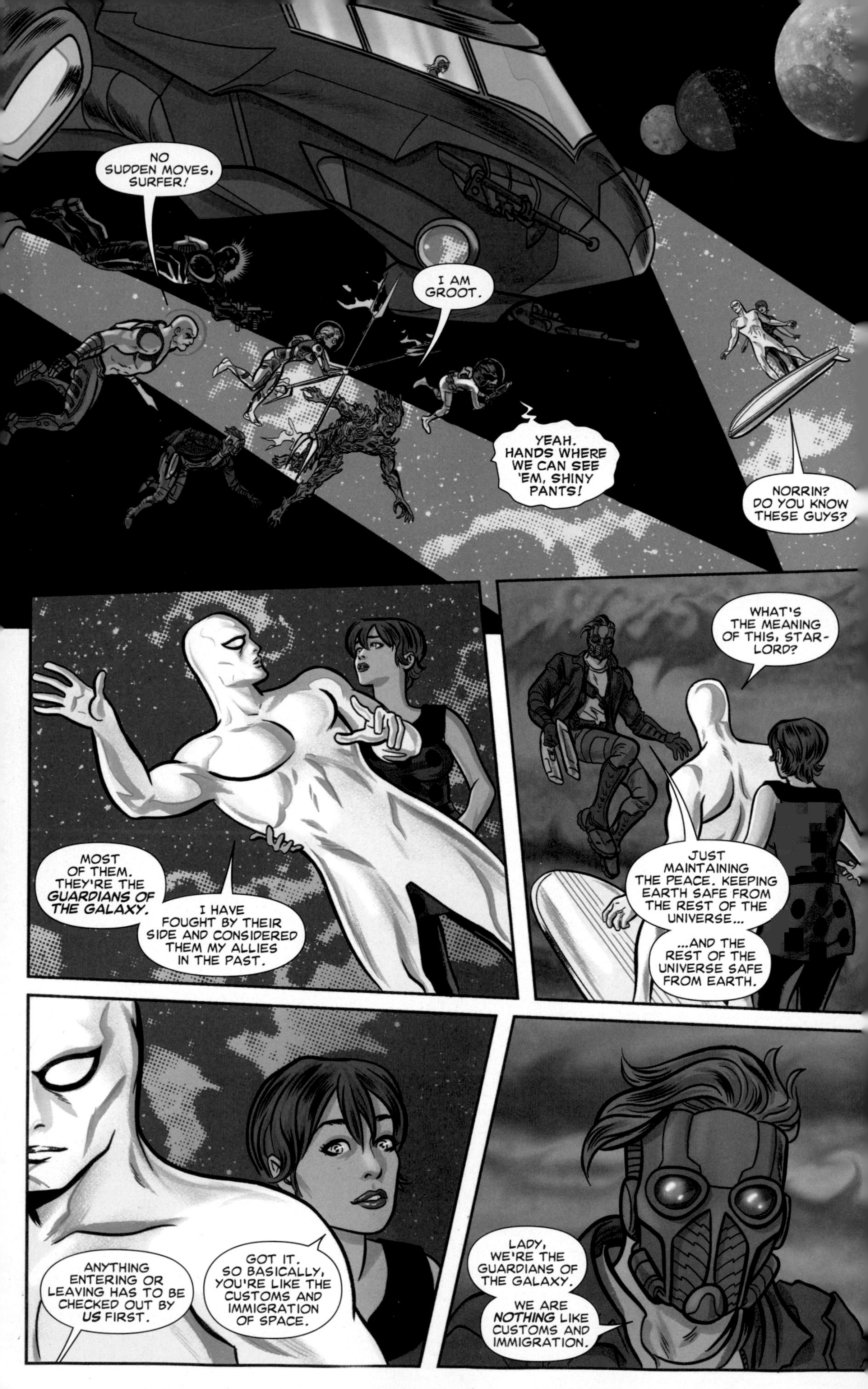
NO SUDDEN MOVES, SURFER!
I AM GROOT.
YEAH. HANDS WHERE WE CAN SEE 'EM, SHINY PANTS!
NORRIN? DO YOU KNOW THESE GUYS?
MOST OF THEM. THEY'RE THE *GUARDIANS OF THE GALAXY.*
I HAVE FOUGHT BY THEIR SIDE AND CONSIDERED THEM MY ALLIES IN THE PAST.
WHAT'S THE MEANING OF THIS, STAR-LORD?
JUST MAINTAINING THE PEACE. KEEPING EARTH SAFE FROM THE REST OF THE UNIVERSE...
...AND THE REST OF THE UNIVERSE SAFE FROM EARTH.
ANYTHING ENTERING OR LEAVING HAS TO BE CHECKED OUT BY *US* FIRST.
GOT IT. SO BASICALLY, YOU'RE LIKE THE CUSTOMS AND IMMIGRATION OF SPACE.
LADY, WE'RE THE GUARDIANS OF THE GALAXY.
WE ARE *NOTHING* LIKE CUSTOMS AND IMMIGRATION.

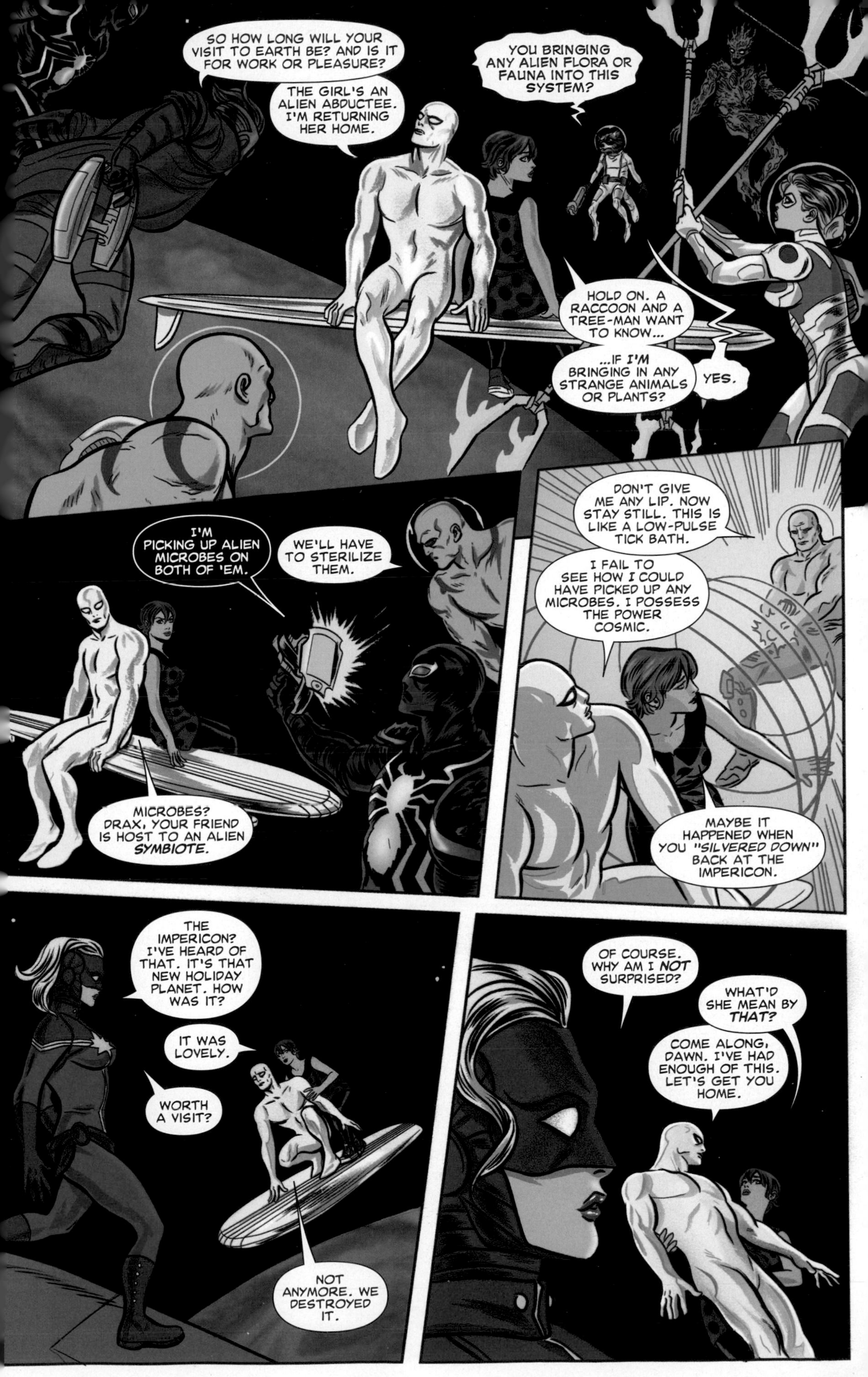
SO HOW LONG WILL YOUR VISIT TO EARTH BE? AND IS IT FOR WORK OR PLEASURE?
THE GIRL'S AN ALIEN ABDUCTEE. I'M RETURNING HER HOME.
YOU BRINGING ANY ALIEN FLORA OR FAUNA INTO THIS SYSTEM?
HOLD ON. A RACCOON AND A TREE-MAN WANT TO KNOW...
...IF I'M BRINGING IN ANY STRANGE ANIMALS OR PLANTS?
YES.
I'M PICKING UP ALIEN MICROBES ON BOTH OF 'EM.
WE'LL HAVE TO STERILIZE THEM.
MICROBES? DRAX, YOUR FRIEND IS HOST TO AN ALIEN SYMBIOTE.
DON'T GIVE ME ANY LIP. NOW STAY STILL. THIS IS LIKE A LOW-PULSE TICK BATH.
I FAIL TO SEE HOW I COULD HAVE PICKED UP ANY MICROBES. I POSSESS THE POWER COSMIC.
MAYBE IT HAPPENED WHEN YOU "SILVERED DOWN" BACK AT THE IMPERICON.
THE IMPERICON? I'VE HEARD OF THAT. IT'S THAT NEW HOLIDAY PLANET. HOW WAS IT?
IT WAS LOVELY.
WORTH A VISIT?
NOT ANYMORE. WE DESTROYED IT.
OF COURSE. WHY AM I NOT SURPRISED?
WHAT'D SHE MEAN BY THAT?
COME ALONG, DAWN. I'VE HAD ENOUGH OF THIS. LET'S GET YOU HOME.

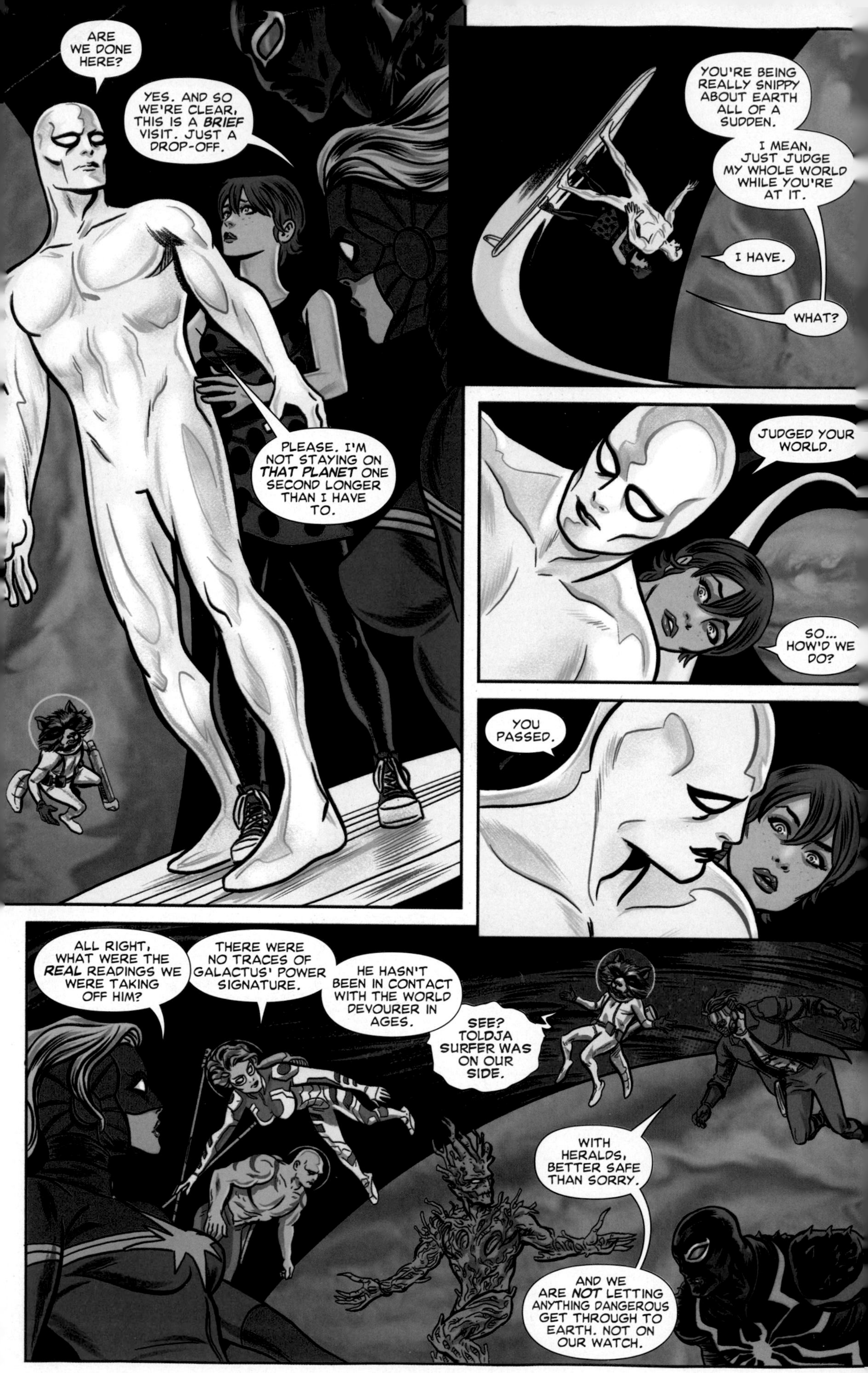

ARE WE DONE HERE?
YES. AND SO WE'RE CLEAR, THIS IS A *BRIEF* VISIT. JUST A DROP-OFF.
PLEASE. I'M NOT STAYING ON *THAT PLANET* ONE SECOND LONGER THAN I HAVE TO.
YOU'RE BEING REALLY SNIPPY ABOUT EARTH ALL OF A SUDDEN.
I MEAN, JUST JUDGE MY WHOLE WORLD WHILE YOU'RE AT IT.
I HAVE.
WHAT?
JUDGED YOUR WORLD.
SO... HOW'D WE DO?
YOU PASSED.
ALL RIGHT, WHAT WERE THE *REAL* READINGS WE WERE TAKING OFF HIM?
THERE WERE NO TRACES OF GALACTUS' POWER SIGNATURE.
HE HASN'T BEEN IN CONTACT WITH THE WORLD DEVOURER IN AGES.
SEE? TOLDJA SURFER WAS ON OUR SIDE.
WITH HERALDS, BETTER SAFE THAN SORRY.
AND WE ARE *NOT* LETTING ANYTHING DANGEROUS GET THROUGH TO EARTH. NOT ON OUR WATCH.

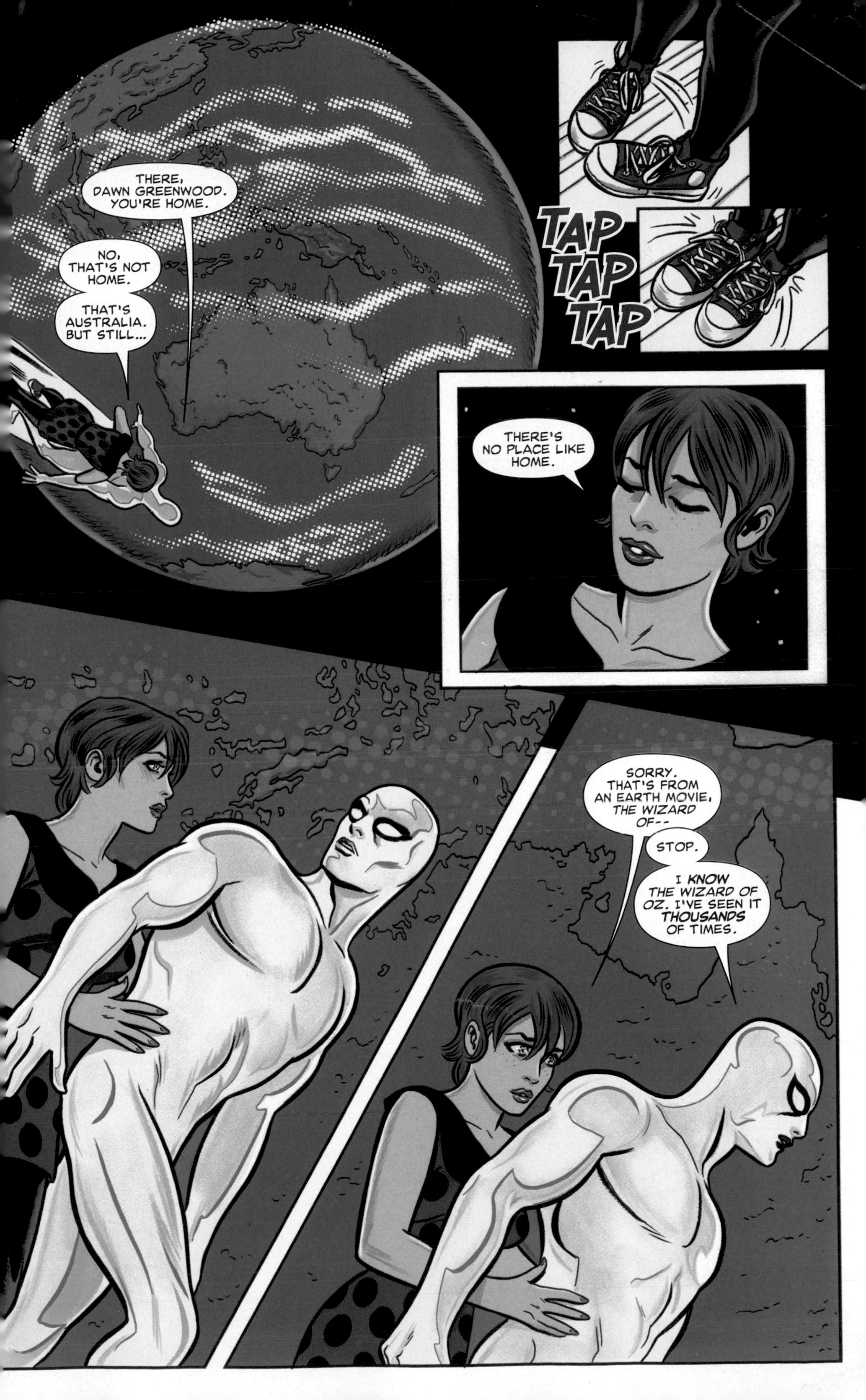
THERE, DAWN GREENWOOD. YOU'RE HOME.
NO, THAT'S NOT HOME.
THAT'S AUSTRALIA. BUT STILL...
TAP TAP TAP
THERE'S NO PLACE LIKE HOME.
SORRY. THAT'S FROM AN EARTH MOVIE, THE WIZARD OF--
STOP.
I KNOW THE WIZARD OF OZ. I'VE SEEN IT THOUSANDS OF TIMES.

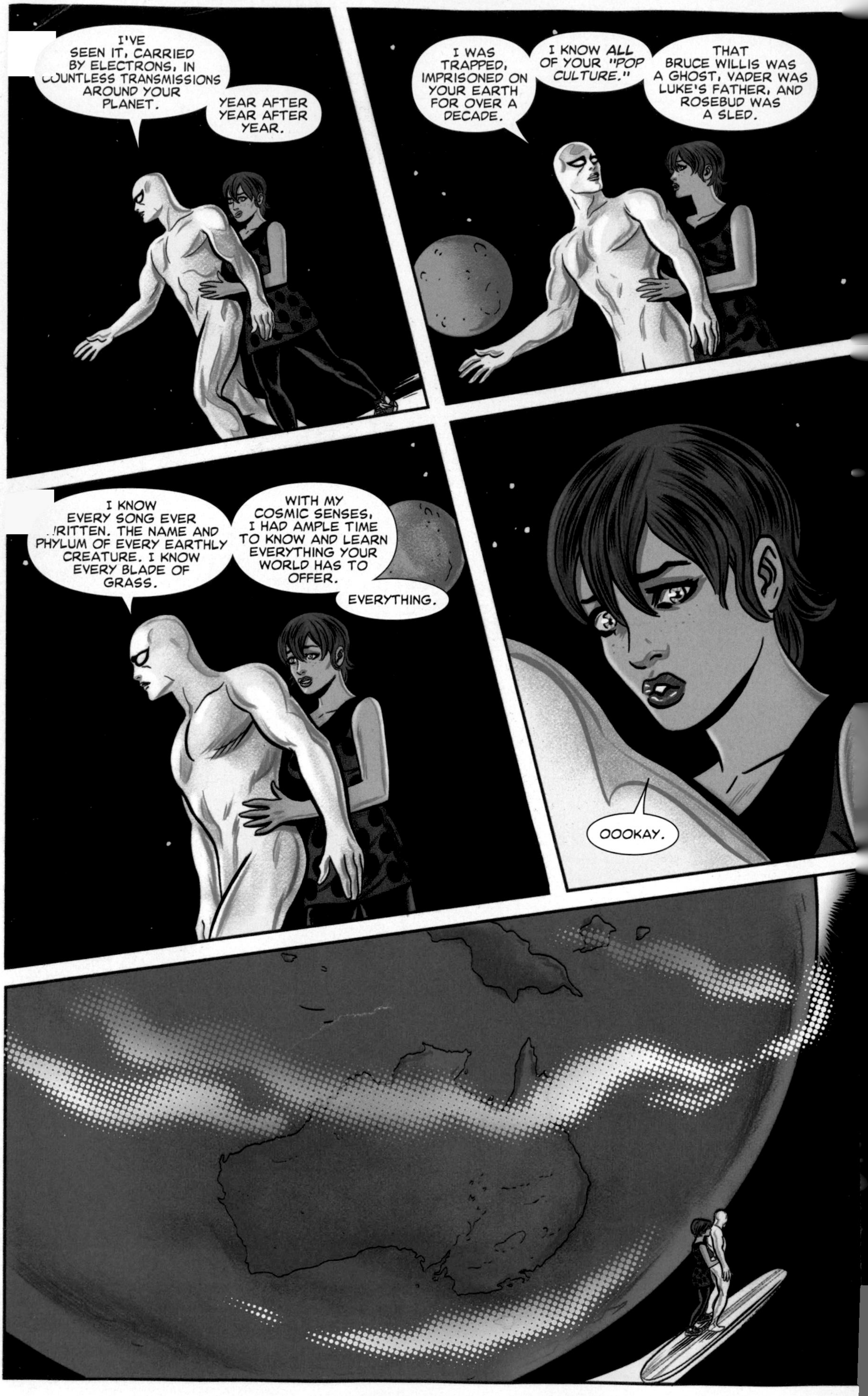
I'VE SEEN IT, CARRIED BY ELECTRONS, IN COUNTLESS TRANSMISSIONS AROUND YOUR PLANET.
YEAR AFTER YEAR AFTER YEAR.
I WAS TRAPPED, IMPRISONED ON YOUR EARTH FOR OVER A DECADE.
I KNOW ALL OF YOUR "POP CULTURE."
THAT BRUCE WILLIS WAS A GHOST, VADER WAS LUKE'S FATHER, AND ROSEBUD WAS A SLED.
I KNOW EVERY SONG EVER WRITTEN. THE NAME AND PHYLUM OF EVERY EARTHLY CREATURE. I KNOW EVERY BLADE OF GRASS.
WITH MY COSMIC SENSES, I HAD AMPLE TIME TO KNOW AND LEARN EVERYTHING YOUR WORLD HAS TO OFFER.
EVERYTHING.
OOOKAY.

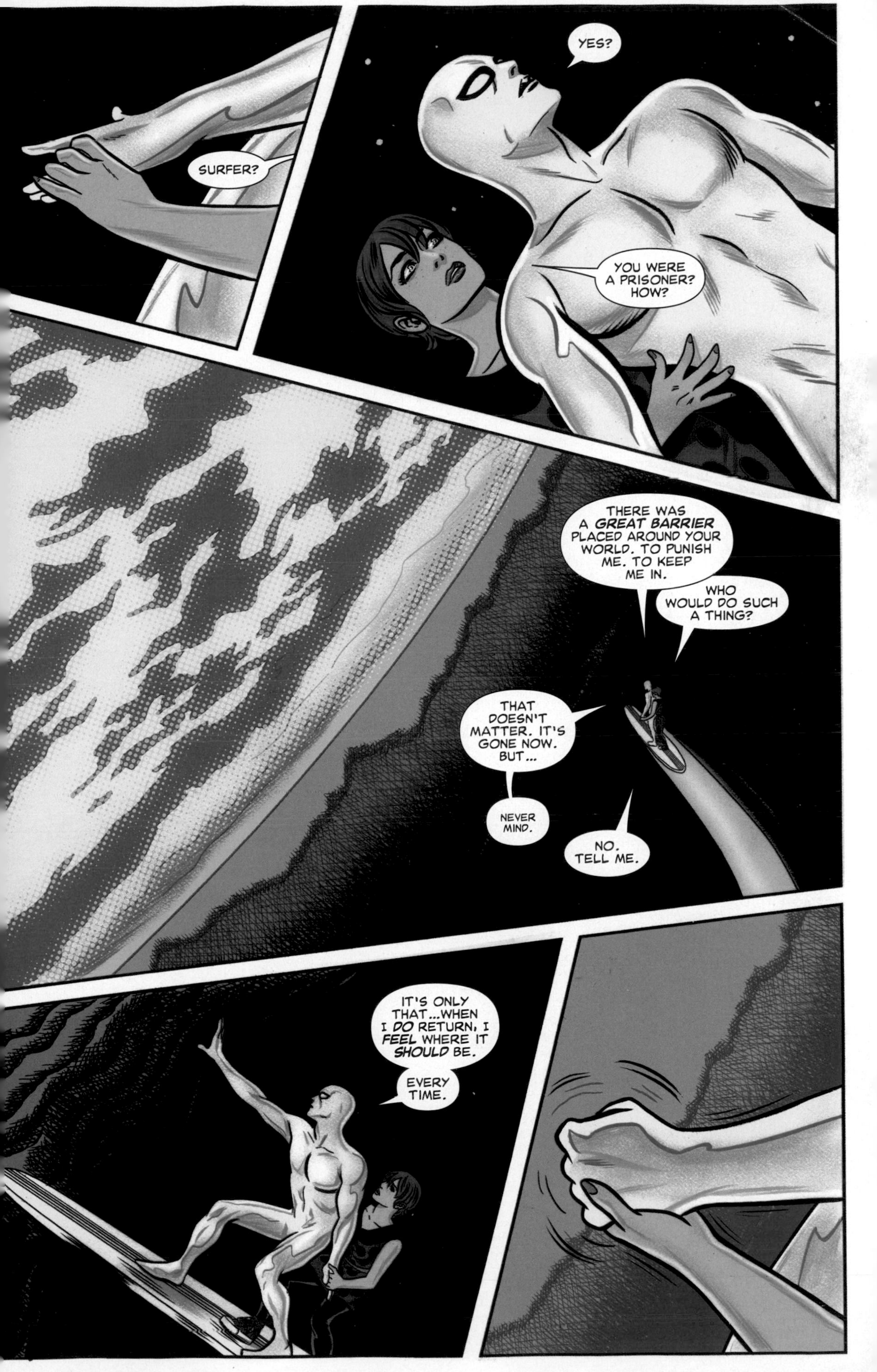
SURFER?
YES?
YOU WERE A PRISONER? HOW?
THERE WAS A GREAT BARRIER PLACED AROUND YOUR WORLD. TO PUNISH ME. TO KEEP ME IN.
WHO WOULD DO SUCH A THING?
THAT DOESN'T MATTER. IT'S GONE NOW. BUT...
NEVER MIND.
NO. TELL ME.
IT'S ONLY THAT...WHEN I DO RETURN, I FEEL WHERE IT SHOULD BE.
EVERY TIME.

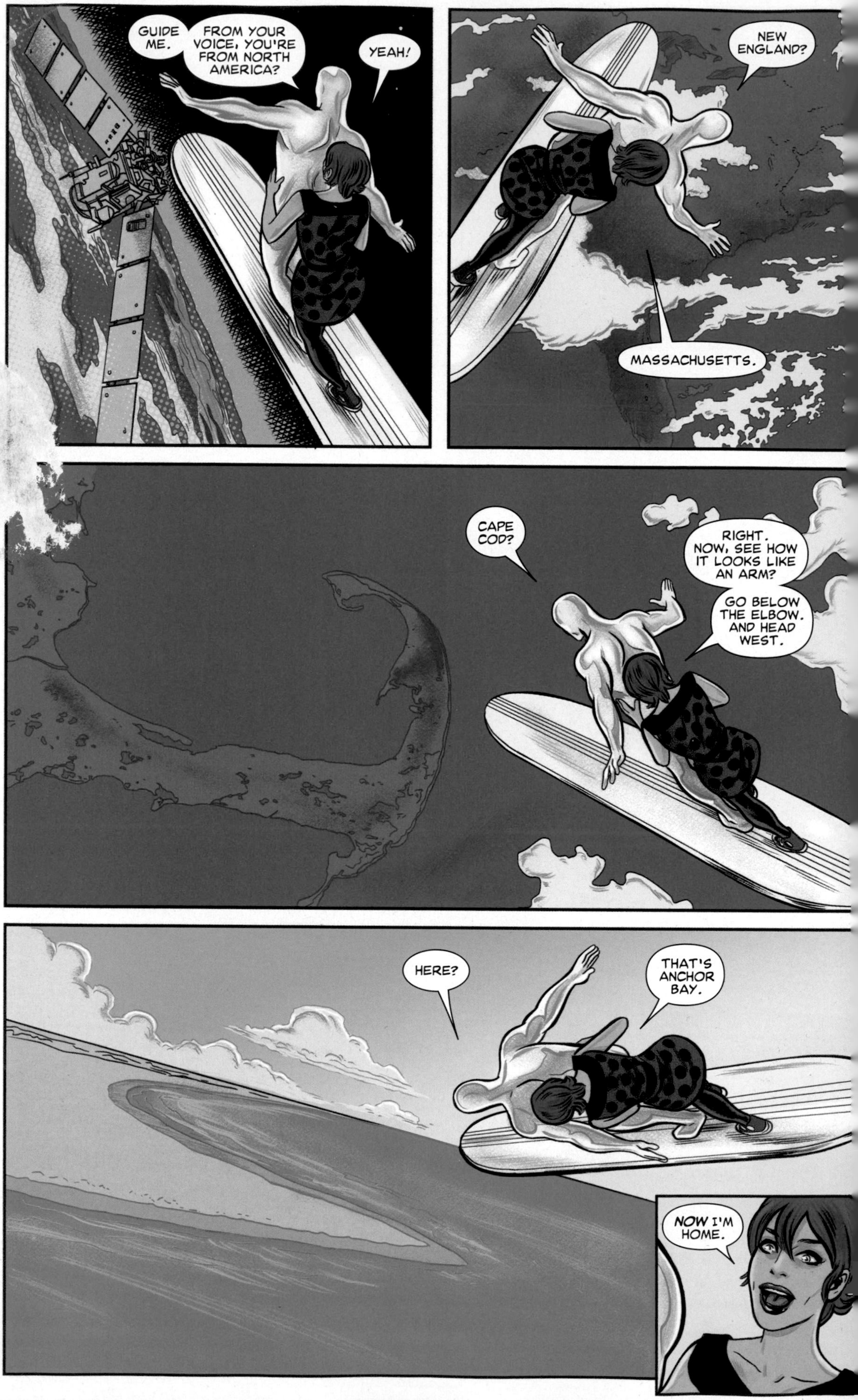
GUIDE ME.
FROM YOUR VOICE, YOU'RE FROM NORTH AMERICA?
YEAH!
NEW ENGLAND?
MASSACHUSETTS.
CAPE COD?
RIGHT. NOW, SEE HOW IT LOOKS LIKE AN ARM?
GO BELOW THE ELBOW. AND HEAD WEST.
HERE?
THAT'S ANCHOR BAY.
NOW I'M HOME.

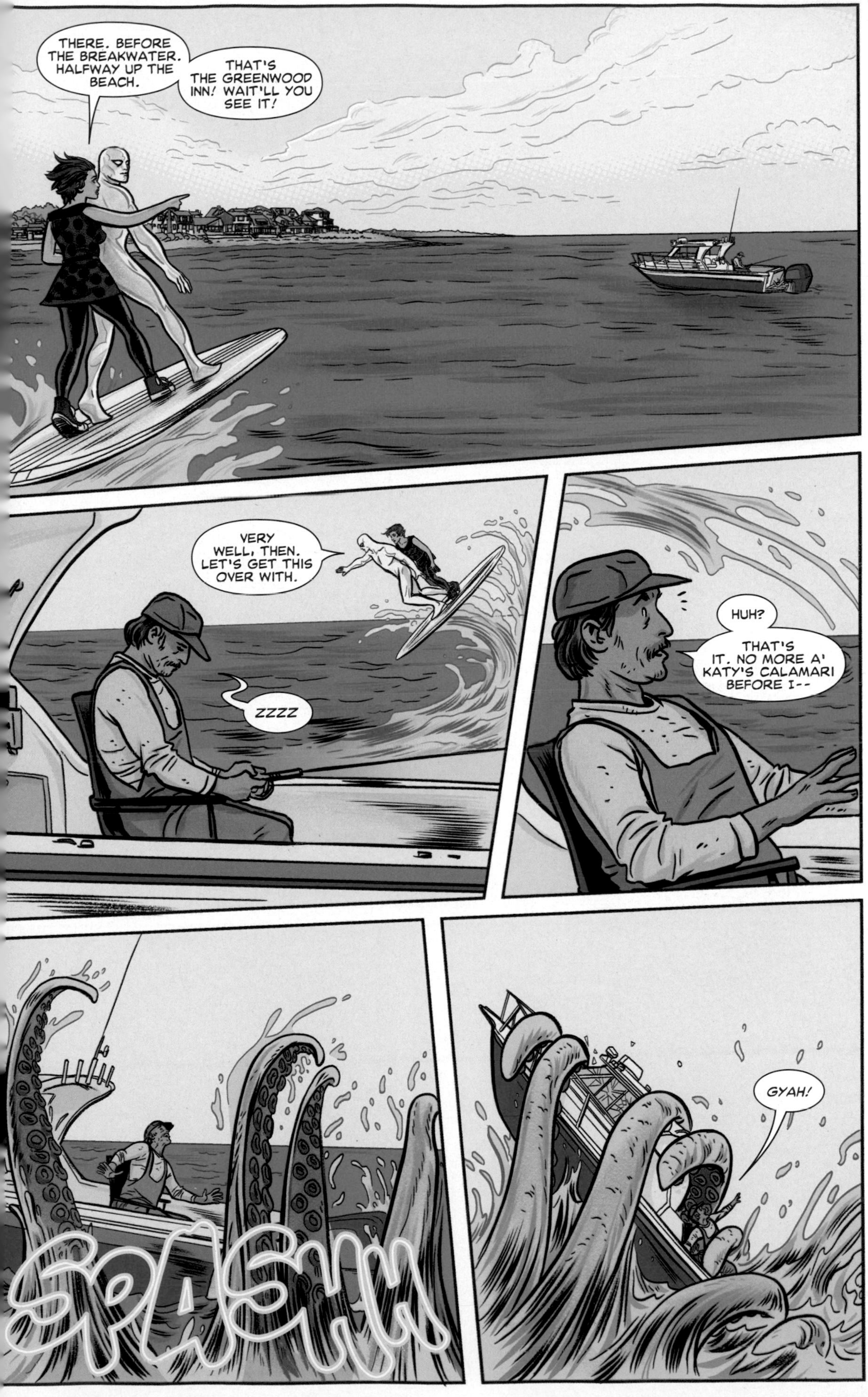
THERE. BEFORE THE BREAKWATER. HALFWAY UP THE BEACH.
THAT'S THE GREENWOOD INN! WAIT'LL YOU SEE IT!
VERY WELL, THEN. LET'S GET THIS OVER WITH.
ZZZZ
HUH?
THAT'S IT. NO MORE A' KATY'S CALAMARI BEFORE I--
SPASHH
GYAH!

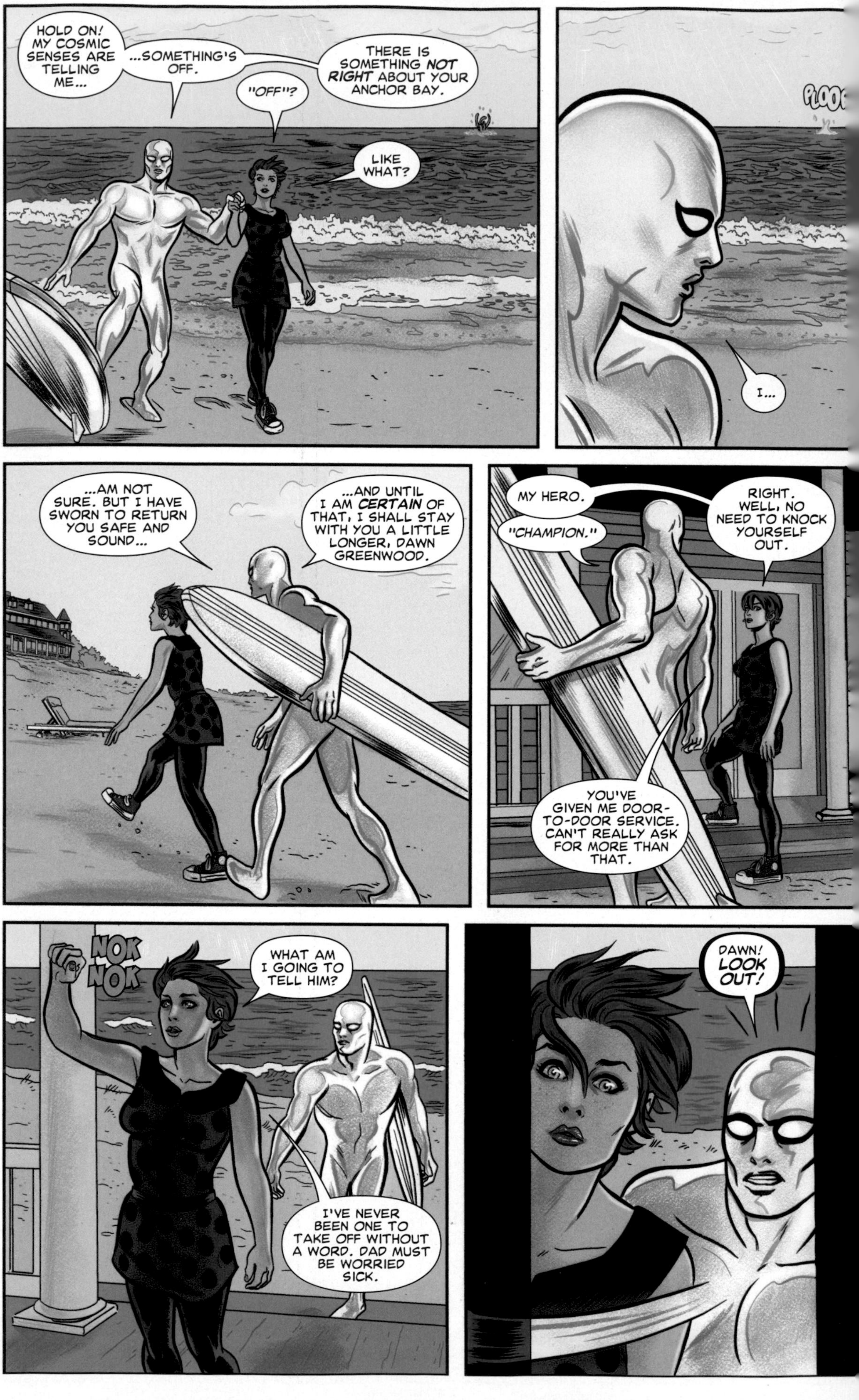

HOLD ON! MY COSMIC SENSES ARE TELLING ME...
...SOMETHING'S OFF.
"OFF"?
THERE IS SOMETHING NOT RIGHT ABOUT YOUR ANCHOR BAY.
LIKE WHAT?
PLOOS
I...
...AM NOT SURE. BUT I HAVE SWORN TO RETURN YOU SAFE AND SOUND...
...AND UNTIL I AM CERTAIN OF THAT, I SHALL STAY WITH YOU A LITTLE LONGER, DAWN GREENWOOD.
MY HERO.
"CHAMPION."
RIGHT. WELL, NO NEED TO KNOCK YOURSELF OUT.
YOU'VE GIVEN ME DOOR-TO-DOOR SERVICE. CAN'T REALLY ASK FOR MORE THAN THAT.
NOK NOK
WHAT AM I GOING TO TELL HIM?
I'VE NEVER BEEN ONE TO TAKE OFF WITHOUT A WORD. DAD MUST BE WORRIED SICK.
DAWN! LOOK OUT!

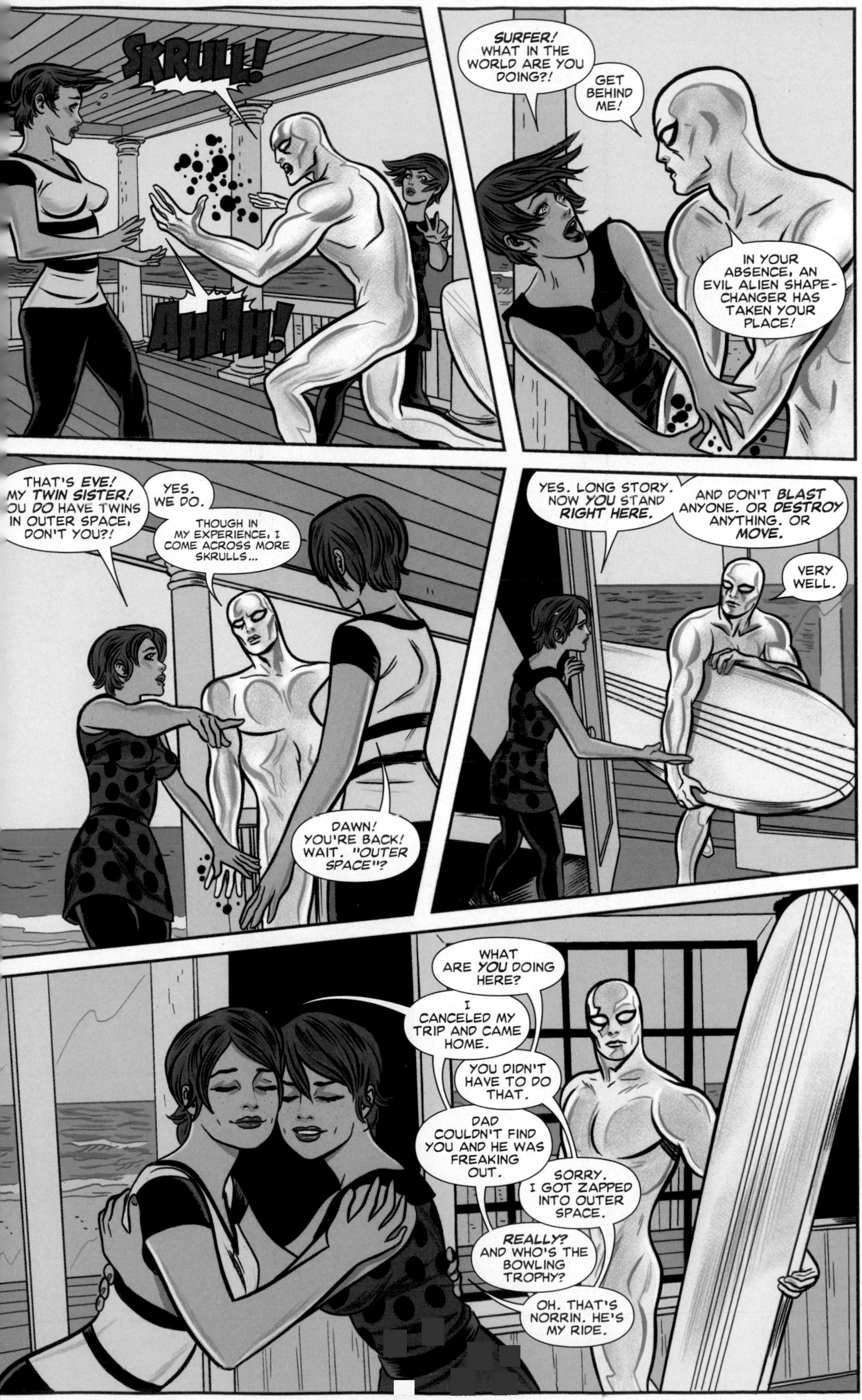
SKRULL!
AHHHH!
SURFER! WHAT IN THE WORLD ARE YOU DOING?!
GET BEHIND ME!
IN YOUR ABSENCE, AN EVIL ALIEN SHAPE-CHANGER HAS TAKEN YOUR PLACE!
THAT'S EVE! MY TWIN SISTER! OU DO HAVE TWINS IN OUTER SPACE, DON'T YOU?!
YES. WE DO.
THOUGH IN MY EXPERIENCE, I COME ACROSS MORE SKRULLS...
DAWN! YOU'RE BACK! WAIT. "OUTER SPACE"?
YES. LONG STORY. NOW YOU STAND RIGHT HERE.
AND DON'T BLAST ANYONE. OR DESTROY ANYTHING. OR MOVE.
VERY WELL.
WHAT ARE YOU DOING HERE?
I CANCELED MY TRIP AND CAME HOME.
YOU DIDN'T HAVE TO DO THAT.
DAD COULDN'T FIND YOU AND HE WAS FREAKING OUT.
SORRY. I GOT ZAPPED INTO OUTER SPACE.
REALLY? AND WHO'S THE BOWLING TROPHY?
OH. THAT'S NORRIN. HE'S MY RIDE.

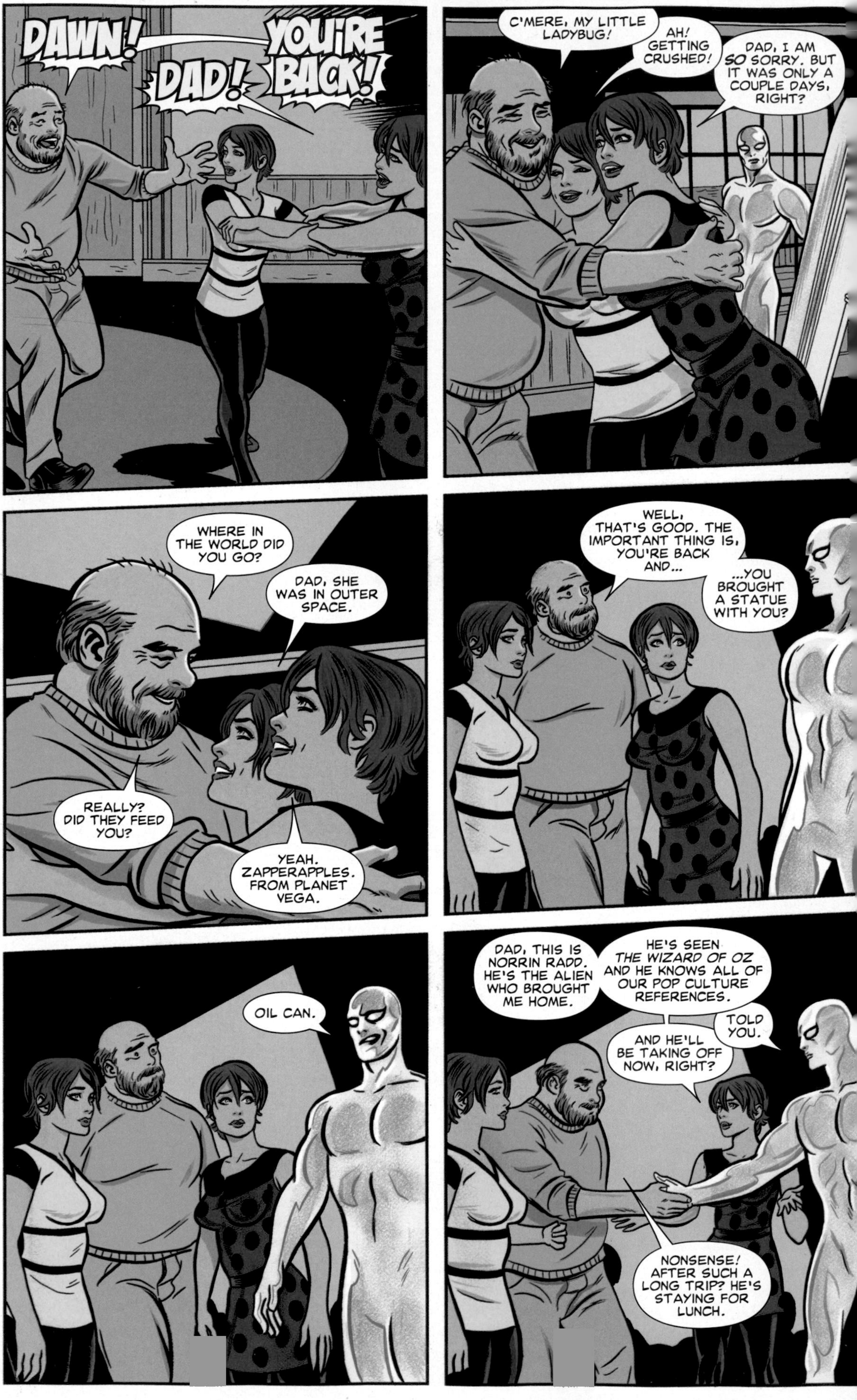
DAWN!
DAD!
YOU'RE BACK!
C'MERE, MY LITTLE LADYBUG!
AH! GETTING CRUSHED!
DAD, I AM SO SORRY. BUT IT WAS ONLY A COUPLE DAYS, RIGHT?
WHERE IN THE WORLD DID YOU GO?
DAD, SHE WAS IN OUTER SPACE.
REALLY? DID THEY FEED YOU?
YEAH. ZAPPERAPPLES. FROM PLANET VEGA.
WELL, THAT'S GOOD. THE IMPORTANT THING IS, YOU'RE BACK AND...
...YOU BROUGHT A STATUE WITH YOU?
OIL CAN.
DAD, THIS IS NORRIN RADD. HE'S THE ALIEN WHO BROUGHT ME HOME.
HE'S SEEN THE WIZARD OF OZ AND HE KNOWS ALL OF OUR POP CULTURE REFERENCES.
TOLD YOU.
AND HE'LL BE TAKING OFF NOW, RIGHT?
NONSENSE! AFTER SUCH A LONG TRIP? HE'S STAYING FOR LUNCH.

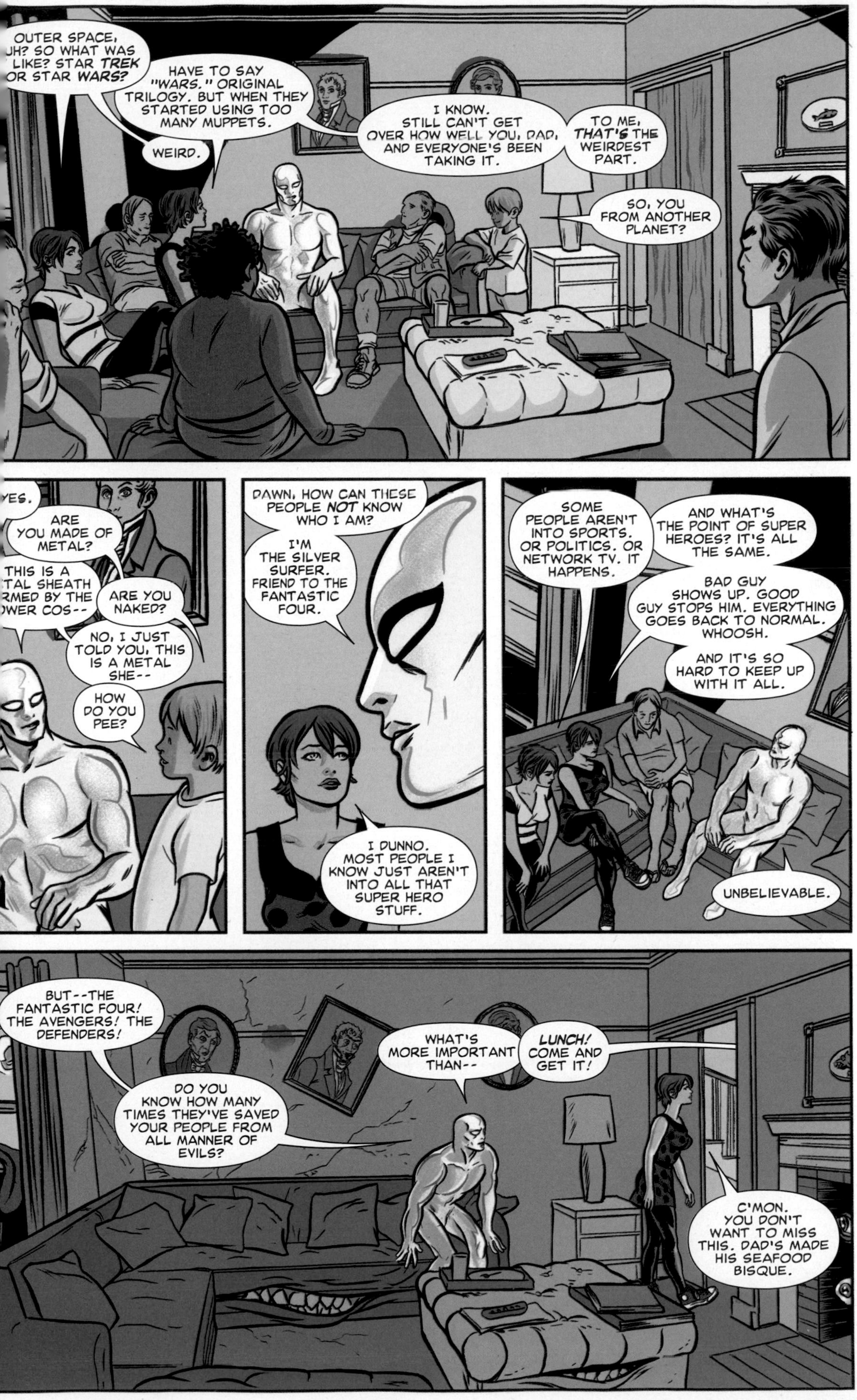

OUTER SPACE, UH? SO WHAT WAS IT LIKE? STAR TREK OR STAR WARS?
HAVE TO SAY "WARS." ORIGINAL TRILOGY. BUT WHEN THEY STARTED USING TOO MANY MUPPETS.
WEIRD.
I KNOW. STILL CAN'T GET OVER HOW WELL YOU, DAD, AND EVERYONE'S BEEN TAKING IT.
TO ME, THAT'S THE WEIRDEST PART.
SO, YOU FROM ANOTHER PLANET?
YES.
ARE YOU MADE OF METAL?
THIS IS A ...TAL SHEATH ...RMED BY THE ...OWER COS--
ARE YOU NAKED?
NO, I JUST TOLD YOU, THIS IS A METAL SHE--
HOW DO YOU PEE?
DAWN, HOW CAN THESE PEOPLE NOT KNOW WHO I AM?
I'M THE SILVER SURFER. FRIEND TO THE FANTASTIC FOUR.
I DUNNO. MOST PEOPLE I KNOW JUST AREN'T INTO ALL THAT SUPER HERO STUFF.
SOME PEOPLE AREN'T INTO SPORTS. OR POLITICS. OR NETWORK TV. IT HAPPENS.
AND WHAT'S THE POINT OF SUPER HEROES? IT'S ALL THE SAME.
BAD GUY SHOWS UP. GOOD GUY STOPS HIM. EVERYTHING GOES BACK TO NORMAL. WHOOSH.
AND IT'S SO HARD TO KEEP UP WITH IT ALL.
UNBELIEVABLE.
BUT--THE FANTASTIC FOUR! THE AVENGERS! THE DEFENDERS!
DO YOU KNOW HOW MANY TIMES THEY'VE SAVED YOUR PEOPLE FROM ALL MANNER OF EVILS?
WHAT'S MORE IMPORTANT THAN--
LUNCH! COME AND GET IT!
C'MON. YOU DON'T WANT TO MISS THIS. DAD'S MADE HIS SEAFOOD BISQUE.

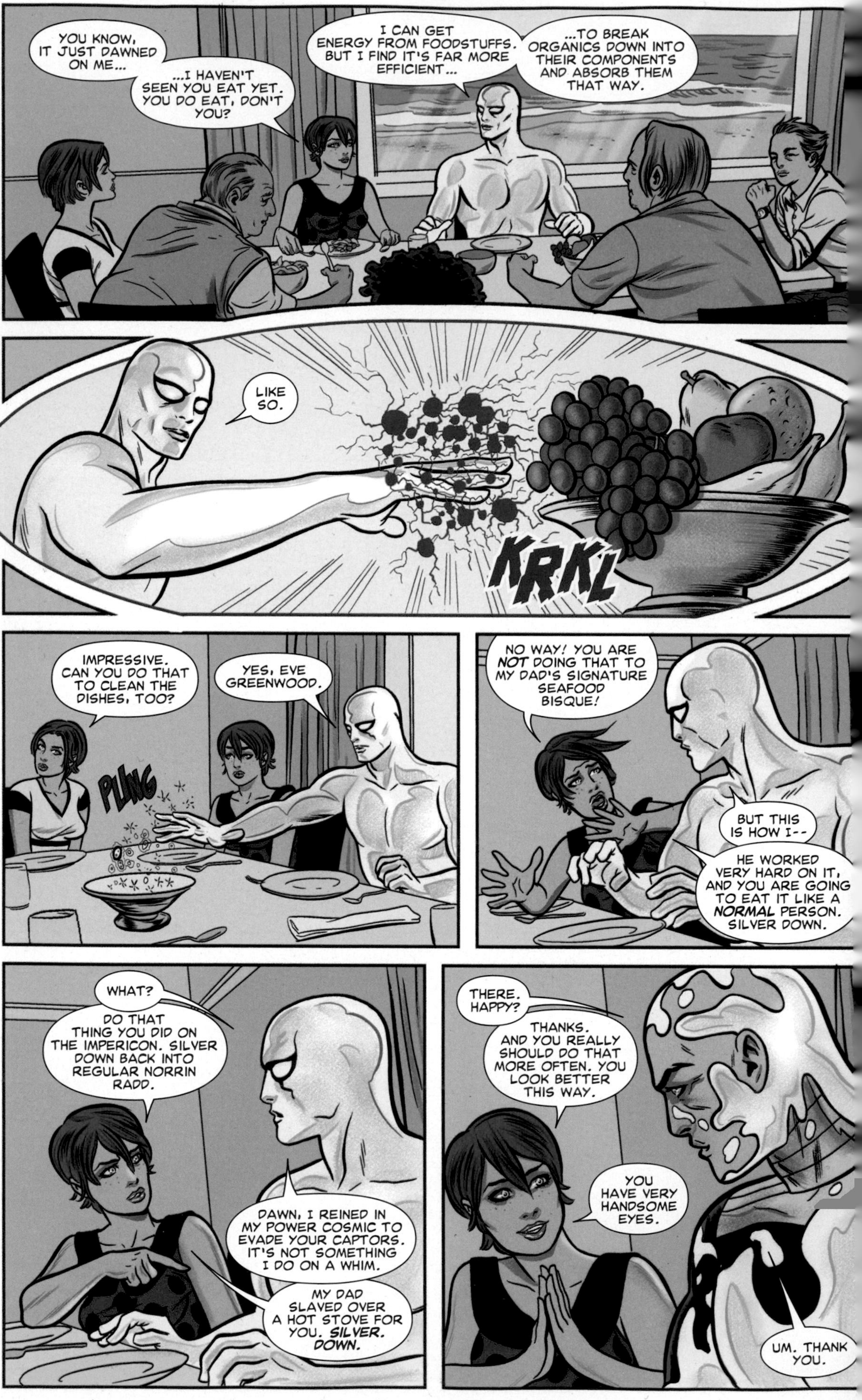
YOU KNOW, IT JUST DAWNED ON ME...
...I HAVEN'T SEEN YOU EAT YET. YOU DO EAT, DON'T YOU?
I CAN GET ENERGY FROM FOODSTUFFS. BUT I FIND IT'S FAR MORE EFFICIENT...
...TO BREAK ORGANICS DOWN INTO THEIR COMPONENTS AND ABSORB THEM THAT WAY.
LIKE SO.
KRKL
IMPRESSIVE. CAN YOU DO THAT TO CLEAN THE DISHES, TOO?
YES, EVE GREENWOOD.
PLING
NO WAY! YOU ARE NOT DOING THAT TO MY DAD'S SIGNATURE SEAFOOD BISQUE!
BUT THIS IS HOW I--
HE WORKED VERY HARD ON IT, AND YOU ARE GOING TO EAT IT LIKE A NORMAL PERSON. SILVER DOWN.
WHAT?
DO THAT THING YOU DID ON THE IMPERICON. SILVER DOWN BACK INTO REGULAR NORRIN RADD.
DAWN, I REINED IN MY POWER COSMIC TO EVADE YOUR CAPTORS. IT'S NOT SOMETHING I DO ON A WHIM.
MY DAD SLAVED OVER A HOT STOVE FOR YOU. SILVER. DOWN.
THERE. HAPPY?
THANKS. AND YOU REALLY SHOULD DO THAT MORE OFTEN. YOU LOOK BETTER THIS WAY.
YOU HAVE VERY HANDSOME EYES.
UM. THANK YOU.

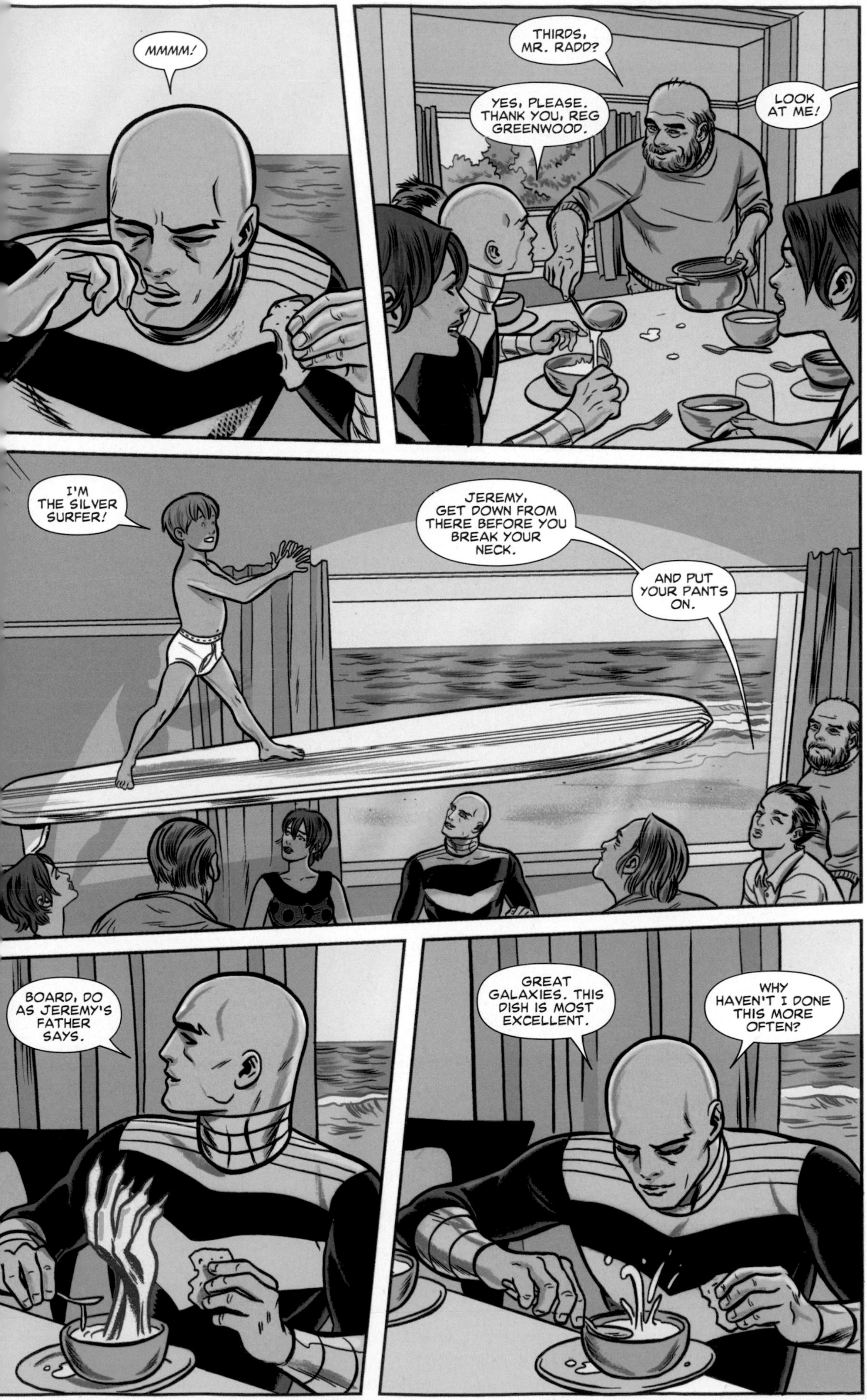
MMMM!
THIRDS, MR. RADD?
YES, PLEASE. THANK YOU, REG GREENWOOD.
LOOK AT ME!
I'M THE SILVER SURFER!
JEREMY, GET DOWN FROM THERE BEFORE YOU BREAK YOUR NECK.
AND PUT YOUR PANTS ON.
BOARD, DO AS JEREMY'S FATHER SAYS.
GREAT GALAXIES. THIS DISH IS MOST EXCELLENT.
WHY HAVEN'T I DONE THIS MORE OFTEN?

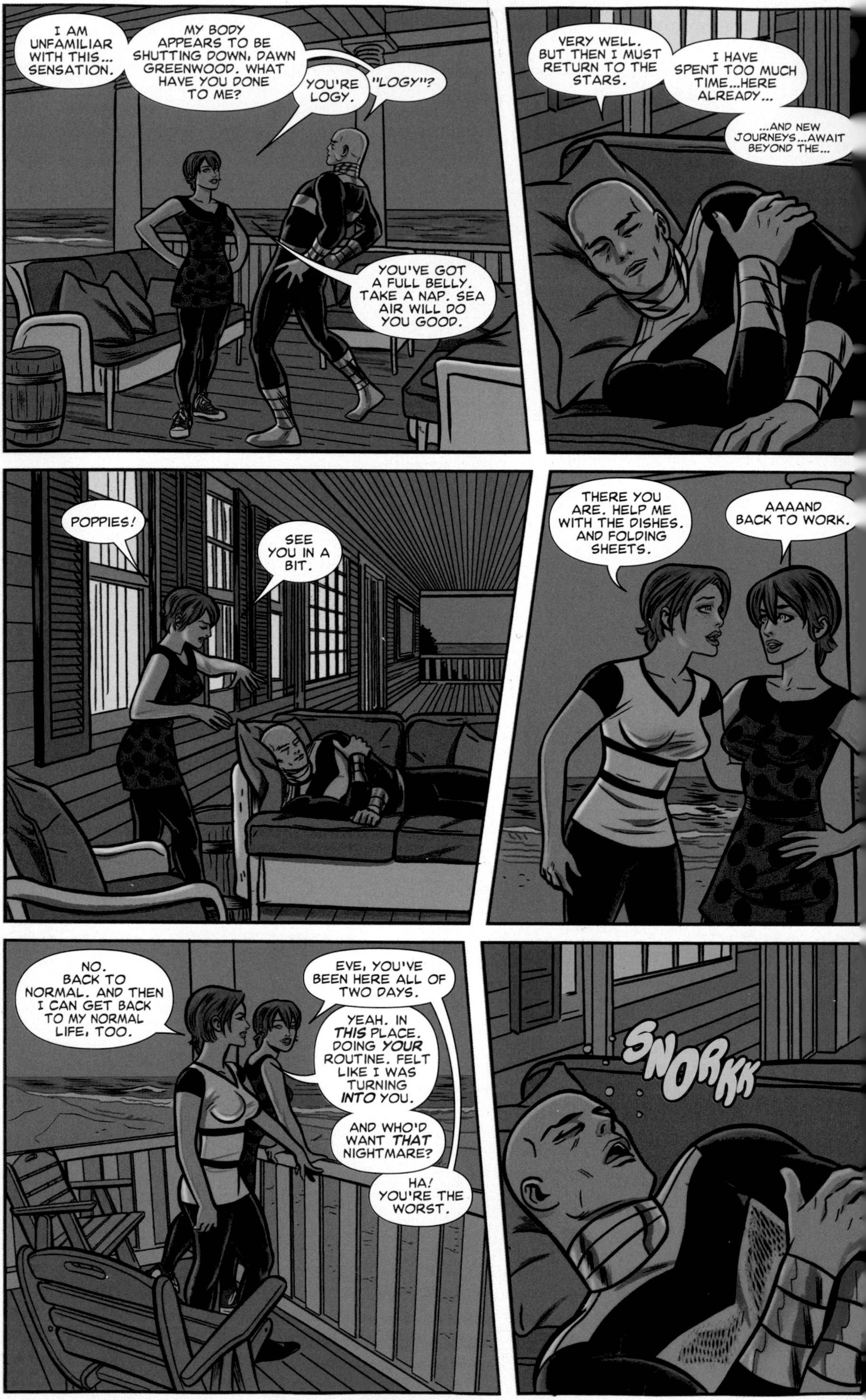
I AM UNFAMILIAR WITH THIS... SENSATION.
MY BODY APPEARS TO BE SHUTTING DOWN, DAWN GREENWOOD. WHAT HAVE YOU DONE TO ME?
YOU'RE LOGY.
"LOGY"?
YOU'VE GOT A FULL BELLY. TAKE A NAP. SEA AIR WILL DO YOU GOOD.
VERY WELL. BUT THEN I MUST RETURN TO THE STARS.
I HAVE SPENT TOO MUCH TIME...HERE ALREADY...
...AND NEW JOURNEYS...AWAIT BEYOND THE...
POPPIES!
SEE YOU IN A BIT.
THERE YOU ARE. HELP ME WITH THE DISHES. AND FOLDING SHEETS.
AAAAND BACK TO WORK.
NO. BACK TO NORMAL. AND THEN I CAN GET BACK TO MY NORMAL LIFE, TOO.
EVE, YOU'VE BEEN HERE ALL OF TWO DAYS.
YEAH. IN THIS PLACE. DOING YOUR ROUTINE. FELT LIKE I WAS TURNING INTO YOU.
AND WHO'D WANT THAT NIGHTMARE?
HA! YOU'RE THE WORST.
SNORKK

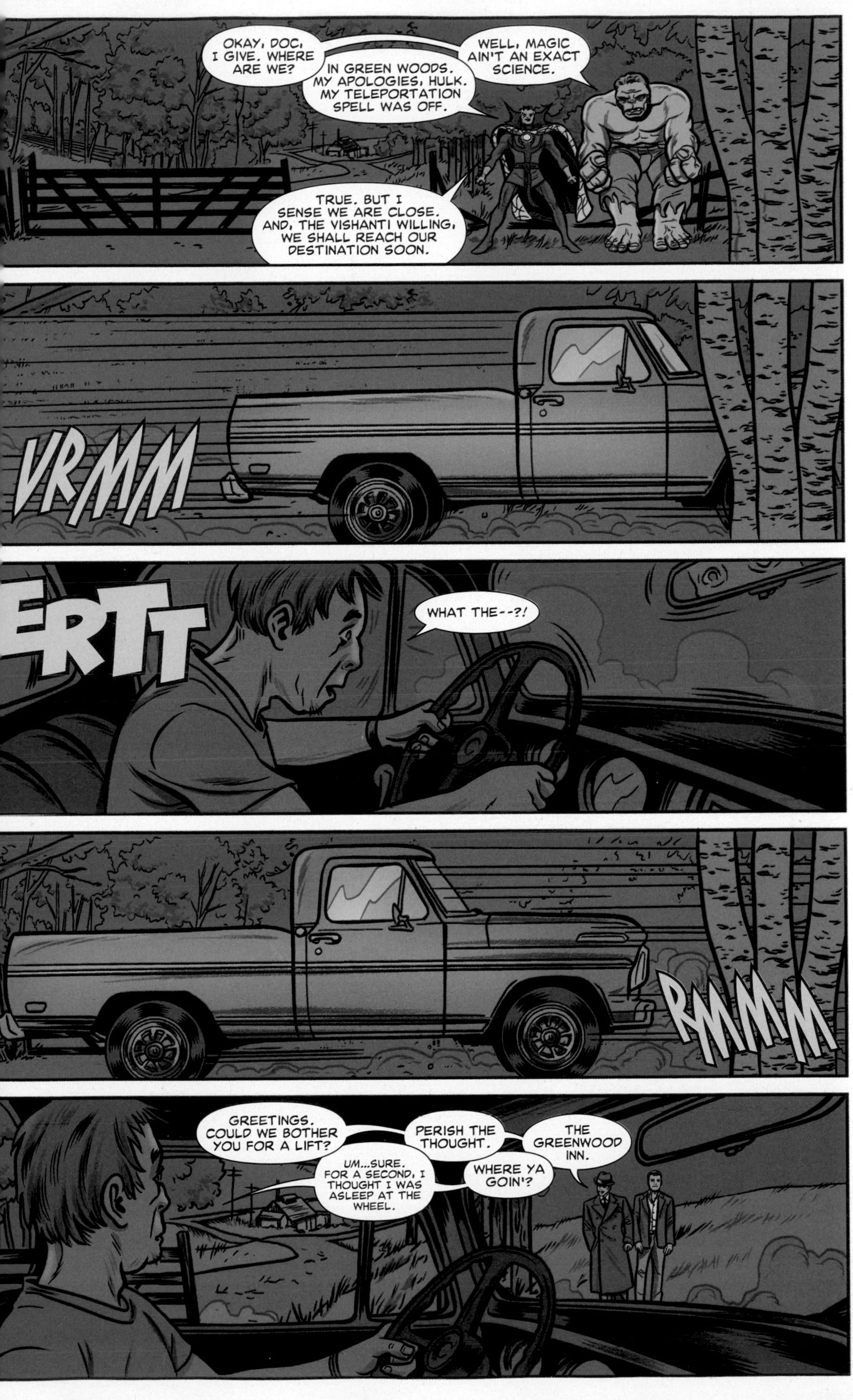
OKAY, DOC, I GIVE. WHERE ARE WE?
IN GREEN WOODS. MY APOLOGIES, HULK. MY TELEPORTATION SPELL WAS OFF.
WELL, MAGIC AIN'T AN EXACT SCIENCE.
TRUE. BUT I SENSE WE ARE CLOSE. AND, THE VISHANTI WILLING, WE SHALL REACH OUR DESTINATION SOON.
VRMM
ERTT
WHAT THE--?!
RMMM
GREETINGS. COULD WE BOTHER YOU FOR A LIFT?
UM...SURE. FOR A SECOND, I THOUGHT I WAS ASLEEP AT THE WHEEL.
PERISH THE THOUGHT.
WHERE YA GOIN'?
THE GREENWOOD INN.

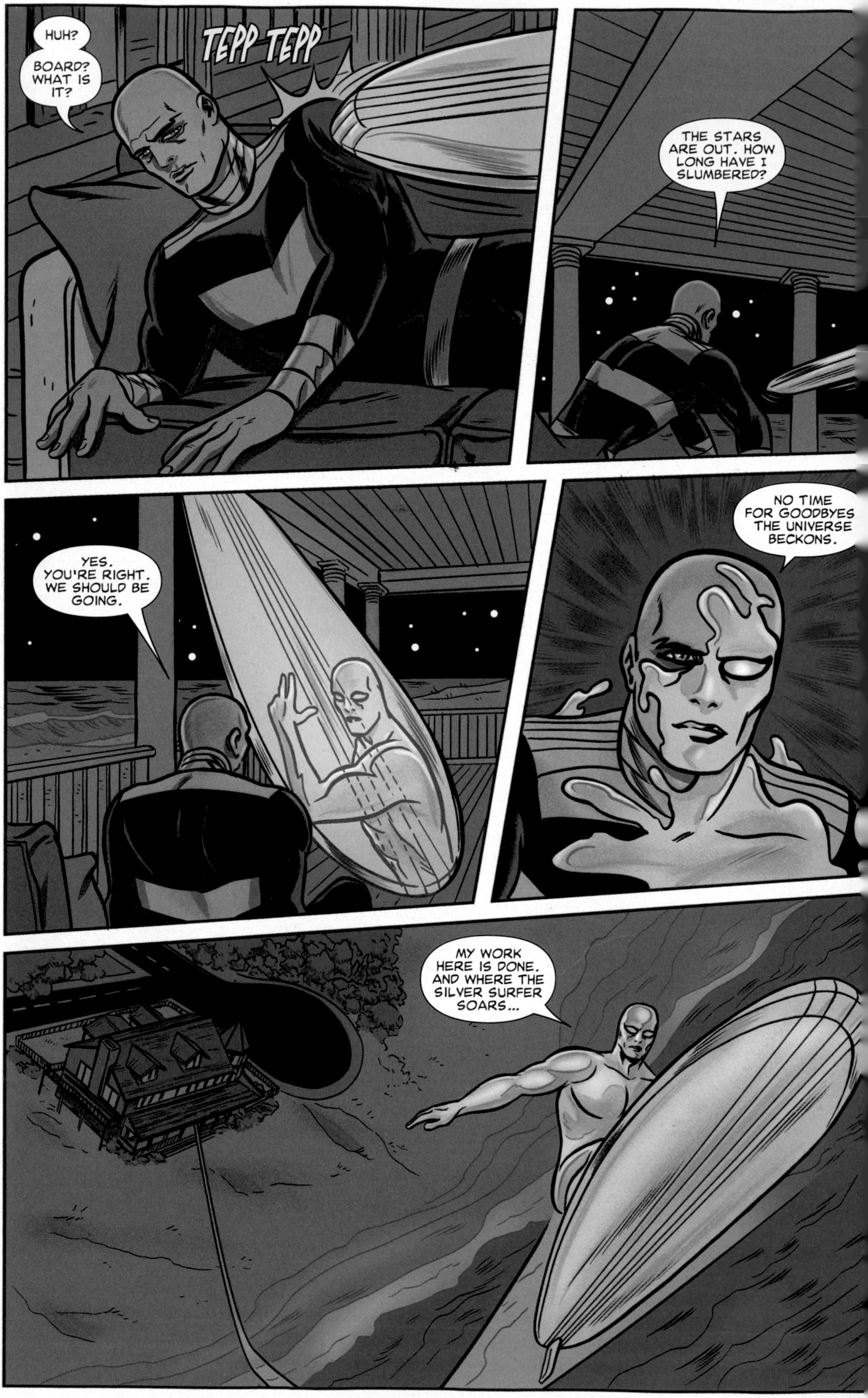
HUH?
BOARD? WHAT IS IT?
TEPP TEPP
THE STARS ARE OUT. HOW LONG HAVE I SLUMBERED?
YES. YOU'RE RIGHT. WE SHOULD BE GOING.
NO TIME FOR GOODBYES THE UNIVERSE BECKONS.
MY WORK HERE IS DONE. AND WHERE THE SILVER SURFER SOARS...

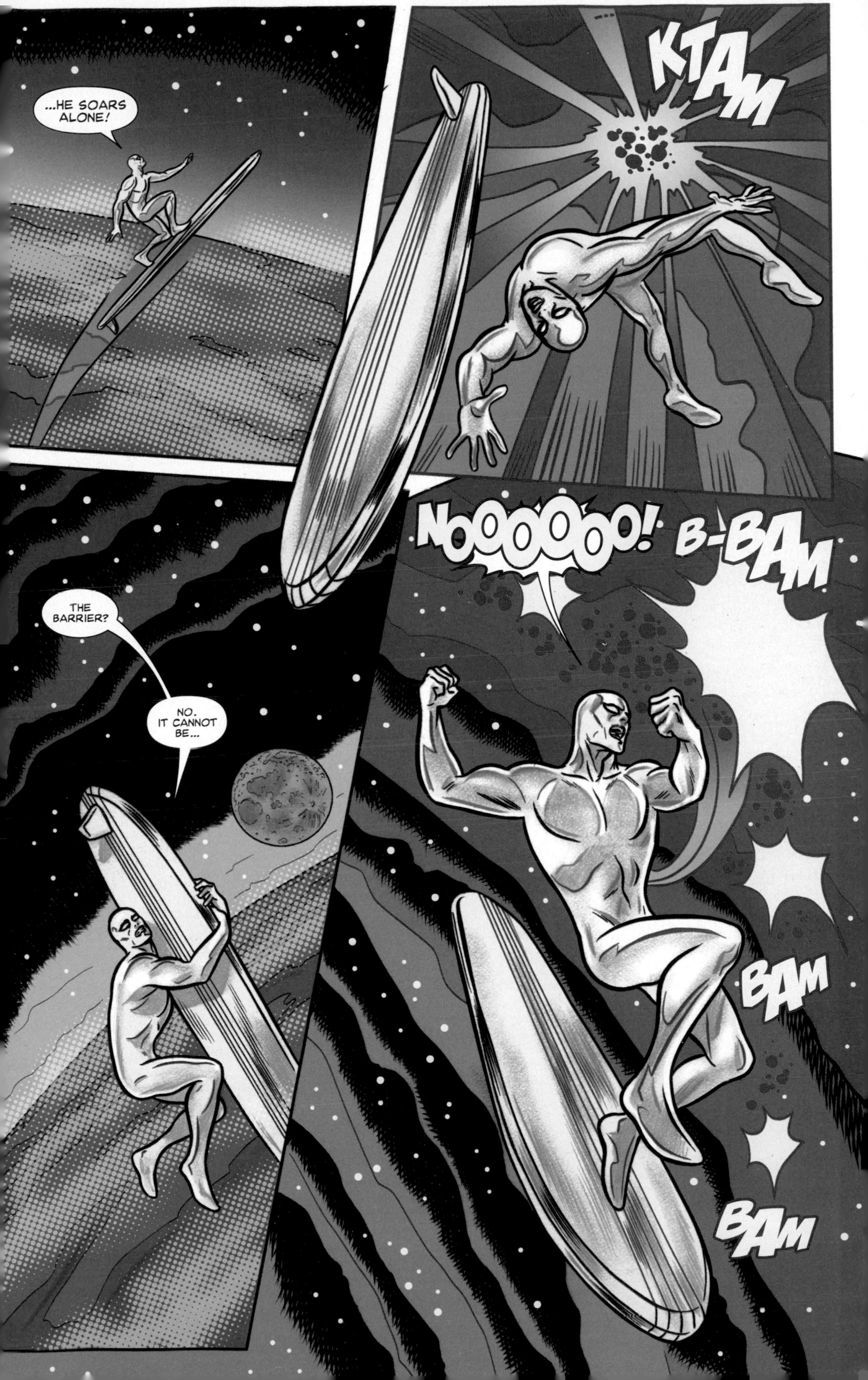
...HE SOARS ALONE!
KTAM
THE BARRIER?
NO. IT CANNOT BE...
NOOOOOO!
B-BAM
BAM
BAM

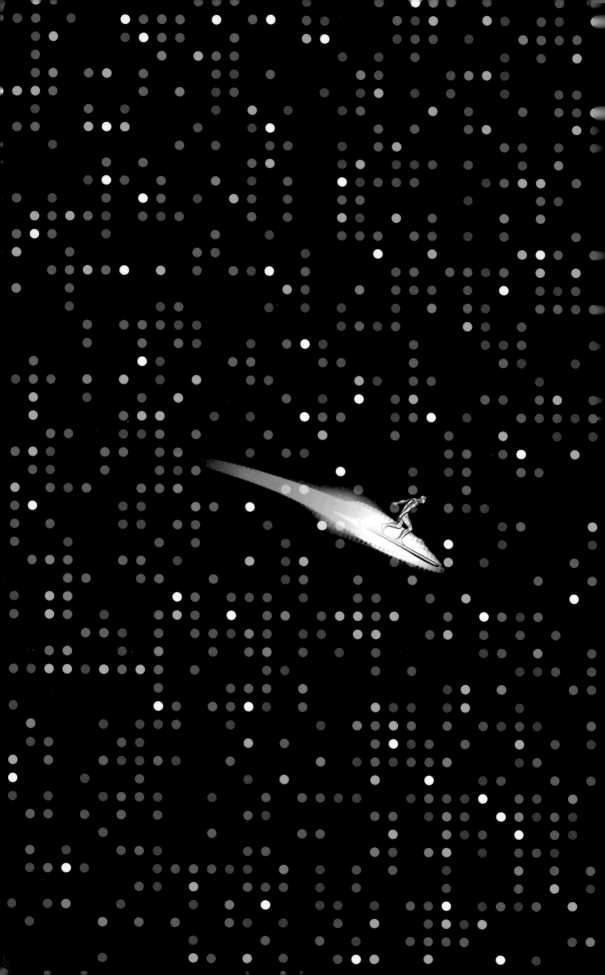

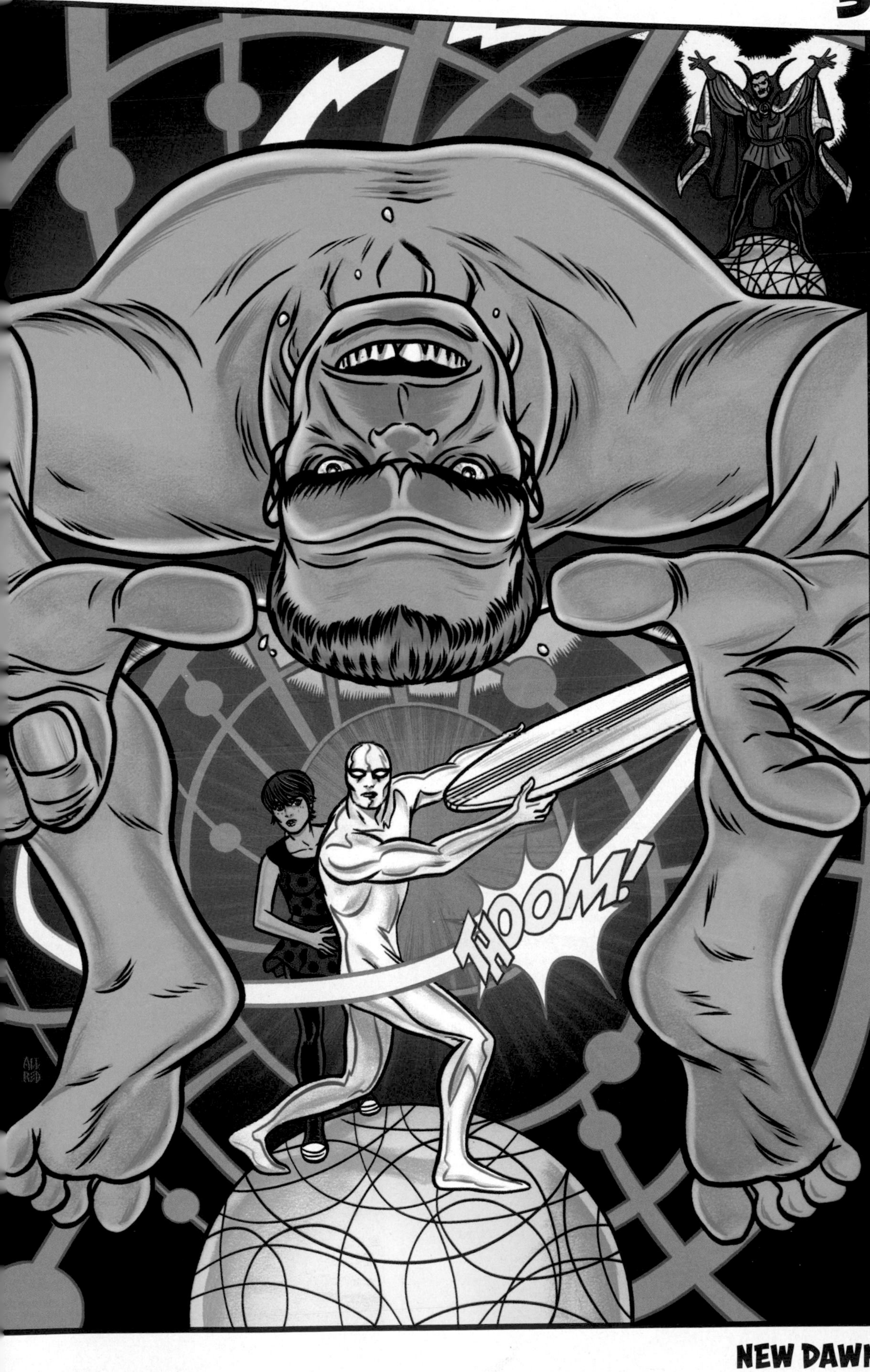
THOOM!

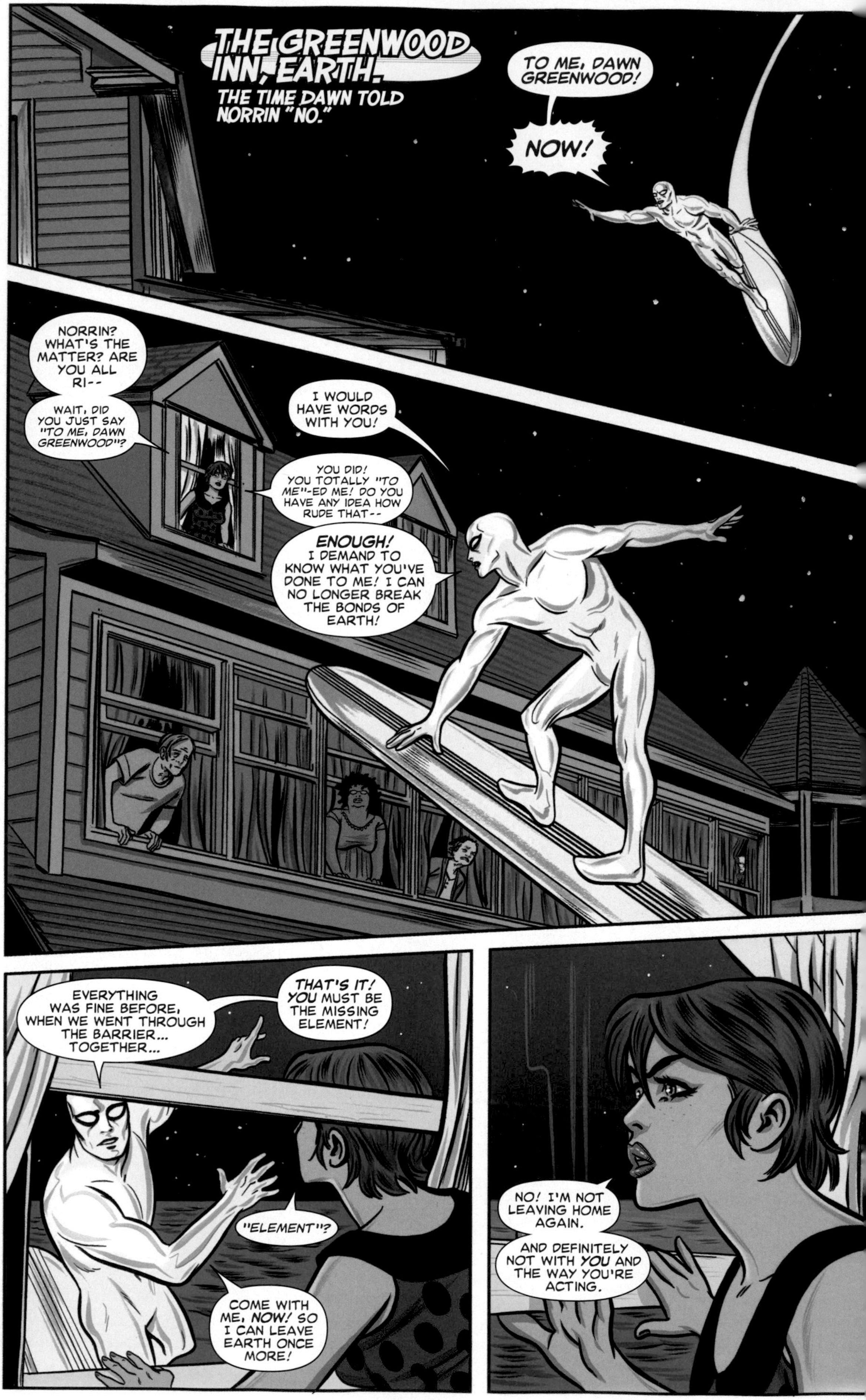
THE GREENWOOD INN, EARTH.
THE TIME DAWN TOLD NORRIN "NO."
TO ME, DAWN GREENWOOD!
NOW!
NORRIN? WHAT'S THE MATTER? ARE YOU ALL RI--
WAIT, DID YOU JUST SAY "TO ME, DAWN GREENWOOD"?
I WOULD HAVE WORDS WITH YOU!
YOU DID! YOU TOTALLY "TO ME"-ED ME! DO YOU HAVE ANY IDEA HOW RUDE THAT--
ENOUGH! I DEMAND TO KNOW WHAT YOU'VE DONE TO ME! I CAN NO LONGER BREAK THE BONDS OF EARTH!
EVERYTHING WAS FINE BEFORE, WHEN WE WENT THROUGH THE BARRIER... TOGETHER...
THAT'S IT! YOU MUST BE THE MISSING ELEMENT!
"ELEMENT"?
COME WITH ME, NOW! SO I CAN LEAVE EARTH ONCE MORE!
NO! I'M NOT LEAVING HOME AGAIN.
AND DEFINITELY NOT WITH YOU AND THE WAY YOU'RE ACTING.

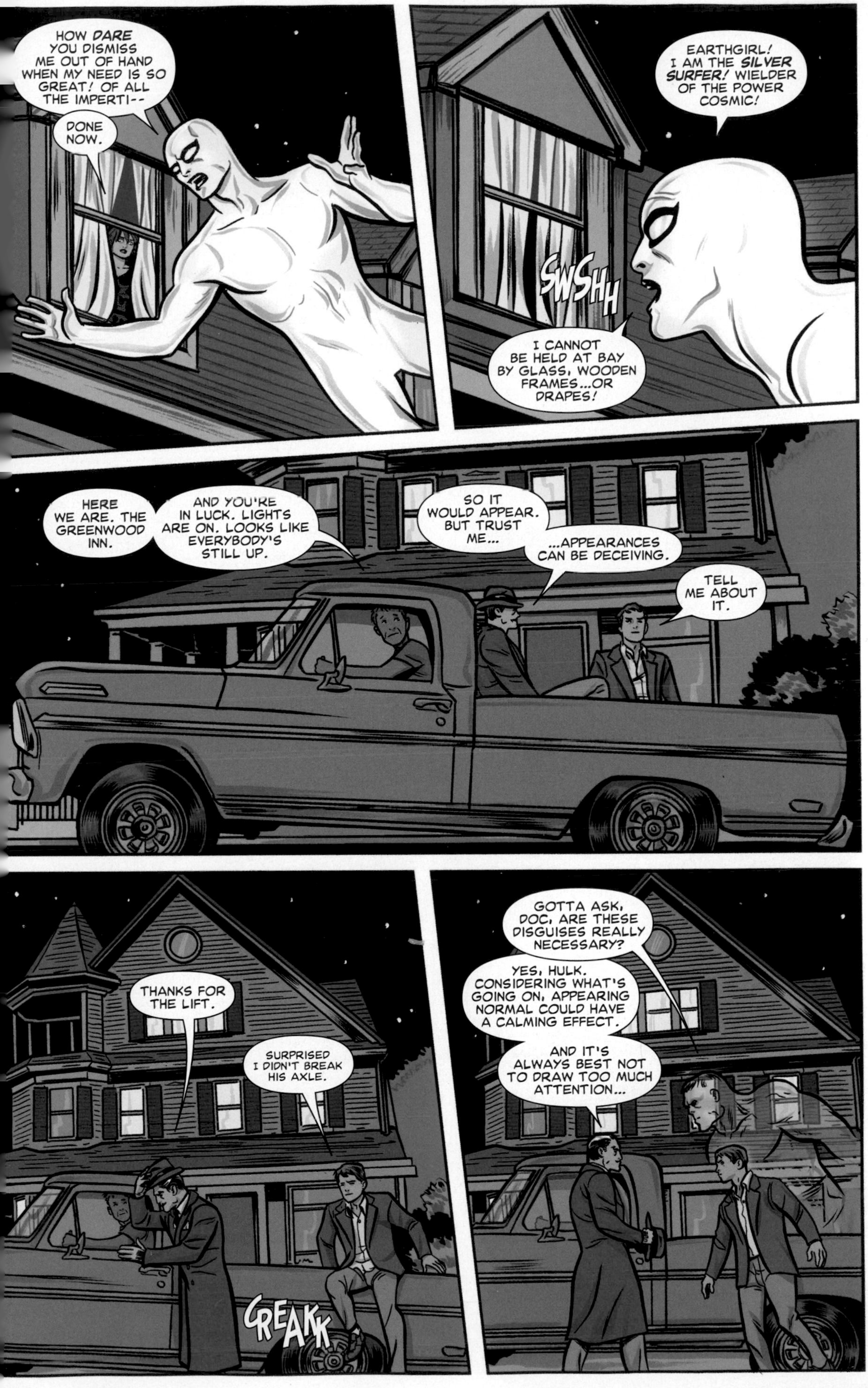
HOW DARE YOU DISMISS ME OUT OF HAND WHEN MY NEED IS SO GREAT! OF ALL THE IMPERTI--
DONE NOW.
EARTHGIRL! I AM THE SILVER SURFER! WIELDER OF THE POWER COSMIC!
SWSHH
I CANNOT BE HELD AT BAY BY GLASS, WOODEN FRAMES...OR DRAPES!
HERE WE ARE. THE GREENWOOD INN.
AND YOU'RE IN LUCK. LIGHTS ARE ON. LOOKS LIKE EVERYBODY'S STILL UP.
SO IT WOULD APPEAR. BUT TRUST ME...
...APPEARANCES CAN BE DECEIVING.
TELL ME ABOUT IT.
THANKS FOR THE LIFT.
SURPRISED I DIDN'T BREAK HIS AXLE.
CREAKK
GOTTA ASK, DOC, ARE THESE DISGUISES REALLY NECESSARY?
YES, HULK. CONSIDERING WHAT'S GOING ON, APPEARING NORMAL COULD HAVE A CALMING EFFECT.
AND IT'S ALWAYS BEST NOT TO DRAW TOO MUCH ATTENTION...

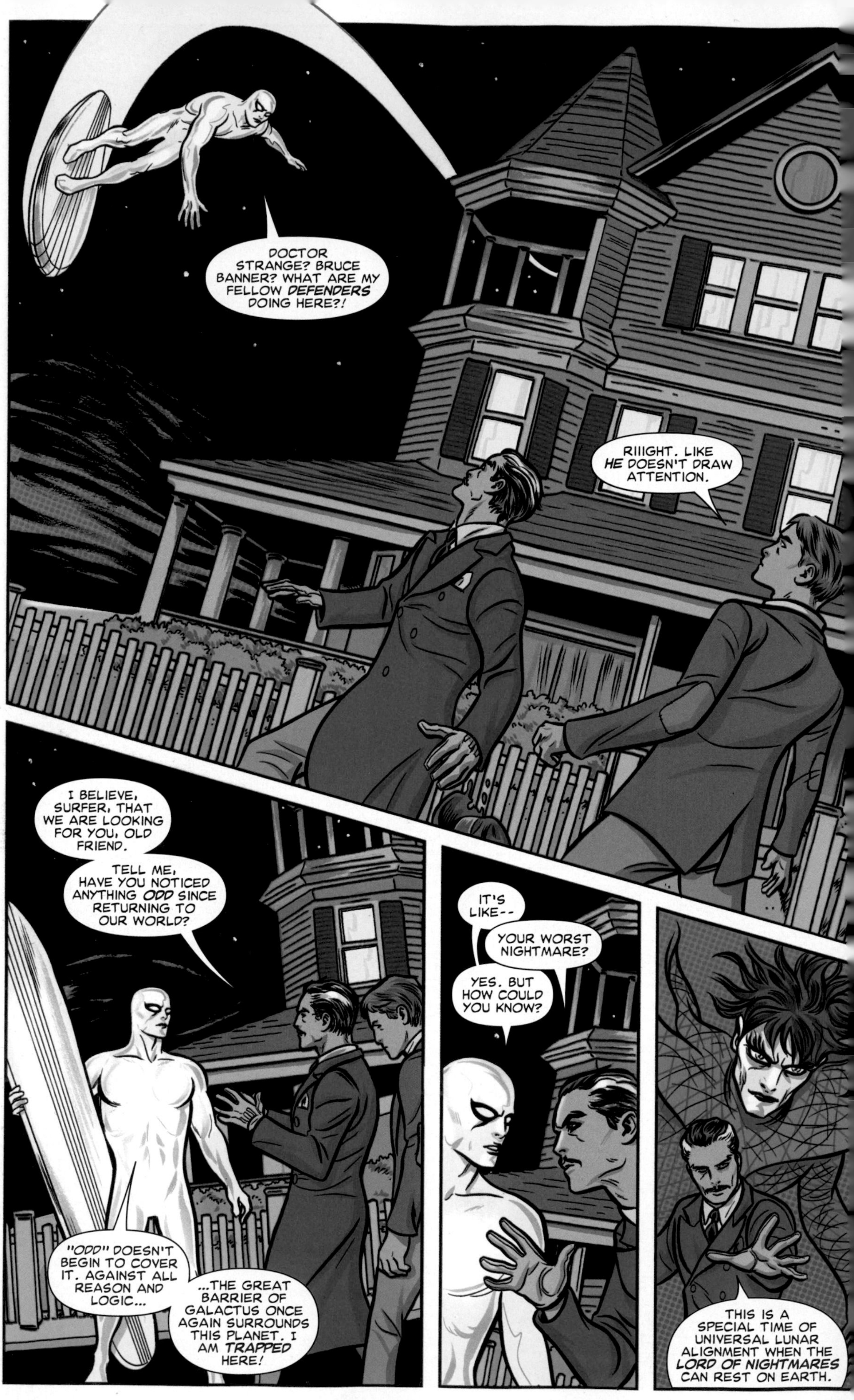

DOCTOR STRANGE? BRUCE BANNER? WHAT ARE MY FELLOW DEFENDERS DOING HERE?!
RIIIGHT. LIKE HE DOESN'T DRAW ATTENTION.
I BELIEVE, SURFER, THAT WE ARE LOOKING FOR YOU, OLD FRIEND.
TELL ME, HAVE YOU NOTICED ANYTHING ODD SINCE RETURNING TO OUR WORLD?
"ODD" DOESN'T BEGIN TO COVER IT. AGAINST ALL REASON AND LOGIC...
...THE GREAT BARRIER OF GALACTUS ONCE AGAIN SURROUNDS THIS PLANET. I AM TRAPPED HERE!
IT'S LIKE--
YOUR WORST NIGHTMARE?
YES. BUT HOW COULD YOU KNOW?
THIS IS A SPECIAL TIME OF UNIVERSAL LUNAR ALIGNMENT WHEN THE LORD OF NIGHTMARES CAN REST ON EARTH.

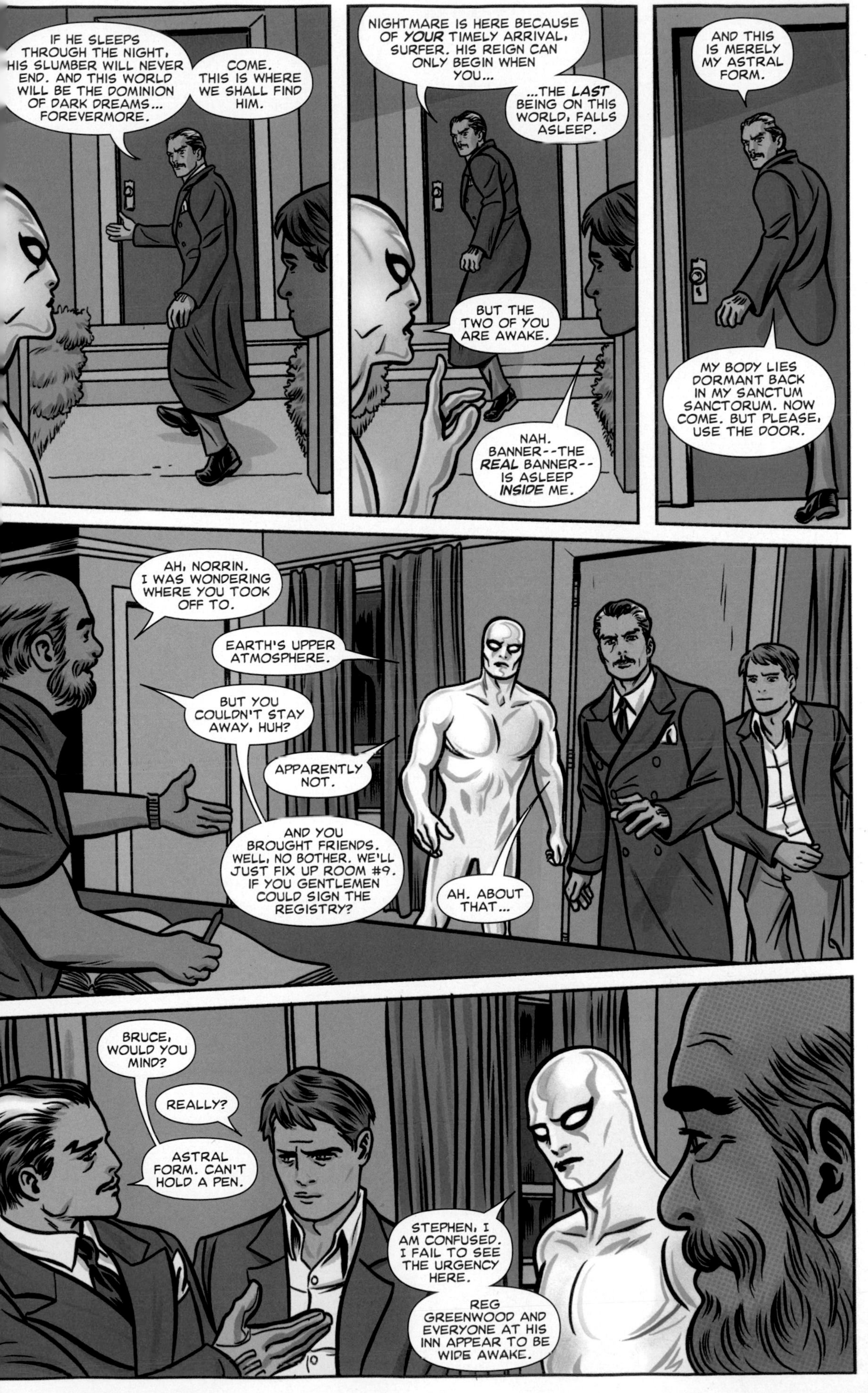
IF HE SLEEPS THROUGH THE NIGHT, HIS SLUMBER WILL NEVER END. AND THIS WORLD WILL BE THE DOMINION OF DARK DREAMS... FOREVERMORE.
COME. THIS IS WHERE WE SHALL FIND HIM.
NIGHTMARE IS HERE BECAUSE OF *YOUR* TIMELY ARRIVAL, SURFER. HIS REIGN CAN ONLY BEGIN WHEN YOU...
...THE *LAST* BEING ON THIS WORLD, FALLS ASLEEP.
BUT THE TWO OF YOU ARE AWAKE.
NAH. BANNER--THE *REAL* BANNER--IS ASLEEP *INSIDE* ME.
AND THIS IS MERELY MY ASTRAL FORM.
MY BODY LIES DORMANT BACK IN MY SANCTUM SANCTORUM. NOW COME. BUT PLEASE, USE THE DOOR.
AH, NORRIN. I WAS WONDERING WHERE YOU TOOK OFF TO.
EARTH'S UPPER ATMOSPHERE.
BUT YOU COULDN'T STAY AWAY, HUH?
APPARENTLY NOT.
AND YOU BROUGHT FRIENDS. WELL, NO BOTHER. WE'LL JUST FIX UP ROOM #9. IF YOU GENTLEMEN COULD SIGN THE REGISTRY?
AH. ABOUT THAT...
BRUCE, WOULD YOU MIND?
REALLY?
ASTRAL FORM. CAN'T HOLD A PEN.
STEPHEN, I AM CONFUSED. I FAIL TO SEE THE URGENCY HERE.
REG GREENWOOD AND EVERYONE AT HIS INN APPEAR TO BE WIDE AWAKE.

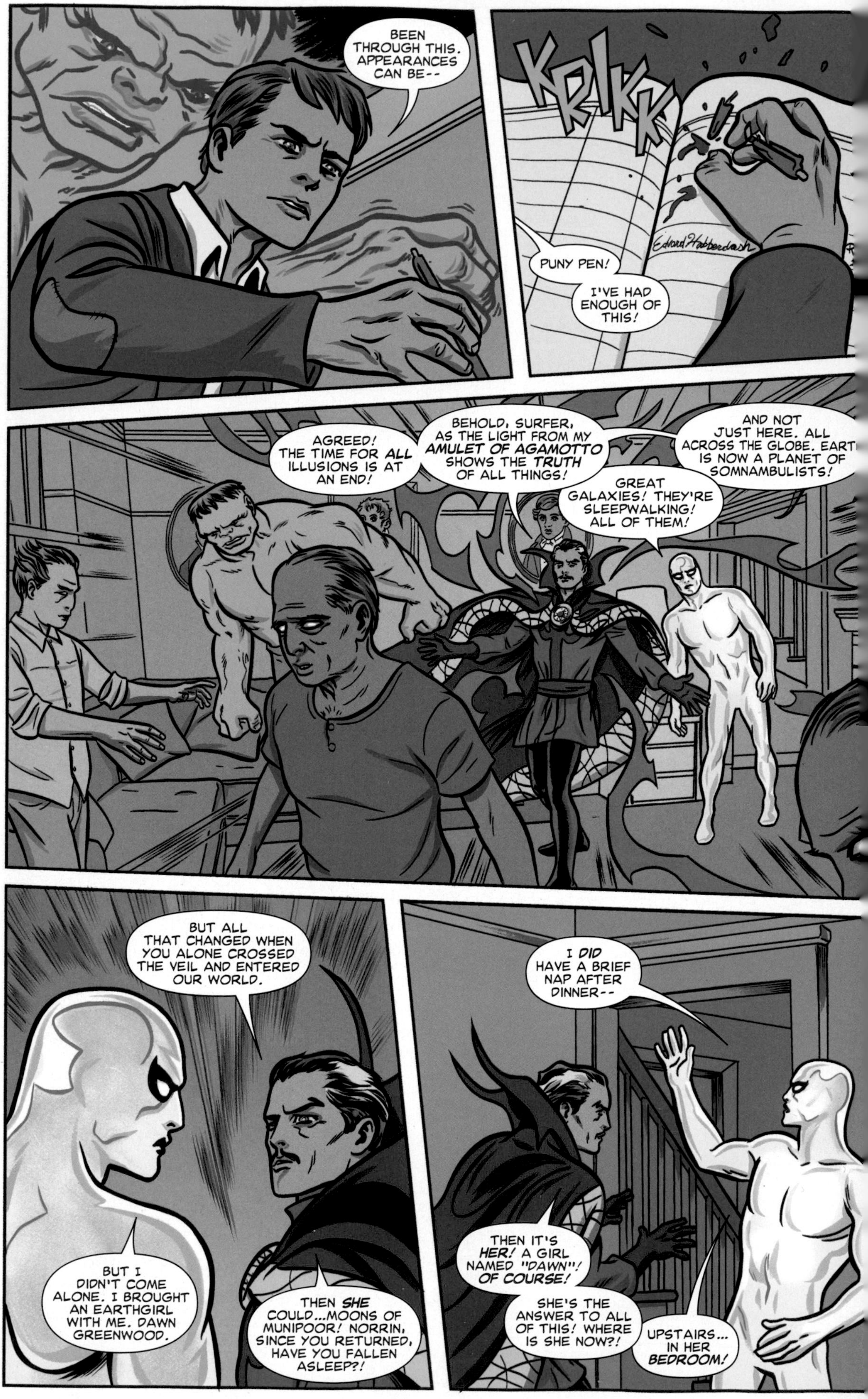
BEEN THROUGH THIS. APPEARANCES CAN BE--
KRIKK
PUNY PEN!
I'VE HAD ENOUGH OF THIS!
AGREED! THE TIME FOR ALL ILLUSIONS IS AT AN END!
BEHOLD, SURFER, AS THE LIGHT FROM MY AMULET OF AGAMOTTO SHOWS THE TRUTH OF ALL THINGS!
GREAT GALAXIES! THEY'RE SLEEPWALKING! ALL OF THEM!
AND NOT JUST HERE. ALL ACROSS THE GLOBE. EART IS NOW A PLANET OF SOMNAMBULISTS!
BUT ALL THAT CHANGED WHEN YOU ALONE CROSSED THE VEIL AND ENTERED OUR WORLD.
BUT I DIDN'T COME ALONE. I BROUGHT AN EARTHGIRL WITH ME. DAWN GREENWOOD.
THEN SHE COULD...MOONS OF MUNIPOOR! NORRIN, SINCE YOU RETURNED, HAVE YOU FALLEN ASLEEP?!
I DID HAVE A BRIEF NAP AFTER DINNER--
THEN IT'S HER! A GIRL NAMED "DAWN"! OF COURSE!
SHE'S THE ANSWER TO ALL OF THIS! WHERE IS SHE NOW?!
UPSTAIRS... IN HER BEDROOM!

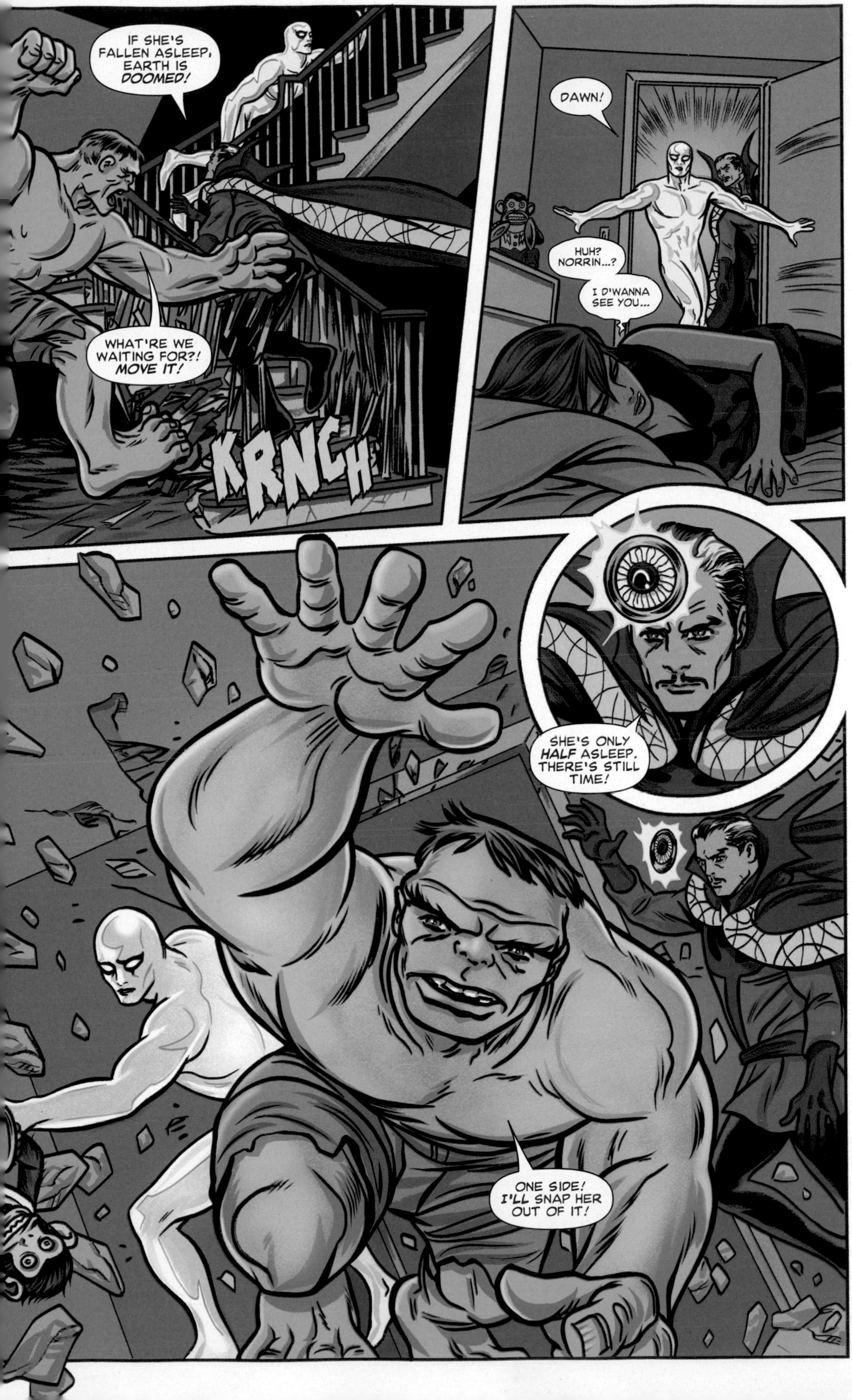
IF SHE'S FALLEN ASLEEP, EARTH IS DOOMED!
WHAT'RE WE WAITING FOR?! MOVE IT!
KRNCH
DAWN!
HUH? NORRIN...?
I D'WANNA SEE YOU...
SHE'S ONLY HALF ASLEEP. THERE'S STILL TIME!
ONE SIDE! I'LL SNAP HER OUT OF IT!

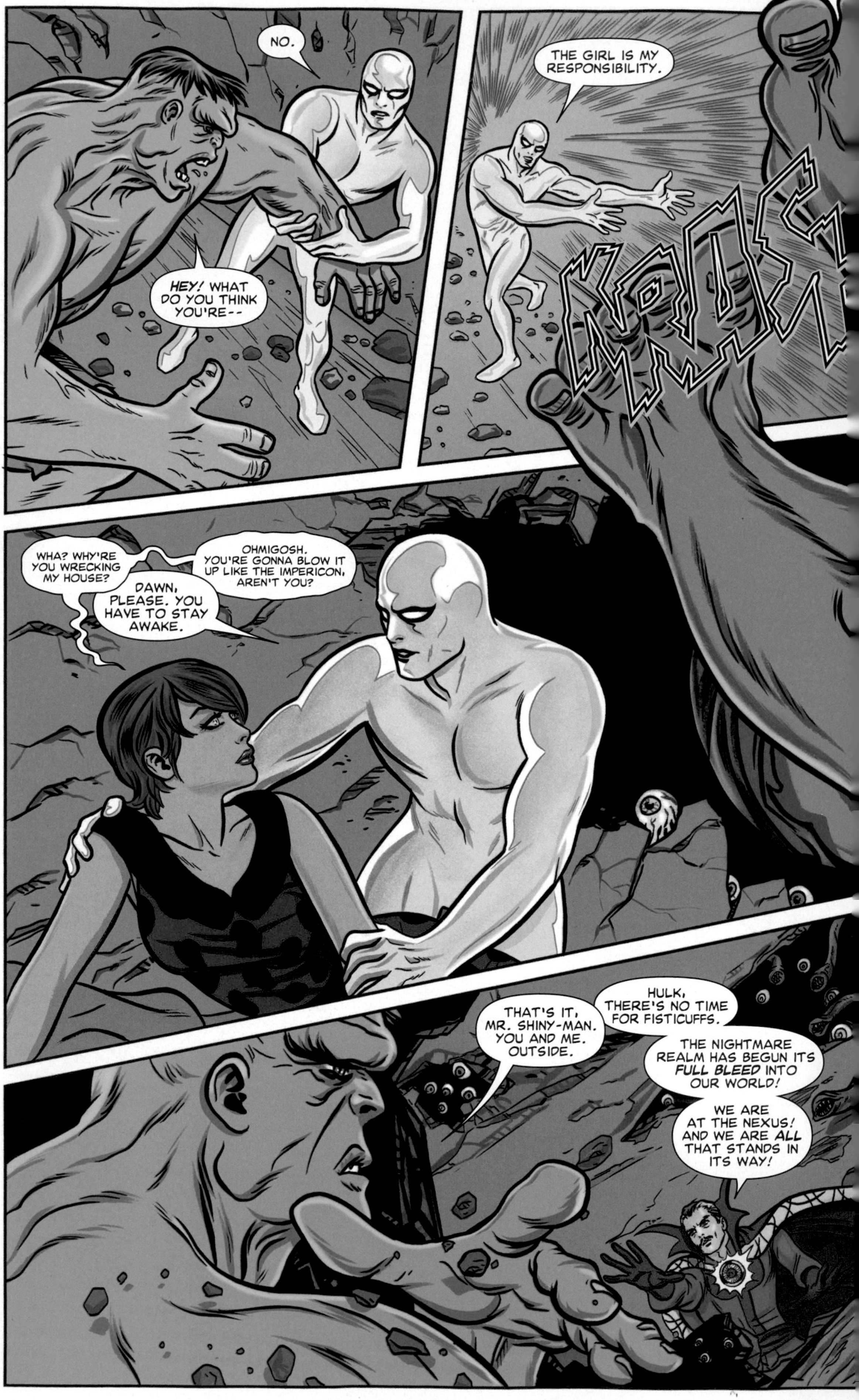

NO.
HEY! WHAT DO YOU THINK YOU'RE--
THE GIRL IS MY RESPONSIBILITY.
KRASH
WHA? WHY'RE YOU WRECKING MY HOUSE?
OHMIGOSH. YOU'RE GONNA BLOW IT UP LIKE THE IMPERICON, AREN'T YOU?
DAWN, PLEASE. YOU HAVE TO STAY AWAKE.
THAT'S IT, MR. SHINY-MAN. YOU AND ME. OUTSIDE.
HULK, THERE'S NO TIME FOR FISTICUFFS.
THE NIGHTMARE REALM HAS BEGUN ITS FULL BLEED INTO OUR WORLD!
WE ARE AT THE NEXUS! AND WE ARE ALL THAT STANDS IN ITS WAY!

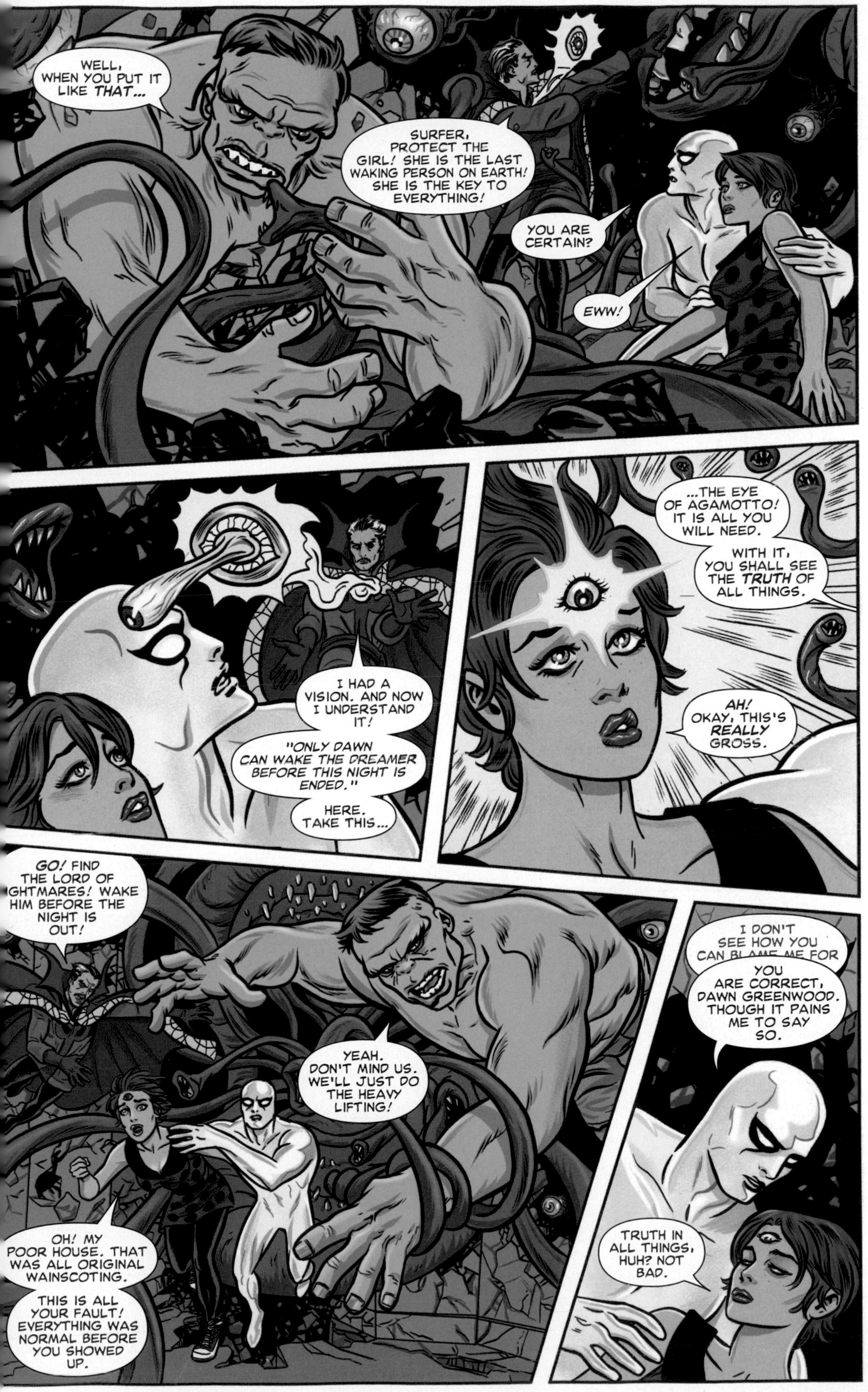
WELL, WHEN YOU PUT IT LIKE THAT...
SURFER, PROTECT THE GIRL! SHE IS THE LAST WAKING PERSON ON EARTH! SHE IS THE KEY TO EVERYTHING!
YOU ARE CERTAIN?
EWW!
I HAD A VISION. AND NOW I UNDERSTAND IT!
"ONLY DAWN CAN WAKE THE DREAMER BEFORE THIS NIGHT IS ENDED."
HERE. TAKE THIS...
...THE EYE OF AGAMOTTO! IT IS ALL YOU WILL NEED.
WITH IT, YOU SHALL SEE THE TRUTH OF ALL THINGS.
AH! OKAY, THIS'S REALLY GROSS.
GO! FIND THE LORD OF GHTMARES! WAKE HIM BEFORE THE NIGHT IS OUT!
YEAH. DON'T MIND US. WE'LL JUST DO THE HEAVY LIFTING!
OH! MY POOR HOUSE. THAT WAS ALL ORIGINAL WAINSCOTING.
THIS IS ALL YOUR FAULT! EVERYTHING WAS NORMAL BEFORE YOU SHOWED UP.
I DON'T SEE HOW YOU CAN BLAME ME FOR
YOU ARE CORRECT, DAWN GREENWOOD. THOUGH IT PAINS ME TO SAY SO.
TRUTH IN ALL THINGS, HUH? NOT BAD.

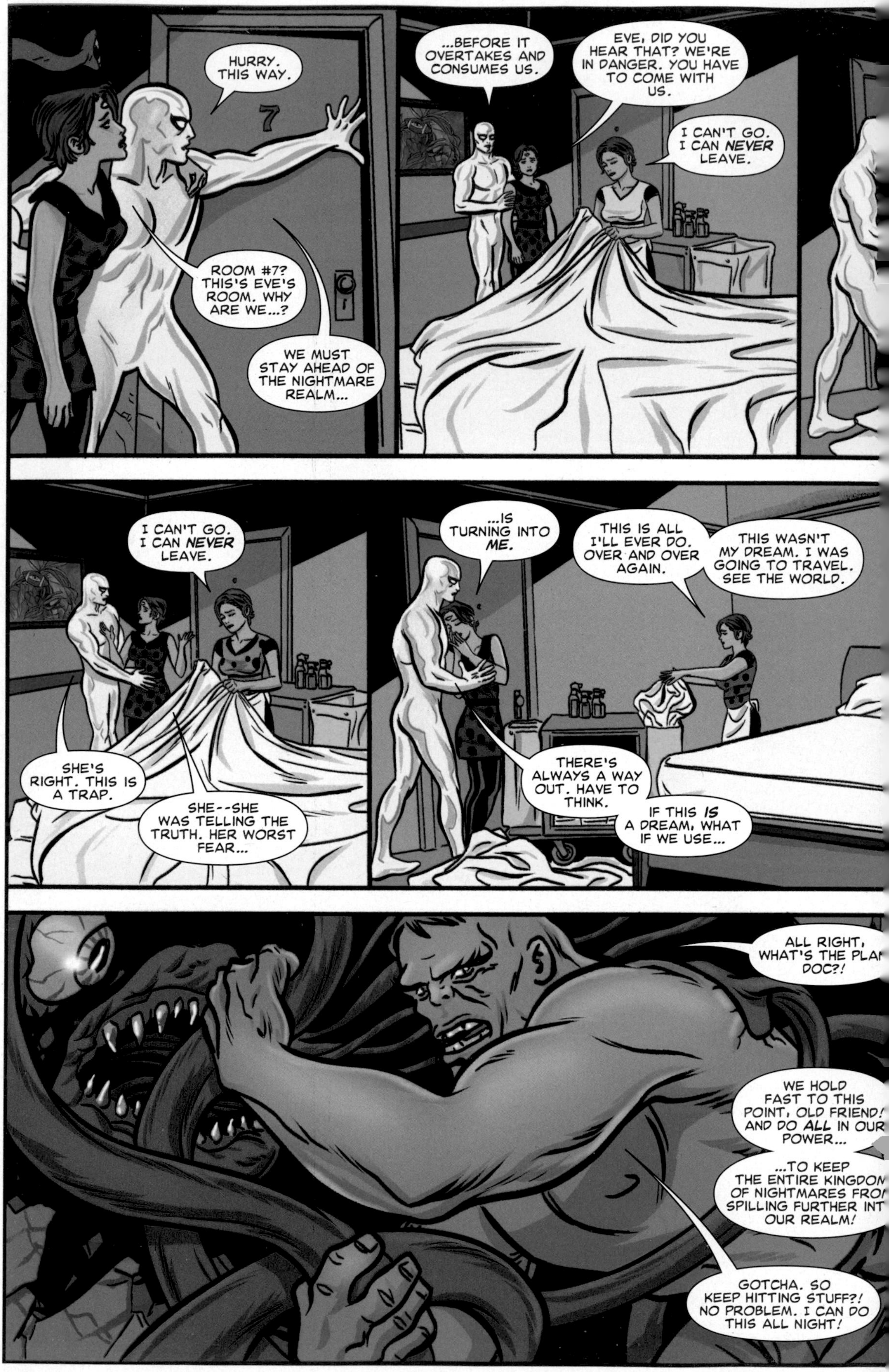
HURRY. THIS WAY.
ROOM #7? THIS'S EVE'S ROOM. WHY ARE WE...?
WE MUST STAY AHEAD OF THE NIGHTMARE REALM...
...BEFORE IT OVERTAKES AND CONSUMES US.
EVE, DID YOU HEAR THAT? WE'RE IN DANGER. YOU HAVE TO COME WITH US.
I CAN'T GO. I CAN NEVER LEAVE.
I CAN'T GO. I CAN NEVER LEAVE.
SHE'S RIGHT. THIS IS A TRAP.
SHE--SHE WAS TELLING THE TRUTH. HER WORST FEAR...
...IS TURNING INTO ME.
THIS IS ALL I'LL EVER DO. OVER AND OVER AGAIN.
THIS WASN'T MY DREAM. I WAS GOING TO TRAVEL. SEE THE WORLD.
THERE'S ALWAYS A WAY OUT. HAVE TO THINK.
IF THIS IS A DREAM, WHAT IF WE USE...
ALL RIGHT, WHAT'S THE PLA DOC?!
WE HOLD FAST TO THIS POINT, OLD FRIEND! AND DO ALL IN OUR POWER...
...TO KEEP THE ENTIRE KINGDO OF NIGHTMARES FRO SPILLING FURTHER INT OUR REALM!
GOTCHA. SO KEEP HITTING STUFF?! NO PROBLEM. I CAN DO THIS ALL NIGHT!

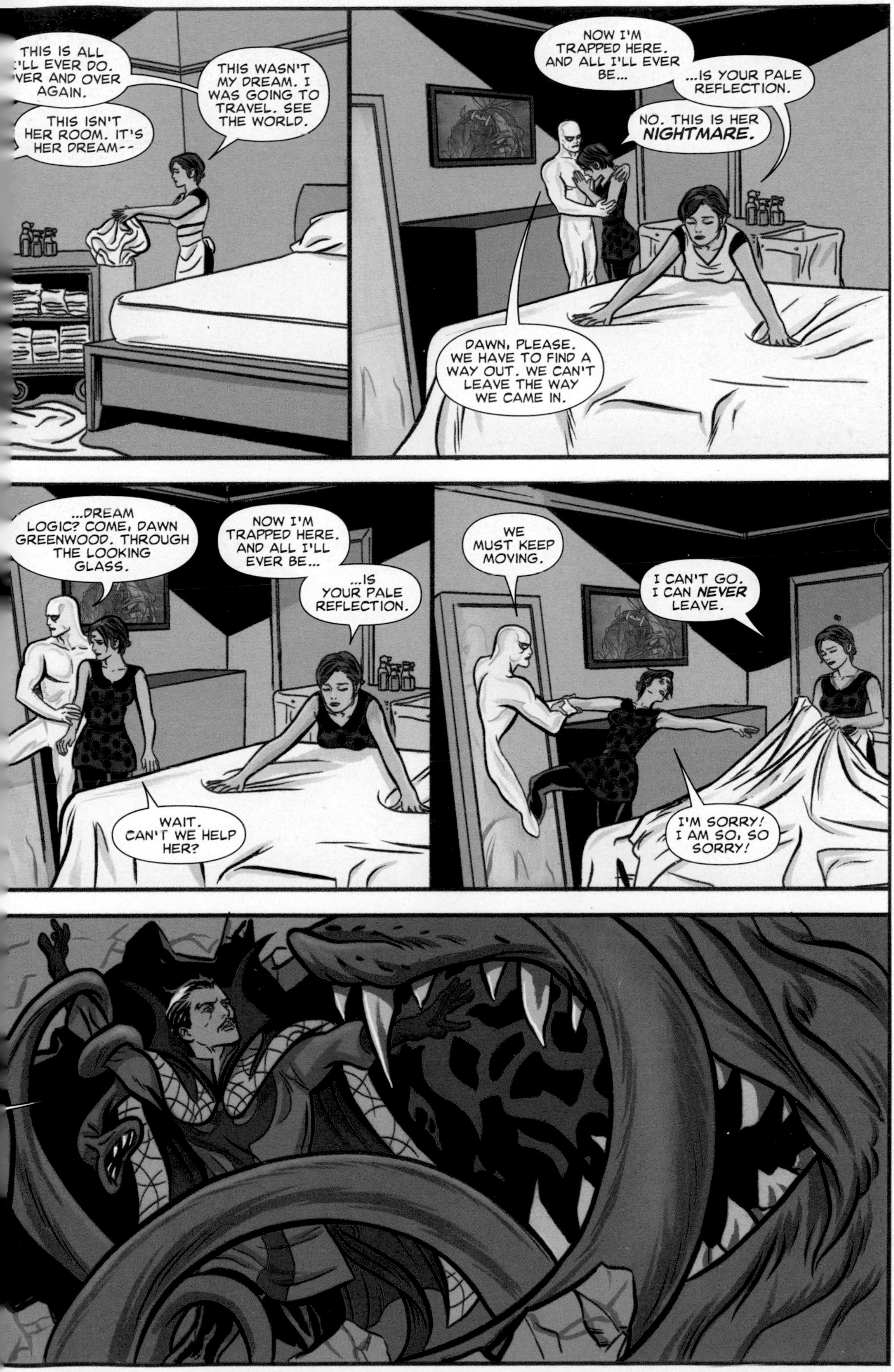

THIS IS ALL I'LL EVER DO. OVER AND OVER AGAIN.
THIS ISN'T HER ROOM. IT'S HER DREAM--
THIS WASN'T MY DREAM. I WAS GOING TO TRAVEL. SEE THE WORLD.
NOW I'M TRAPPED HERE. AND ALL I'LL EVER BE...
...IS YOUR PALE REFLECTION.
NO. THIS IS HER *NIGHTMARE.*
DAWN, PLEASE. WE HAVE TO FIND A WAY OUT. WE CAN'T LEAVE THE WAY WE CAME IN.
...DREAM LOGIC? COME, DAWN GREENWOOD. THROUGH THE LOOKING GLASS.
NOW I'M TRAPPED HERE. AND ALL I'LL EVER BE...
...IS YOUR PALE REFLECTION.
WAIT. CAN'T WE HELP HER?
WE MUST KEEP MOVING.
I CAN'T GO. I CAN *NEVER* LEAVE.
I'M SORRY! I AM SO, SO SORRY!

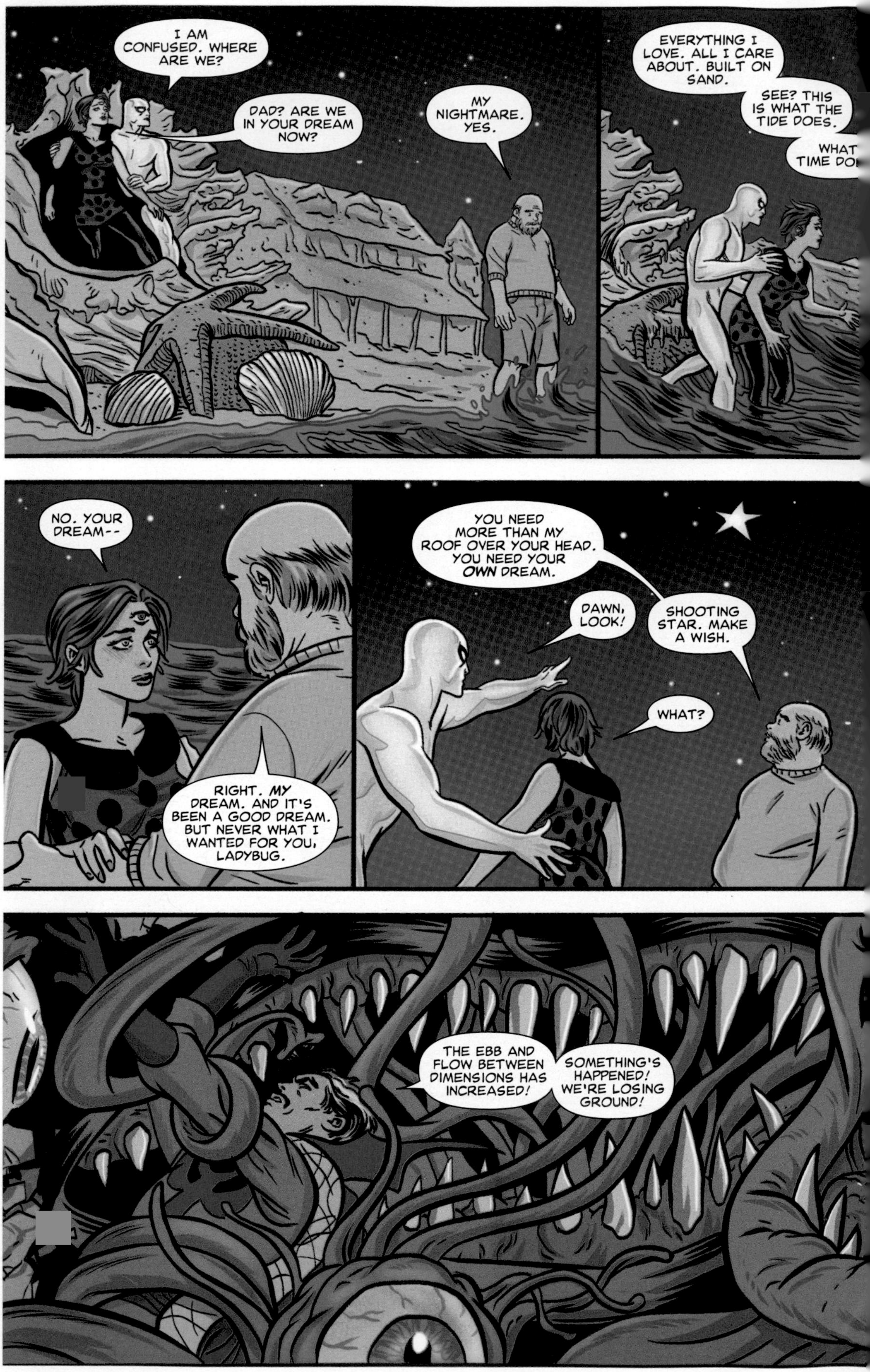
I AM CONFUSED. WHERE ARE WE?
DAD? ARE WE IN YOUR DREAM NOW?
MY NIGHTMARE. YES.
EVERYTHING I LOVE. ALL I CARE ABOUT. BUILT ON SAND.
SEE? THIS IS WHAT THE TIDE DOES.
WHAT TIME DO
NO. YOUR DREAM--
RIGHT. MY DREAM. AND IT'S BEEN A GOOD DREAM. BUT NEVER WHAT I WANTED FOR YOU, LADYBUG.
YOU NEED MORE THAN MY ROOF OVER YOUR HEAD. YOU NEED YOUR OWN DREAM.
DAWN, LOOK!
SHOOTING STAR. MAKE A WISH.
WHAT?
THE EBB AND FLOW BETWEEN DIMENSIONS HAS INCREASED!
SOMETHING'S HAPPENED! WE'RE LOSING GROUND!

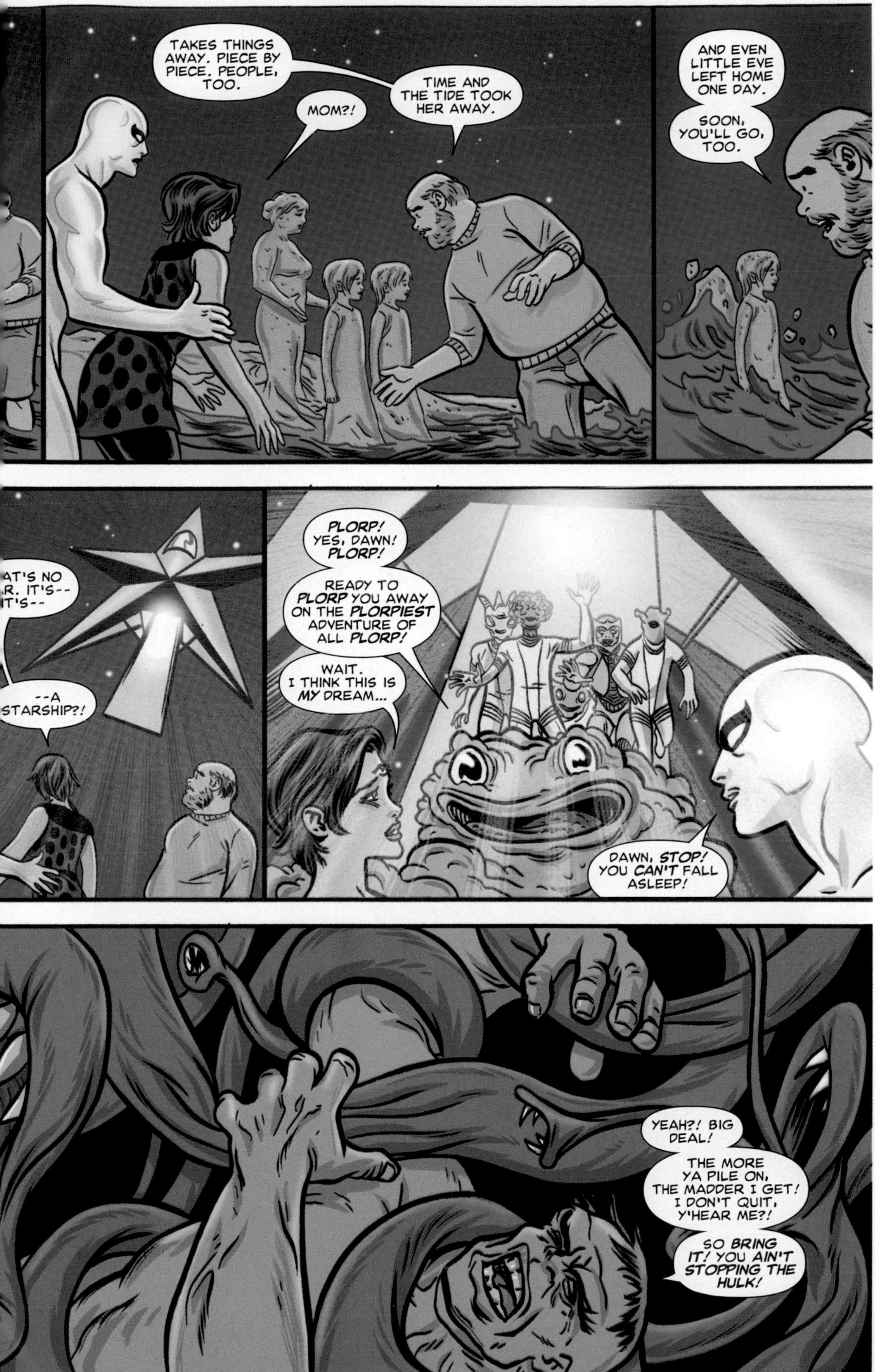
TAKES THINGS AWAY. PIECE BY PIECE. PEOPLE, TOO.
MOM?!
TIME AND THE TIDE TOOK HER AWAY.
AND EVEN LITTLE EVE LEFT HOME ONE DAY.
SOON, YOU'LL GO, TOO.
AT'S NO R. IT'S-- T'S--
--A STARSHIP?!
PLORP! YES, DAWN! PLORP!
READY TO PLORP YOU AWAY ON THE PLORPIEST ADVENTURE OF ALL PLORP!
WAIT. I THINK THIS IS MY DREAM...
DAWN, STOP! YOU CAN'T FALL ASLEEP!
YEAH?! BIG DEAL!
THE MORE YA PILE ON, THE MADDER I GET! I DON'T QUIT, Y'HEAR ME?!
SO BRING IT! YOU AIN'T STOPPING THE HULK!

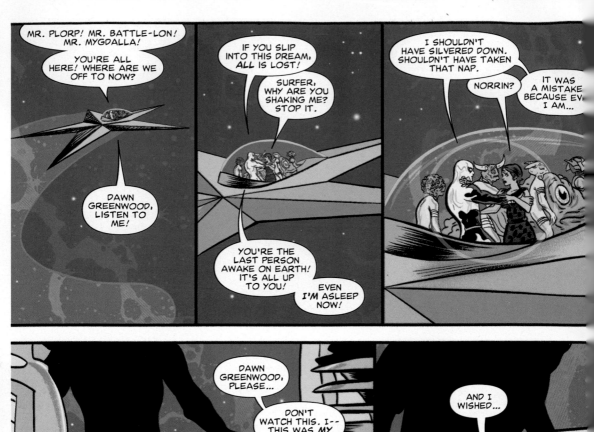

MR. PLORP! MR. BATTLE-LON! MR. MYGDALLA!

YOU'RE ALL HERE! WHERE ARE WE OFF TO NOW?

DAWN GREENWOOD, LISTEN TO ME!

IF YOU SLIP INTO THIS DREAM, ALL IS LOST!

SURFER, WHY ARE YOU SHAKING ME? STOP IT.

YOU'RE THE LAST PERSON AWAKE ON EARTH! IT'S ALL UP TO YOU!

EVEN I'M ASLEEP NOW!

I SHOULDN'T HAVE SILVERED DOWN. SHOULDN'T HAVE TAKEN THAT NAP.

NORRIN?

IT WAS A MISTAKE BECAUSE EV. I AM...

DAWN GREENWOOD, PLEASE...

DON'T WATCH THIS. I-- THIS WAS MY FAULT.

I WAS AN ASTRONOMER. I WAS BORED WITH MY PLANET. I WANTED TO SEE THE STARS AND...

AND I WISHED...

I WISHED...

I DON'T UNDERSTAND, NORRIN. HOW COULD THIS POSSIBLY BE YOUR FAULT?

WHY IS THIS YOUR...

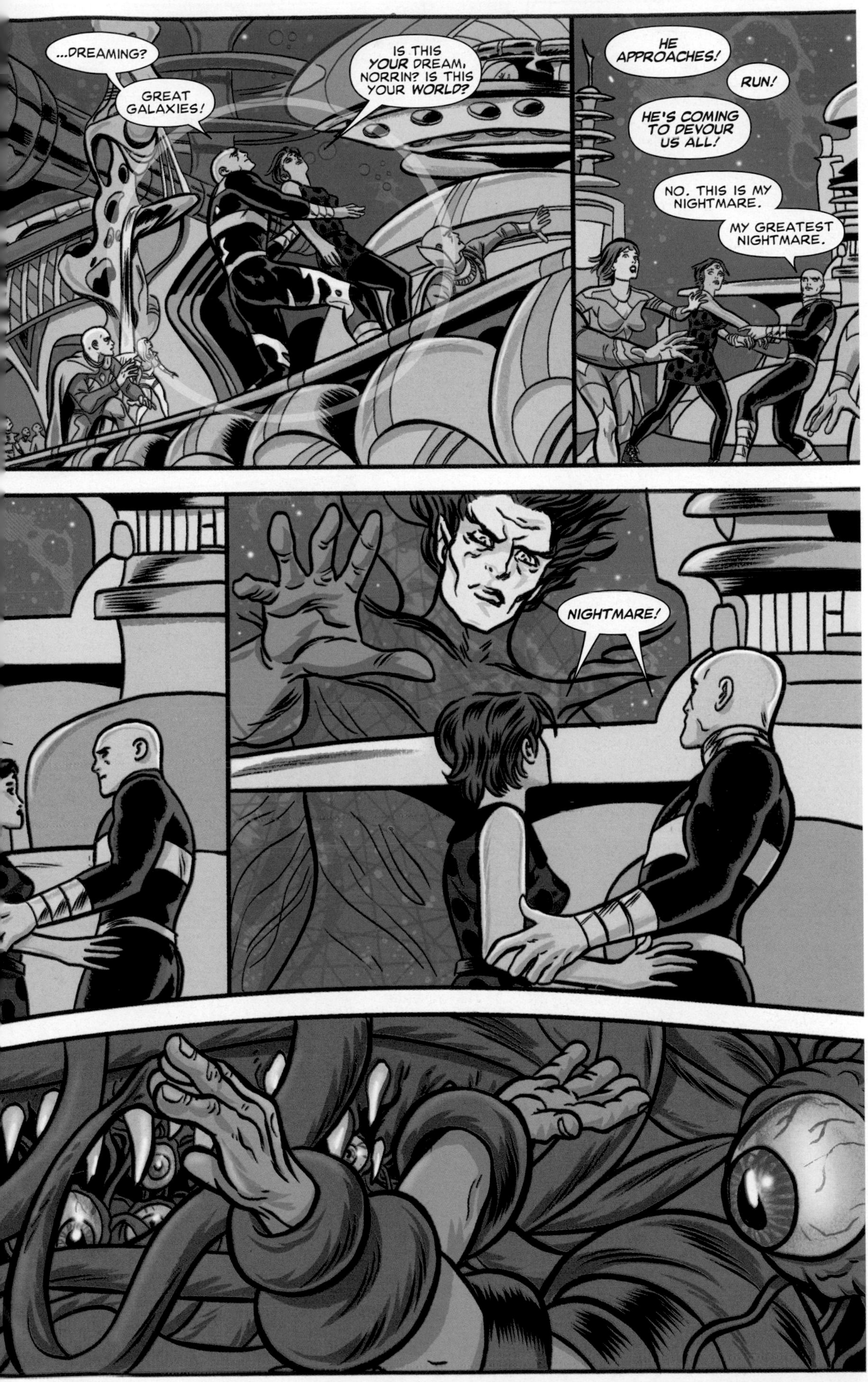
...DREAMING?
GREAT GALAXIES!
IS THIS YOUR DREAM, NORRIN? IS THIS YOUR WORLD?
HE APPROACHES!
RUN!
HE'S COMING TO DEVOUR US ALL!
NO. THIS IS MY NIGHTMARE.
MY GREATEST NIGHTMARE.
NIGHTMARE!

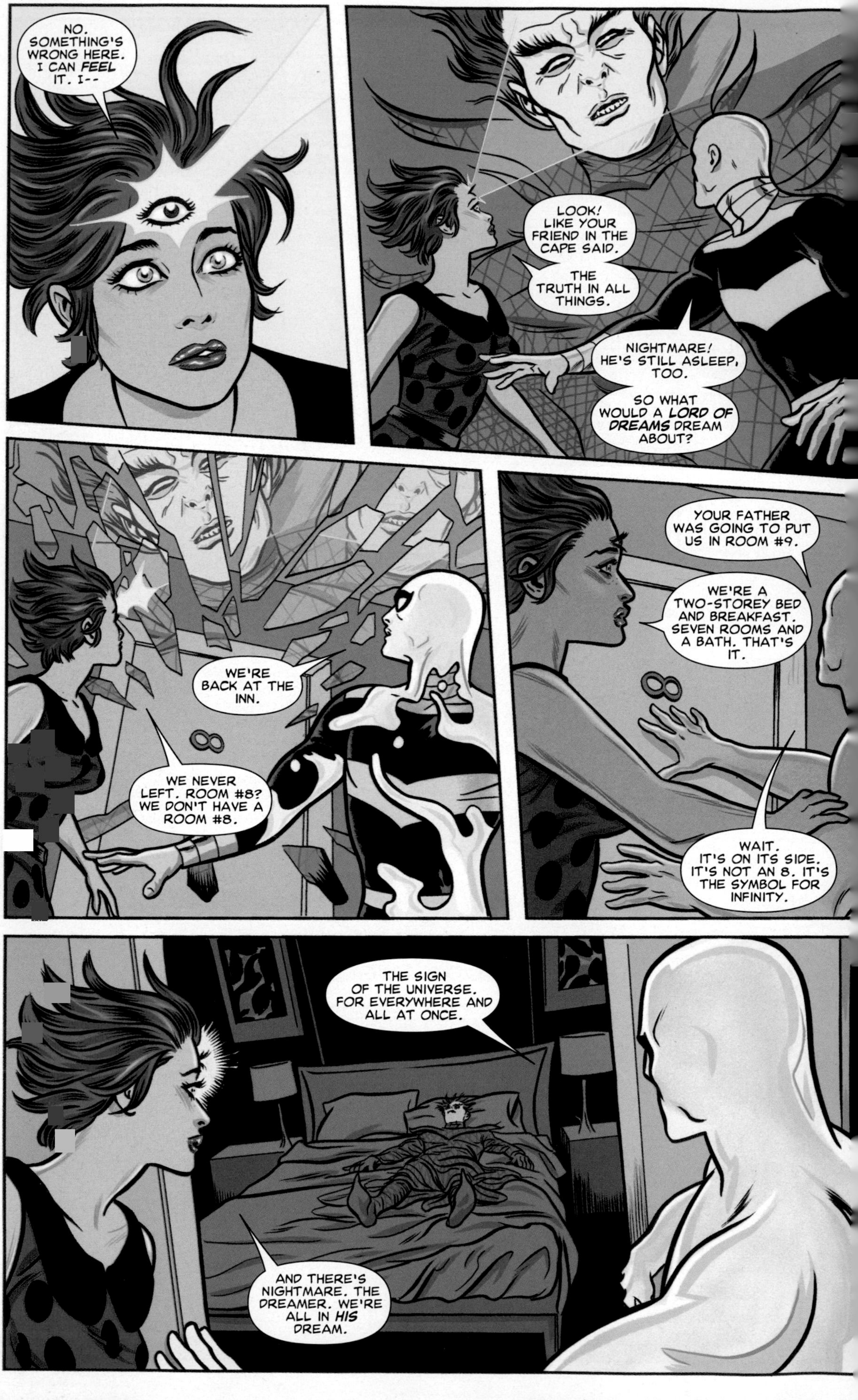

NO. SOMETHING'S WRONG HERE. I CAN FEEL IT. I--
LOOK! LIKE YOUR FRIEND IN THE CAPE SAID.
THE TRUTH IN ALL THINGS.
NIGHTMARE! HE'S STILL ASLEEP, TOO.
SO WHAT WOULD A LORD OF DREAMS DREAM ABOUT?
WE'RE BACK AT THE INN.
WE NEVER LEFT. ROOM #8? WE DON'T HAVE A ROOM #8.
YOUR FATHER WAS GOING TO PUT US IN ROOM #9.
WE'RE A TWO-STOREY BED AND BREAKFAST. SEVEN ROOMS AND A BATH. THAT'S IT.
WAIT. IT'S ON ITS SIDE. IT'S NOT AN 8. IT'S THE SYMBOL FOR INFINITY.
THE SIGN OF THE UNIVERSE. FOR EVERYWHERE AND ALL AT ONCE.
AND THERE'S NIGHTMARE. THE DREAMER. WE'RE ALL IN HIS DREAM.

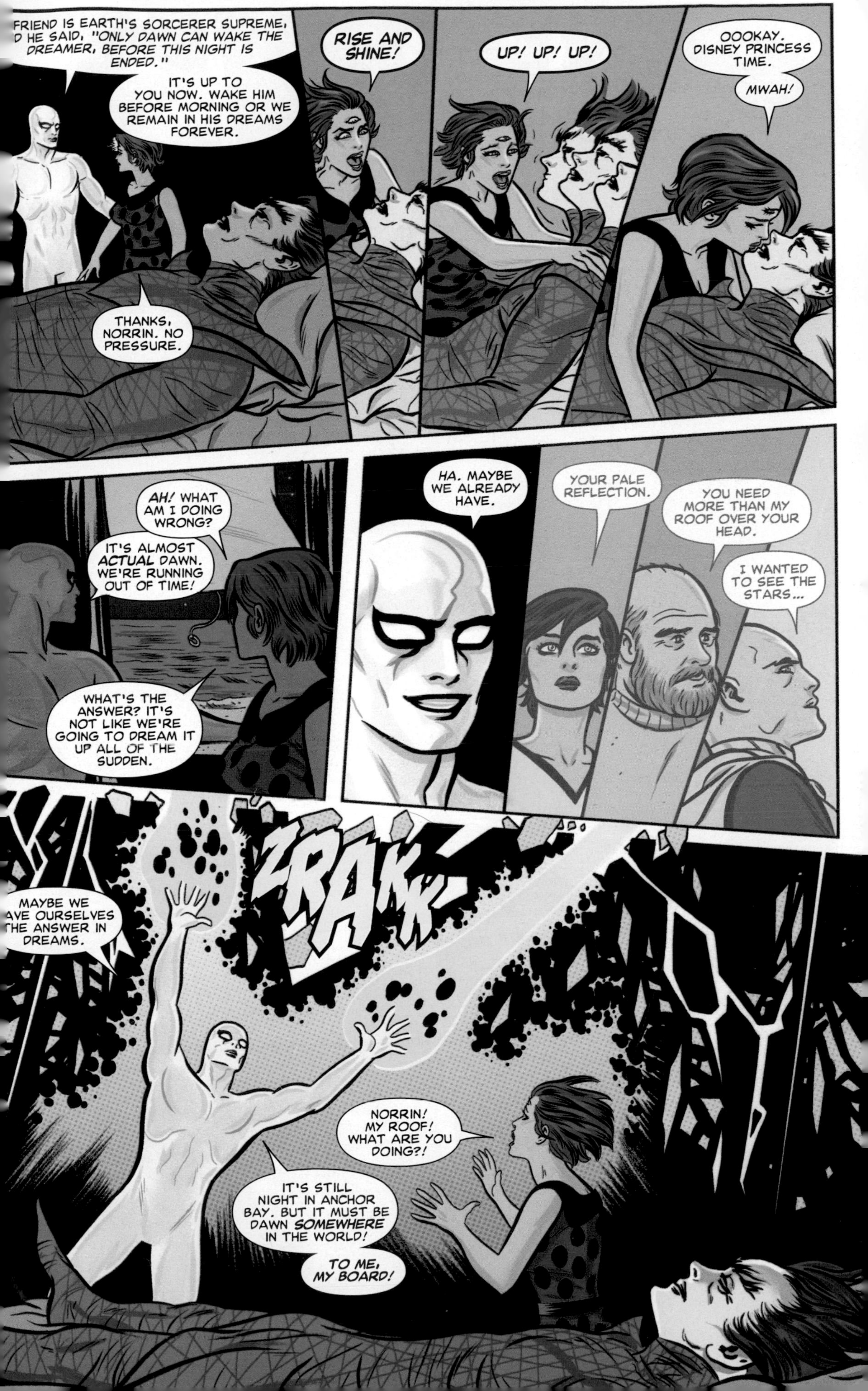
FRIEND IS EARTH'S SORCERER SUPREME, D HE SAID, "ONLY DAWN CAN WAKE THE DREAMER, BEFORE THIS NIGHT IS ENDED."
IT'S UP TO YOU NOW. WAKE HIM BEFORE MORNING OR WE REMAIN IN HIS DREAMS FOREVER.
THANKS, NORRIN. NO PRESSURE.
RISE AND SHINE!
UP! UP! UP!
OOOKAY. DISNEY PRINCESS TIME.
MWAH!
AH! WHAT AM I DOING WRONG?
IT'S ALMOST ACTUAL DAWN. WE'RE RUNNING OUT OF TIME!
WHAT'S THE ANSWER? IT'S NOT LIKE WE'RE GOING TO DREAM IT UP ALL OF THE SUDDEN.
HA. MAYBE WE ALREADY HAVE.
YOUR PALE REFLECTION.
YOU NEED MORE THAN MY ROOF OVER YOUR HEAD.
I WANTED TO SEE THE STARS...
ZRAKK
MAYBE WE AVE OURSELVES THE ANSWER IN DREAMS.
NORRIN! MY ROOF! WHAT ARE YOU DOING?!
IT'S STILL NIGHT IN ANCHOR BAY. BUT IT MUST BE DAWN SOMEWHERE IN THE WORLD!
TO ME, MY BOARD!

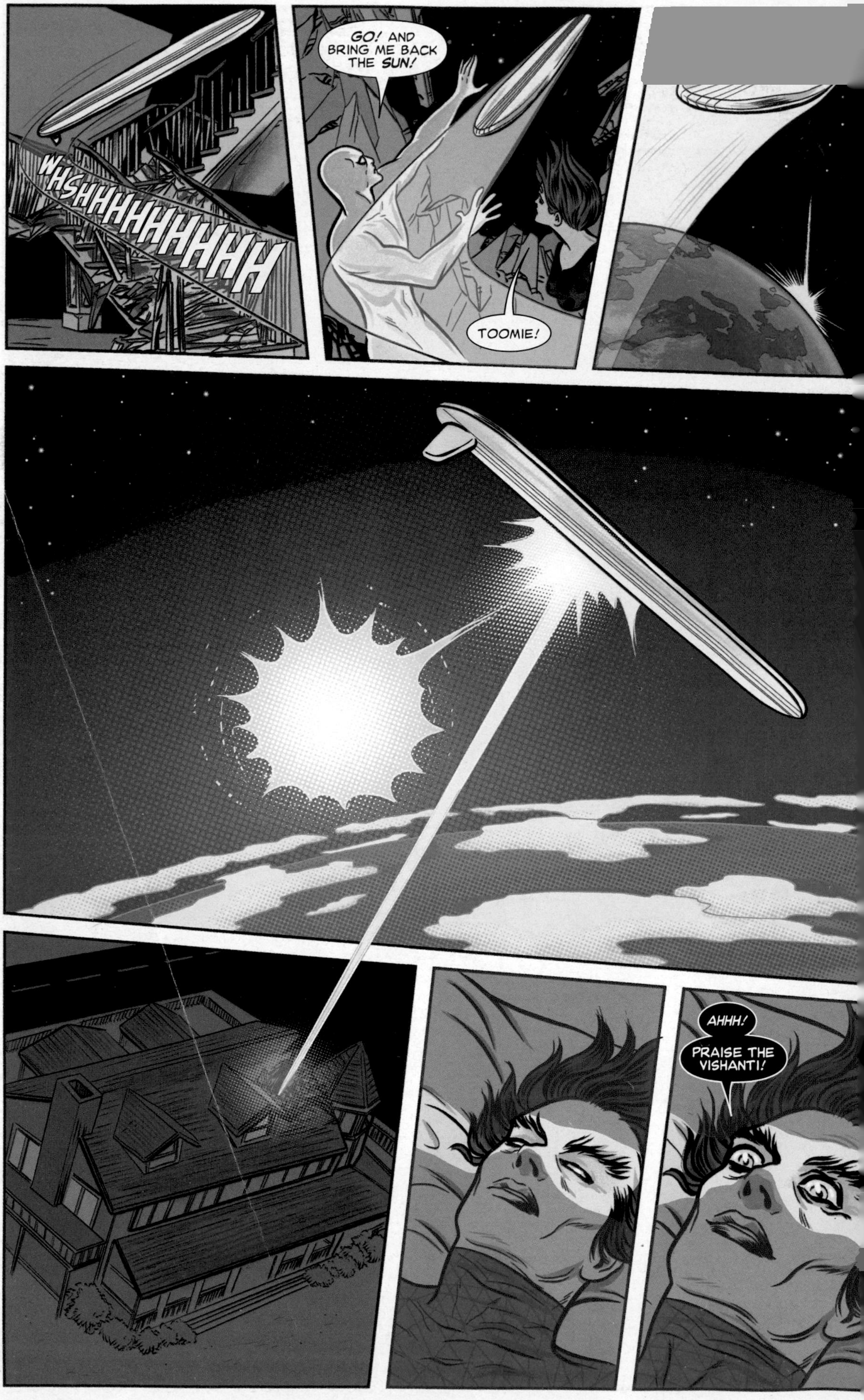
WHSHHHHHHHHHH
GO! AND BRING ME BACK THE SUN!
TOOMIE!
AHHH!
PRAISE THE VISHANTI!

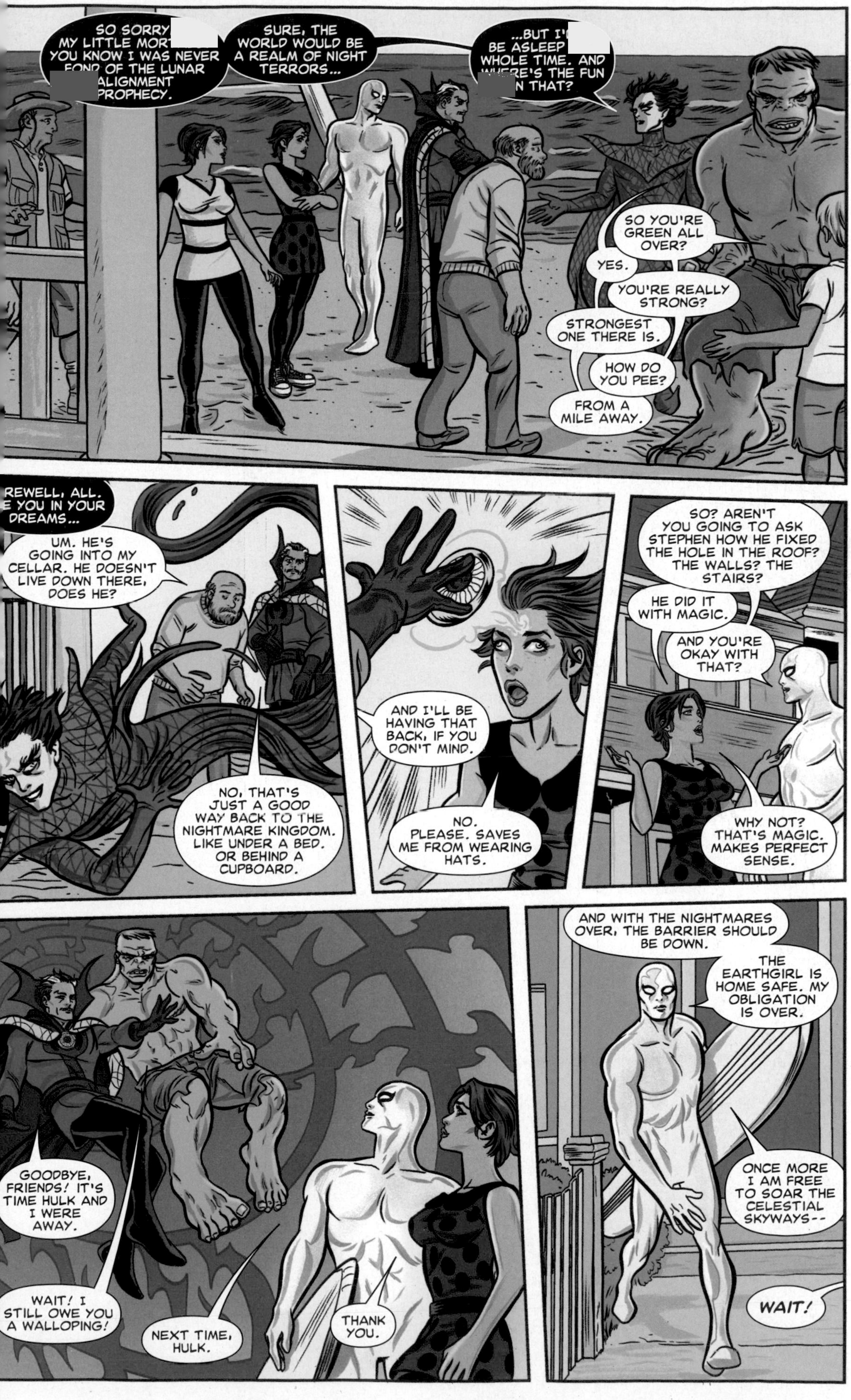

SO SORRY MY LITTLE MORT YOU KNOW I WAS NEVER FOND OF THE LUNAR ALIGNMENT PROPHECY.
SURE, THE WORLD WOULD BE A REALM OF NIGHT TERRORS...
...BUT I' BE ASLEEP WHOLE TIME. AND WHERE'S THE FUN N THAT?
SO YOU'RE GREEN ALL OVER?
YES.
YOU'RE REALLY STRONG?
STRONGEST ONE THERE IS.
HOW DO YOU PEE?
FROM A MILE AWAY.
REWELL, ALL. E YOU IN YOUR DREAMS...
UM. HE'S GOING INTO MY CELLAR. HE DOESN'T LIVE DOWN THERE, DOES HE?
NO, THAT'S JUST A GOOD WAY BACK TO THE NIGHTMARE KINGDOM. LIKE UNDER A BED. OR BEHIND A CUPBOARD.
AND I'LL BE HAVING THAT BACK, IF YOU DON'T MIND.
NO. PLEASE. SAVES ME FROM WEARING HATS.
SO? AREN'T YOU GOING TO ASK STEPHEN HOW HE FIXED THE HOLE IN THE ROOF? THE WALLS? THE STAIRS?
HE DID IT WITH MAGIC.
AND YOU'RE OKAY WITH THAT?
WHY NOT? THAT'S MAGIC. MAKES PERFECT SENSE.
GOODBYE, FRIENDS! IT'S TIME HULK AND I WERE AWAY.
WAIT! I STILL OWE YOU A WALLOPING!
NEXT TIME, HULK.
THANK YOU.
AND WITH THE NIGHTMARES OVER, THE BARRIER SHOULD BE DOWN.
THE EARTHGIRL IS HOME SAFE. MY OBLIGATION IS OVER.
ONCE MORE I AM FREE TO SOAR THE CELESTIAL SKYWAYS--
WAIT!

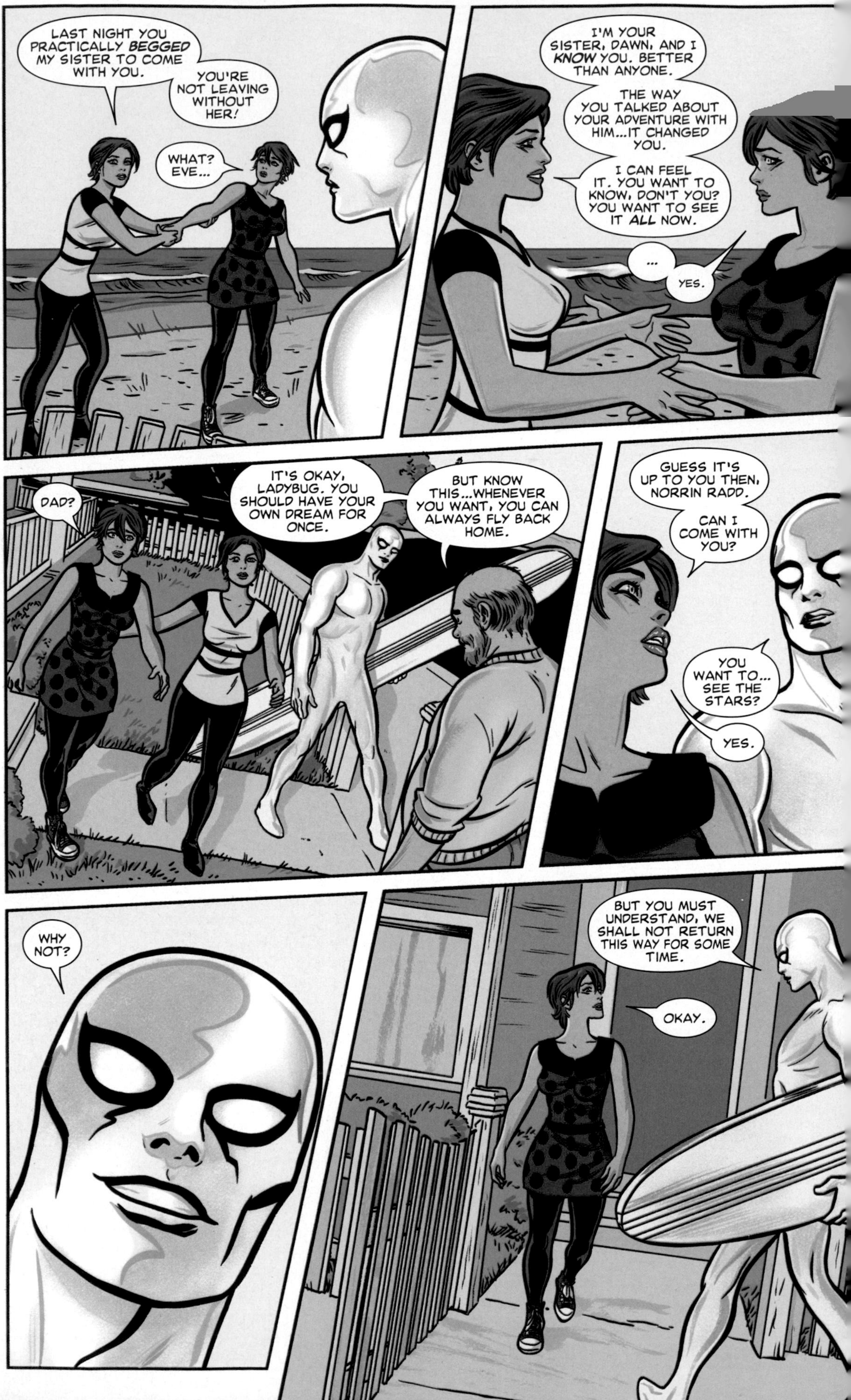
LAST NIGHT YOU PRACTICALLY *BEGGED* MY SISTER TO COME WITH YOU.
YOU'RE NOT LEAVING WITHOUT HER!
WHAT? EVE...
I'M YOUR SISTER, DAWN, AND I *KNOW* YOU. BETTER THAN ANYONE.
THE WAY YOU TALKED ABOUT YOUR ADVENTURE WITH HIM...IT CHANGED YOU.
I CAN FEEL IT. YOU WANT TO KNOW, DON'T YOU? YOU WANT TO SEE IT *ALL* NOW.
...
YES.
DAD?
IT'S OKAY, LADYBUG. YOU SHOULD HAVE YOUR OWN DREAM FOR ONCE.
BUT KNOW THIS...WHENEVER YOU WANT, YOU CAN ALWAYS FLY BACK HOME.
GUESS IT'S UP TO YOU THEN, NORRIN RADD.
CAN I COME WITH YOU?
YOU WANT TO... SEE THE STARS?
YES.
WHY NOT?
BUT YOU MUST UNDERSTAND, WE SHALL NOT RETURN THIS WAY FOR SOME TIME.
OKAY.

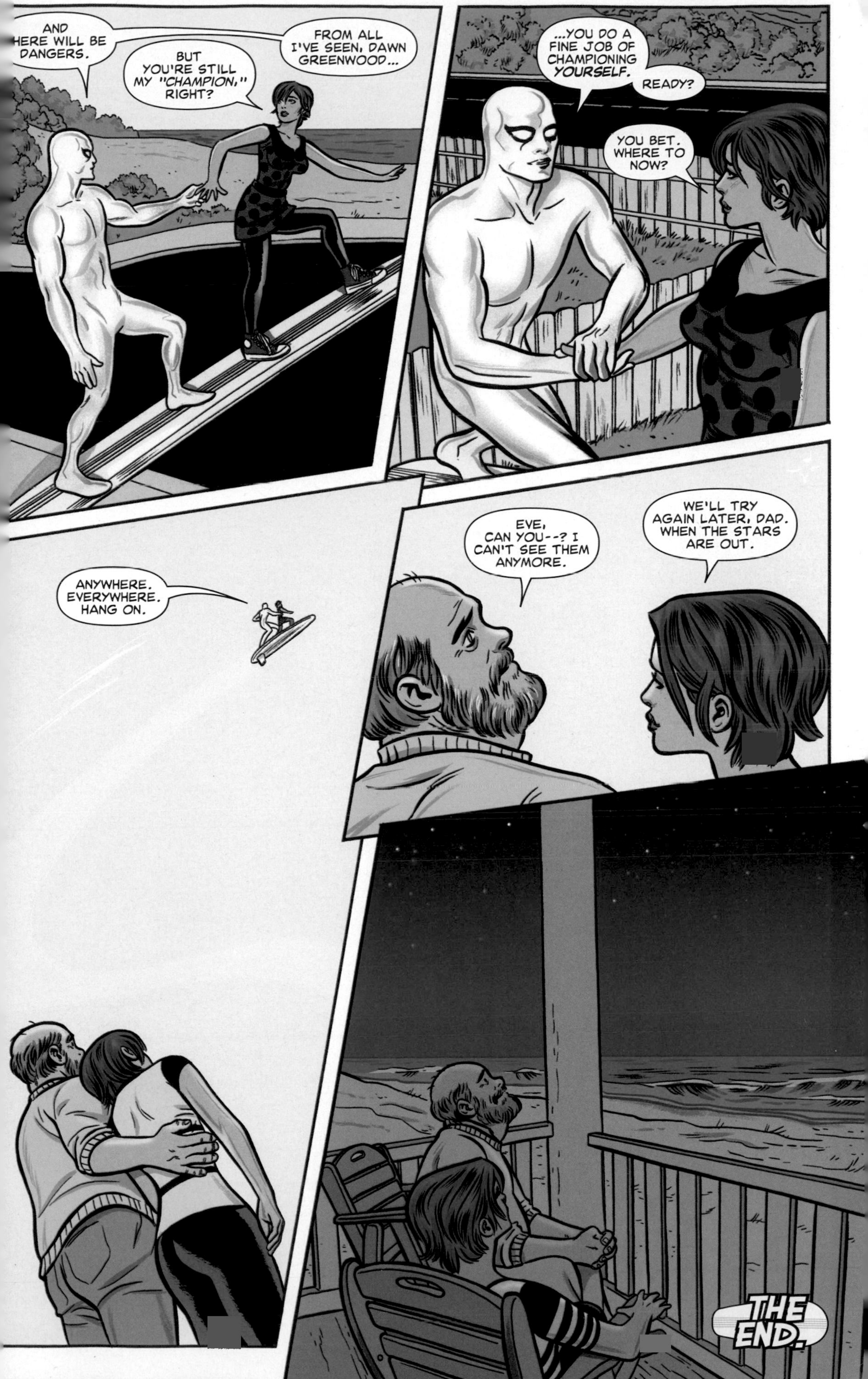

AND HERE WILL BE DANGERS.
BUT YOU'RE STILL MY "CHAMPION," RIGHT?
FROM ALL I'VE SEEN, DAWN GREENWOOD...
...YOU DO A FINE JOB OF CHAMPIONING YOURSELF.
READY?
YOU BET. WHERE TO NOW?
ANYWHERE. EVERYWHERE. HANG ON.
EVE, CAN YOU--? I CAN'T SEE THEM ANYMORE.
WE'LL TRY AGAIN LATER, DAD. WHEN THE STARS ARE OUT.
THE END.

ALL-NEW MARVEL NOW! POINT ONE #1

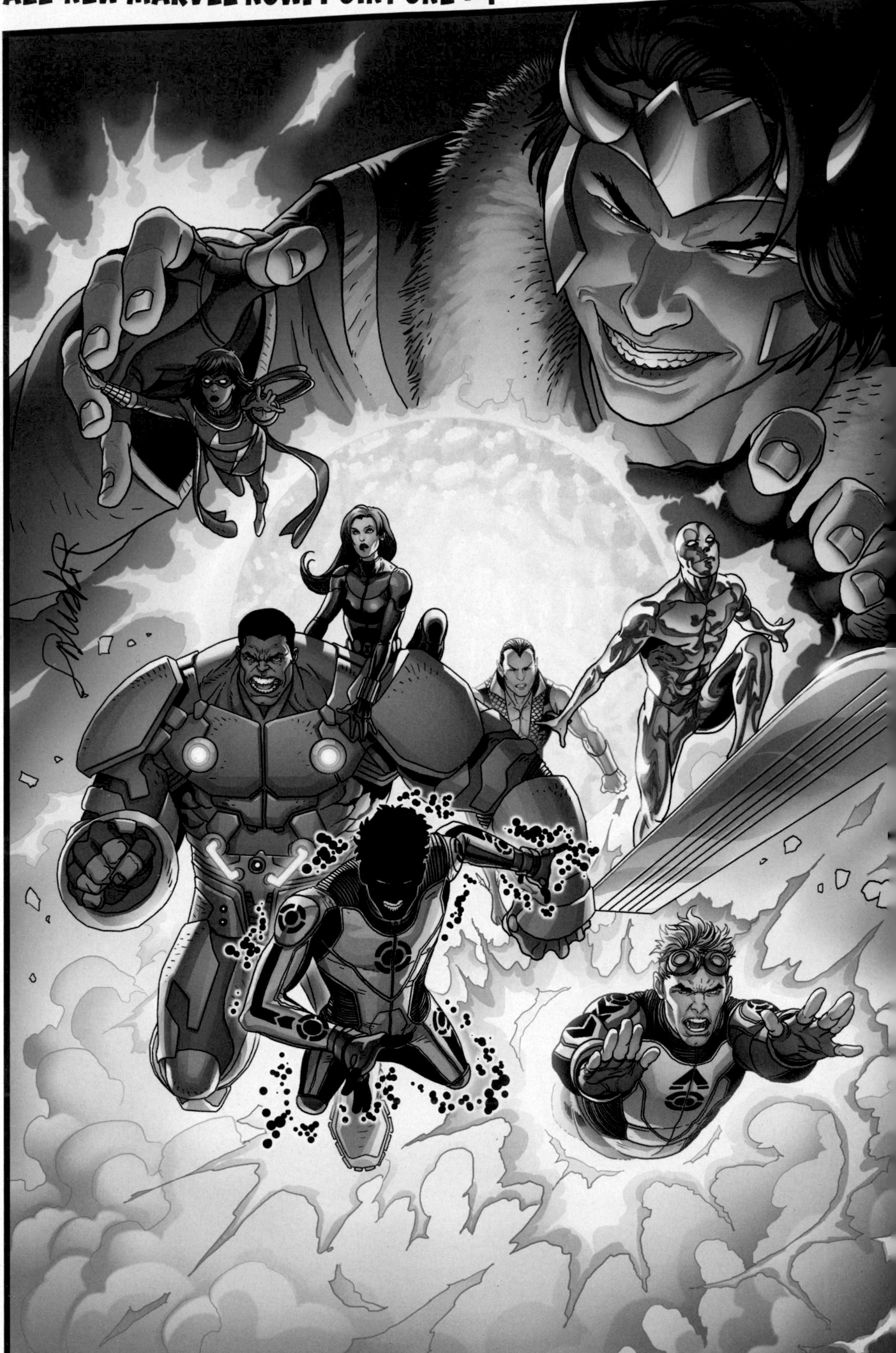

GIRL ON BOARD

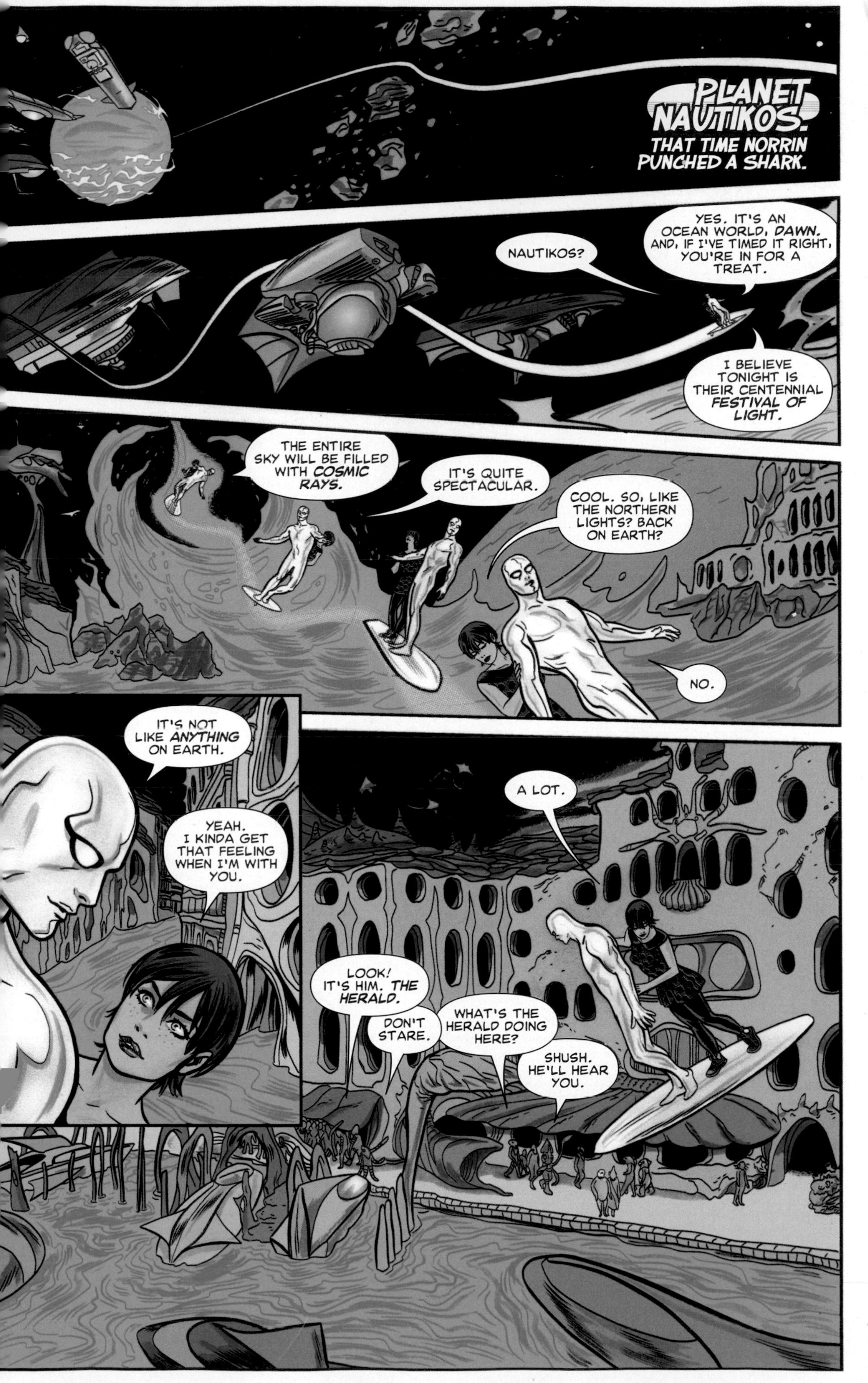
PLANET NAUTIKOS.
THAT TIME NORRIN PUNCHED A SHARK.
NAUTIKOS?
YES. IT'S AN OCEAN WORLD, DAWN. AND, IF I'VE TIMED IT RIGHT, YOU'RE IN FOR A TREAT.
I BELIEVE TONIGHT IS THEIR CENTENNIAL FESTIVAL OF LIGHT.
THE ENTIRE SKY WILL BE FILLED WITH COSMIC RAYS.
IT'S QUITE SPECTACULAR.
COOL. SO, LIKE THE NORTHERN LIGHTS? BACK ON EARTH?
NO.
IT'S NOT LIKE ANYTHING ON EARTH.
YEAH. I KINDA GET THAT FEELING WHEN I'M WITH YOU.
A LOT.
LOOK! IT'S HIM. THE HERALD.
DON'T STARE.
WHAT'S THE HERALD DOING HERE?
SHUSH. HE'LL HEAR YOU.

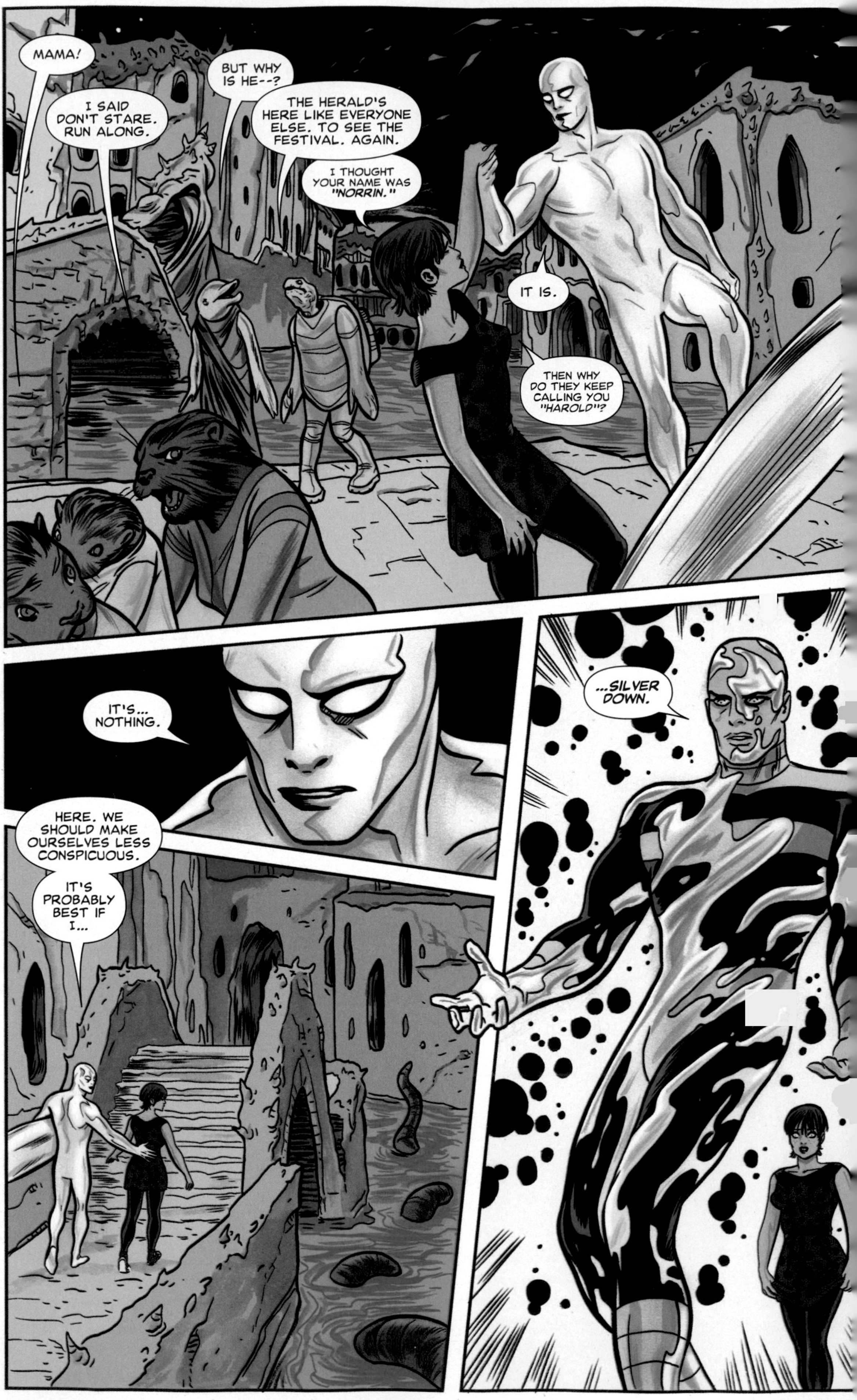
MAMA!
I SAID DON'T STARE. RUN ALONG.
BUT WHY IS HE--?
THE HERALD'S HERE LIKE EVERYONE ELSE. TO SEE THE FESTIVAL. AGAIN.
I THOUGHT YOUR NAME WAS "NORRIN."
IT IS.
THEN WHY DO THEY KEEP CALLING YOU "HAROLD"?
IT'S... NOTHING.
HERE. WE SHOULD MAKE OURSELVES LESS CONSPICUOUS.
IT'S PROBABLY BEST IF I...
...SILVER DOWN.

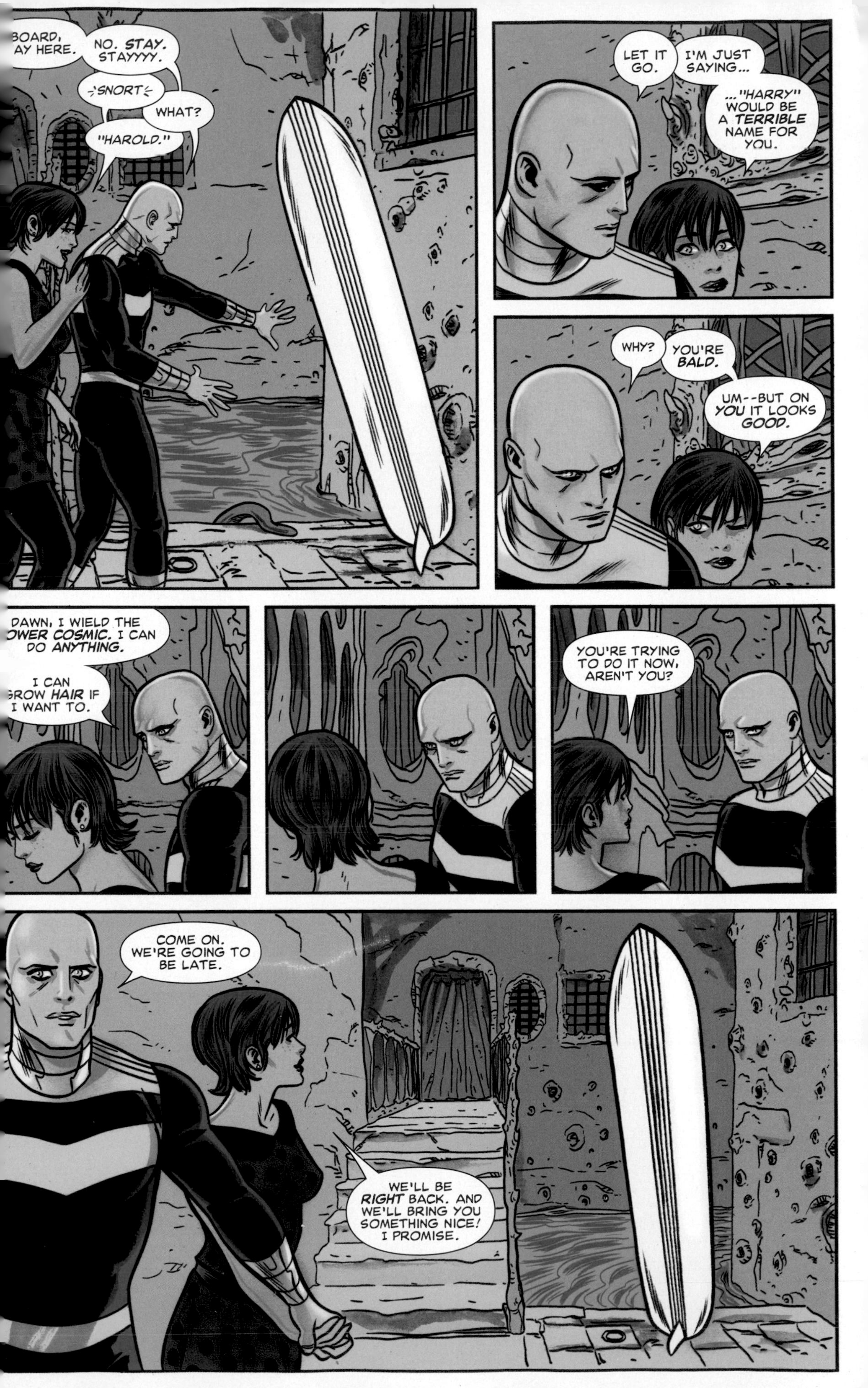

BOARD,
AY HERE.
NO. STAY. STAYYYY.
SNORT
WHAT?
"HAROLD."
LET IT GO.
I'M JUST SAYING...
..."HARRY" WOULD BE A TERRIBLE NAME FOR YOU.
WHY?
YOU'RE BALD.
UM--BUT ON YOU IT LOOKS GOOD.
DAWN, I WIELD THE
OWER COSMIC. I CAN DO ANYTHING.
I CAN
GROW HAIR IF I WANT TO.
YOU'RE TRYING TO DO IT NOW, AREN'T YOU?
COME ON. WE'RE GOING TO BE LATE.
WE'LL BE RIGHT BACK. AND WE'LL BRING YOU SOMETHING NICE! I PROMISE.

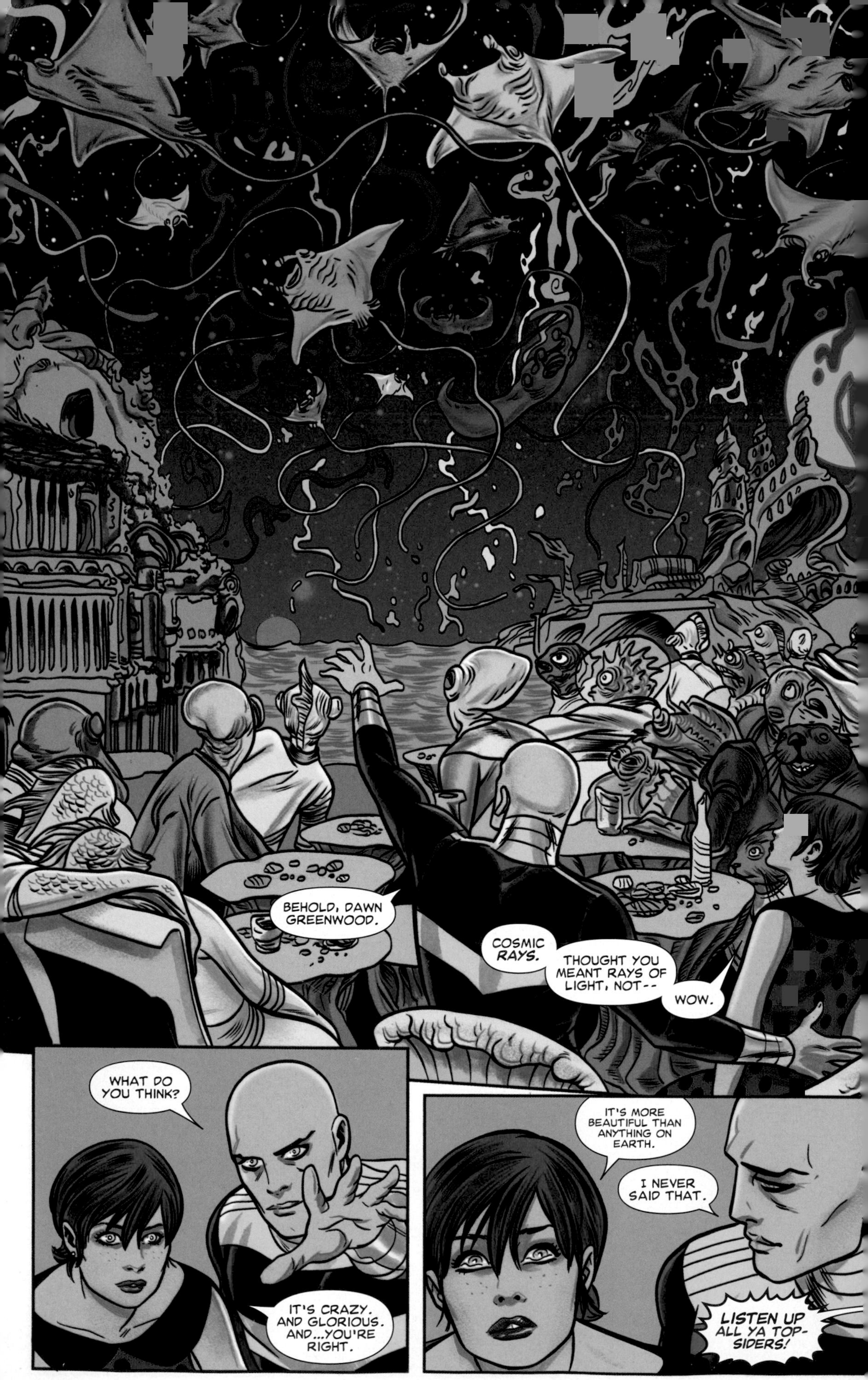
BEHOLD, DAWN GREENWOOD.
COSMIC RAYS.
THOUGHT YOU MEANT RAYS OF LIGHT, NOT--
WOW.
WHAT DO YOU THINK?
IT'S CRAZY. AND GLORIOUS. AND...YOU'RE RIGHT.
IT'S MORE BEAUTIFUL THAN ANYTHING ON EARTH.
I NEVER SAID THAT.
LISTEN UP ALL YA TOP-SIDERS!

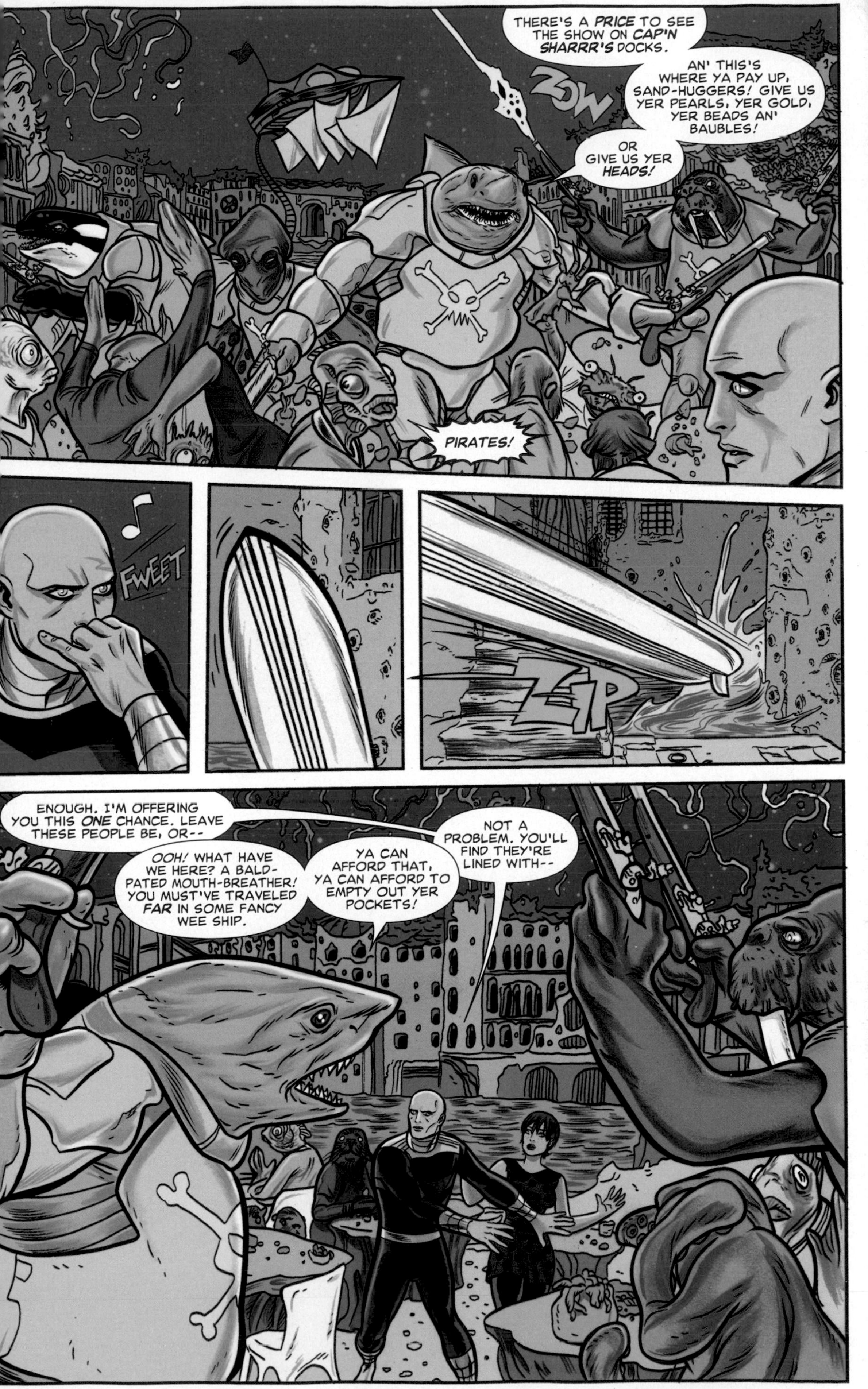
THERE'S A PRICE TO SEE THE SHOW ON CAP'N SHARRR'S DOCKS.
AN' THIS'S WHERE YA PAY UP, SAND-HUGGERS! GIVE US YER PEARLS, YER GOLD, YER BEADS AN' BAUBLES!
ZOW
OR GIVE US YER HEADS!
PIRATES!
FWEET
ZIP
ENOUGH. I'M OFFERING YOU THIS ONE CHANCE. LEAVE THESE PEOPLE BE, OR--
OOH! WHAT HAVE WE HERE? A BALD-PATED MOUTH-BREATHER! YOU MUST'VE TRAVELED FAR IN SOME FANCY WEE SHIP.
YA CAN AFFORD THAT, YA CAN AFFORD TO EMPTY OUT YER POCKETS!
NOT A PROBLEM. YOU'LL FIND THEY'RE LINED WITH--

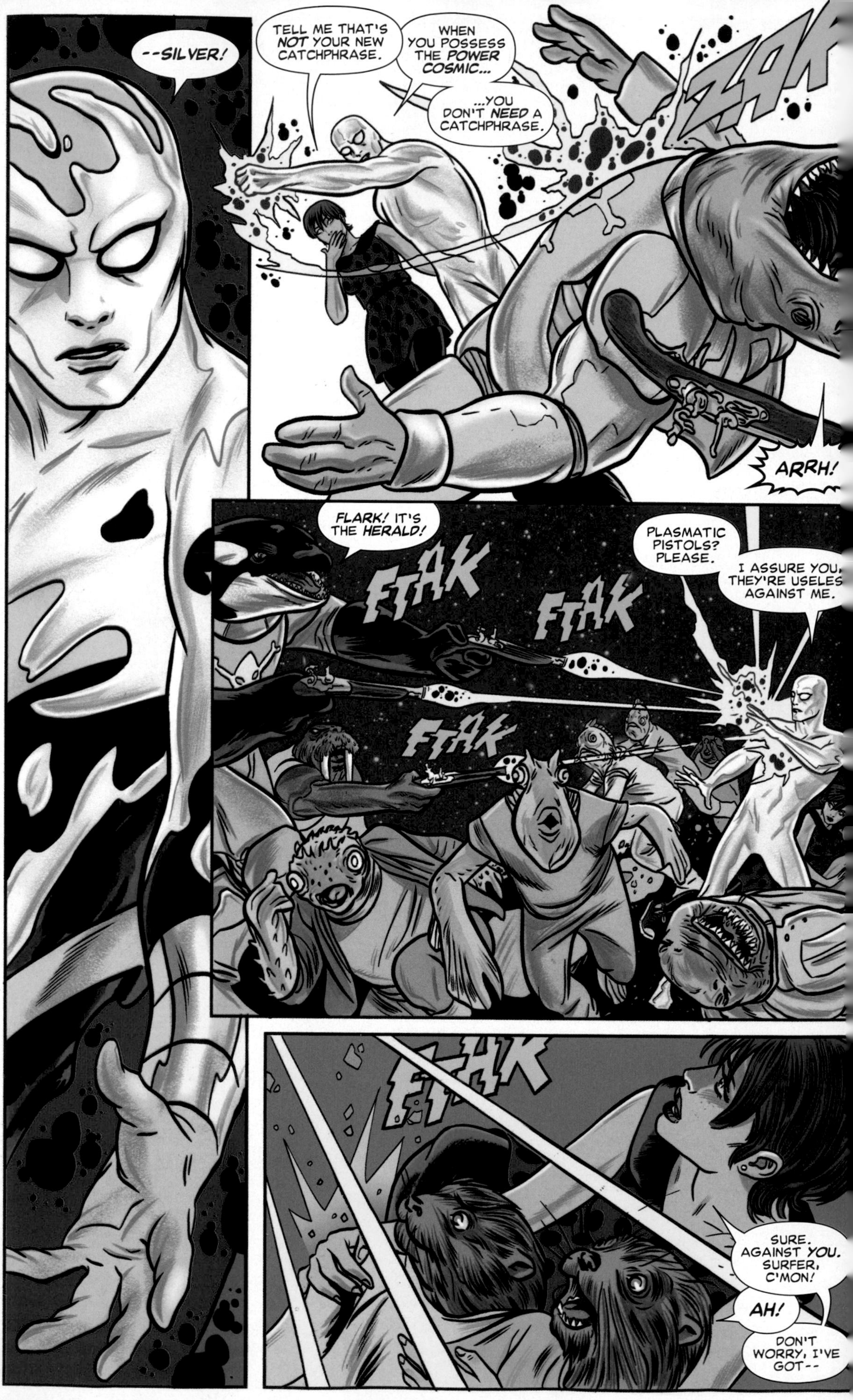
--SILVER!
TELL ME THAT'S NOT YOUR NEW CATCHPHRASE.
WHEN YOU POSSESS THE POWER COSMIC...
...YOU DON'T NEED A CATCHPHRASE.
ZAK
ARRH!
FLARK! IT'S THE HERALD!
FTAK
FTAK
PLASMATIC PISTOLS? PLEASE.
I ASSURE YOU, THEY'RE USELES AGAINST ME.
FTAK
FTAK
SURE. AGAINST YOU. SURFER, C'MON!
AH!
DON'T WORRY, I'VE GOT--

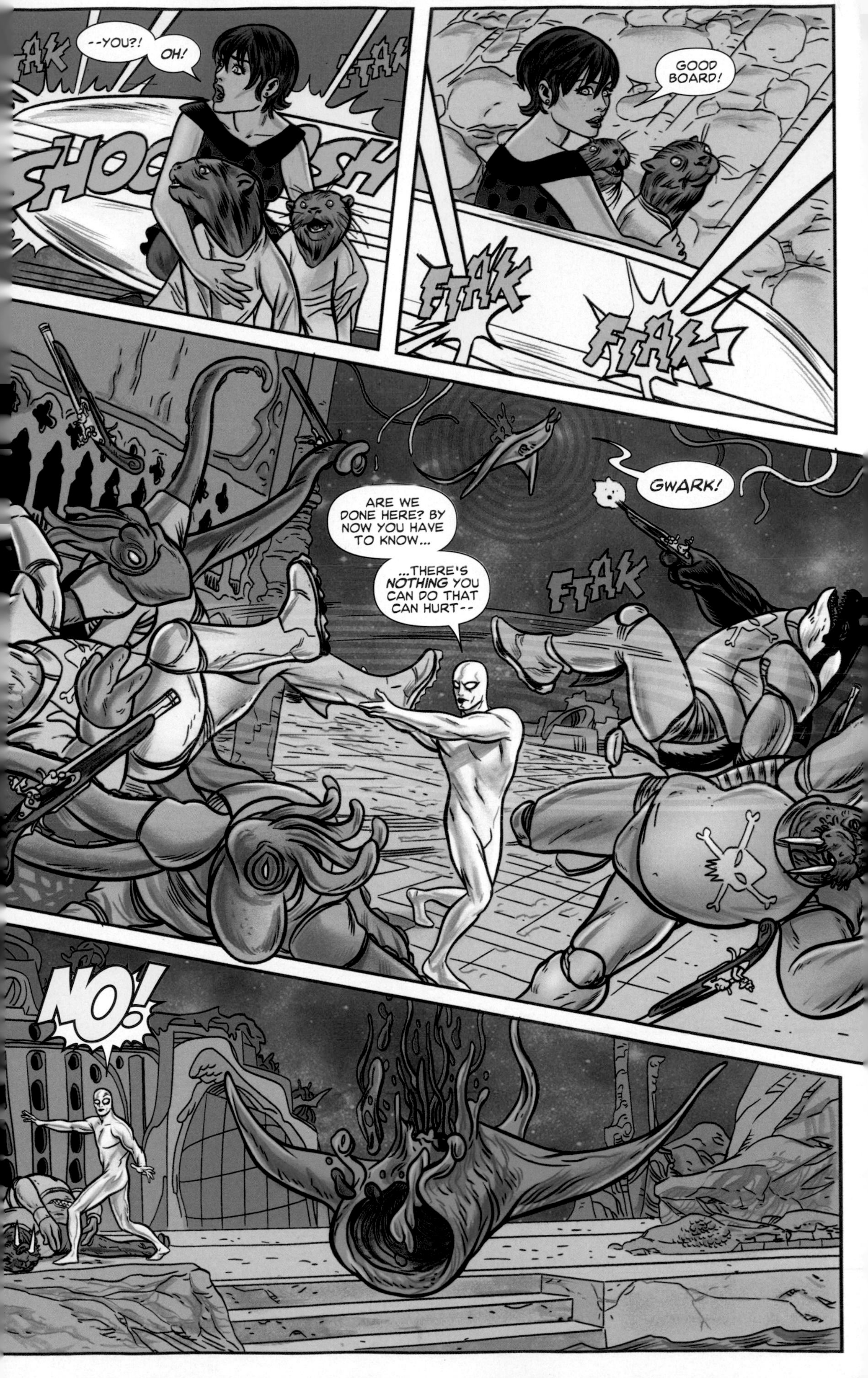
AK
--YOU?!
OH!
FTAK
SHOOOSH
GOOD BOARD!
FTAK
FTAK
GWARK!
ARE WE DONE HERE? BY NOW YOU HAVE TO KNOW...
...THERE'S *NOTHING* YOU CAN DO THAT CAN HURT--
FTAK
NO!

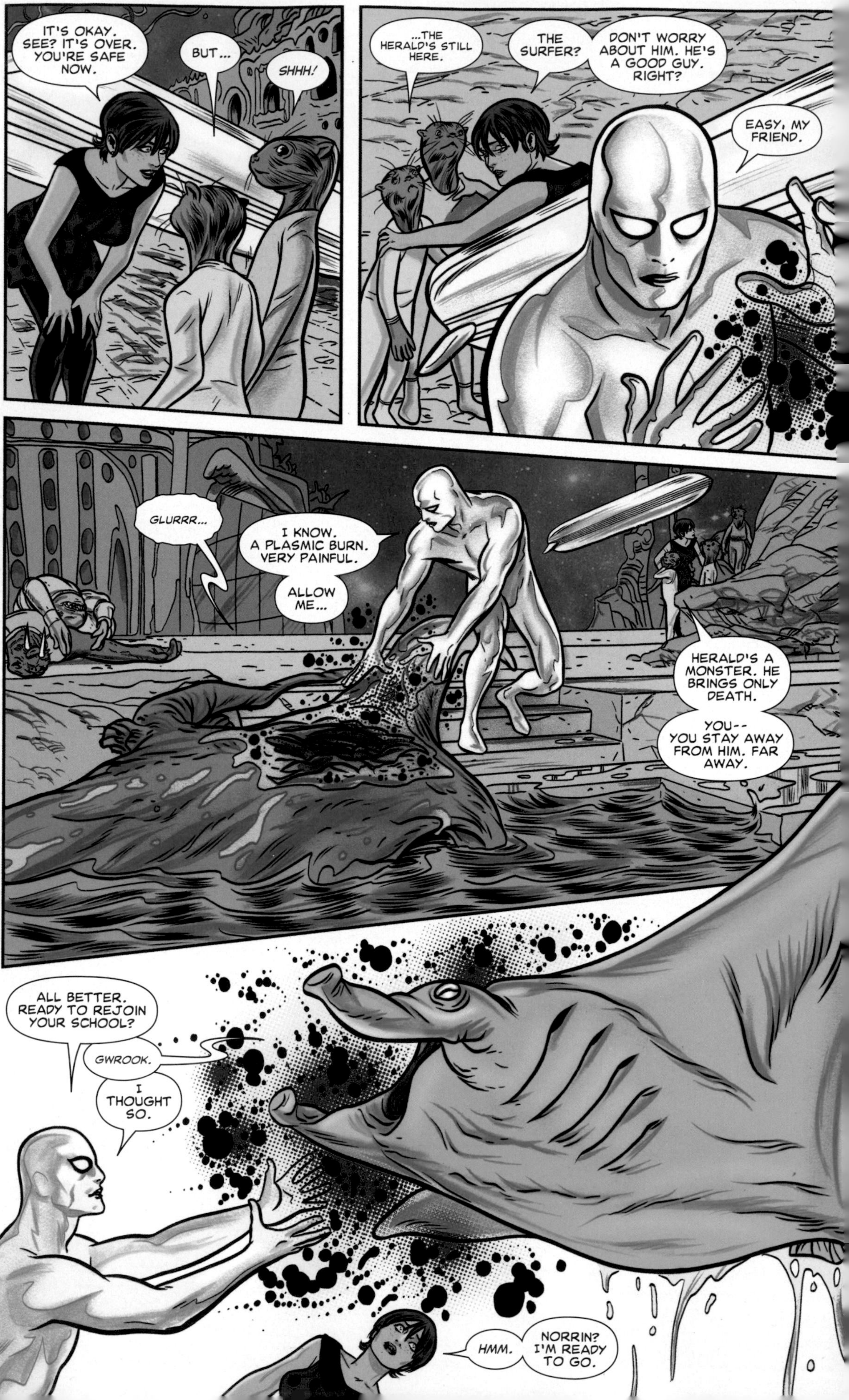
IT'S OKAY. SEE? IT'S OVER. YOU'RE SAFE NOW.
BUT...
SHHH!
...THE HERALD'S STILL HERE.
THE SURFER?
DON'T WORRY ABOUT HIM. HE'S A GOOD GUY. RIGHT?
EASY, MY FRIEND.
GLURRR...
I KNOW. A PLASMIC BURN. VERY PAINFUL.
ALLOW ME...
HERALD'S A MONSTER. HE BRINGS ONLY DEATH.
YOU-- YOU STAY AWAY FROM HIM. FAR AWAY.
ALL BETTER. READY TO REJOIN YOUR SCHOOL?
GWROOK.
I THOUGHT SO.
HMM.
NORRIN? I'M READY TO GO.

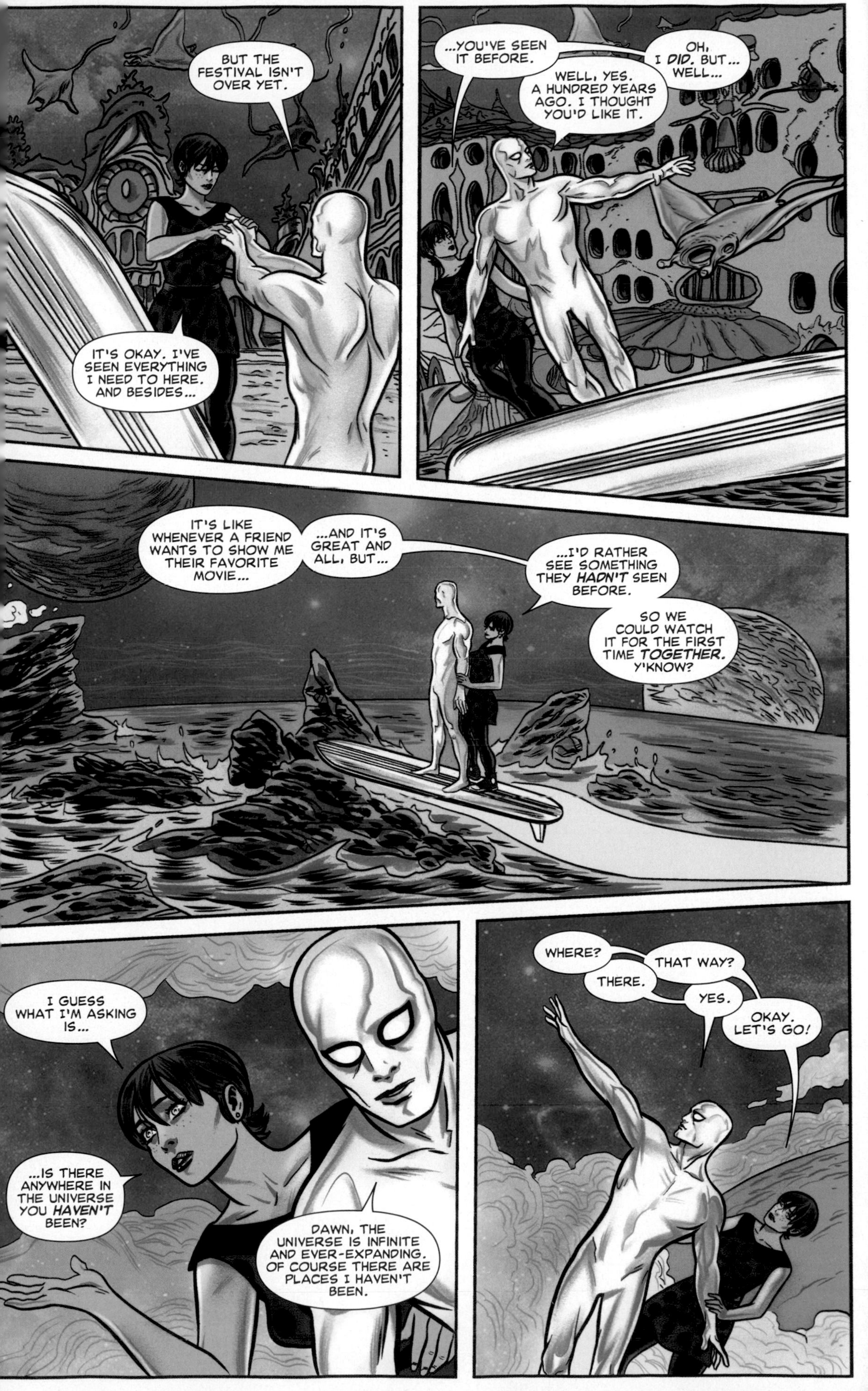
BUT THE FESTIVAL ISN'T OVER YET.
IT'S OKAY. I'VE SEEN EVERYTHING I NEED TO HERE. AND BESIDES...
...YOU'VE SEEN IT BEFORE.
OH, I *DID.* BUT... WELL...
WELL, YES. A HUNDRED YEARS AGO. I THOUGHT YOU'D LIKE IT.
IT'S LIKE WHENEVER A FRIEND WANTS TO SHOW ME THEIR FAVORITE MOVIE...
...AND IT'S GREAT AND ALL, BUT...
...I'D RATHER SEE SOMETHING THEY *HADN'T* SEEN BEFORE.
SO WE COULD WATCH IT FOR THE FIRST TIME *TOGETHER.* Y'KNOW?
I GUESS WHAT I'M ASKING IS...
...IS THERE ANYWHERE IN THE UNIVERSE YOU *HAVEN'T* BEEN?
DAWN, THE UNIVERSE IS INFINITE AND EVER-EXPANDING. OF COURSE THERE ARE PLACES I HAVEN'T BEEN.
WHERE?
THAT WAY?
THERE.
YES.
OKAY. LET'S GO!

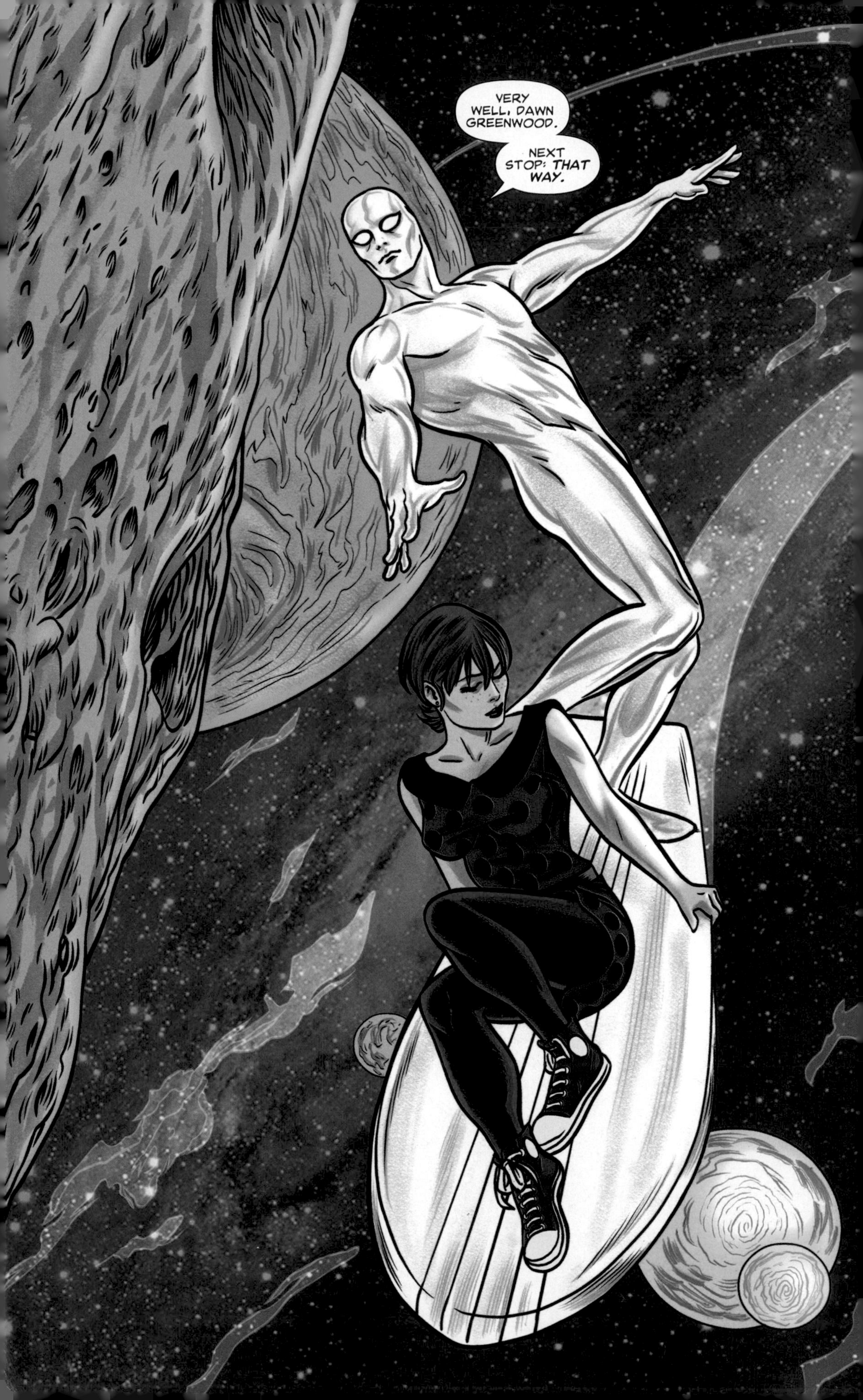
VERY WELL, DAWN GREENWOOD.
NEXT STOP: THAT WAY.

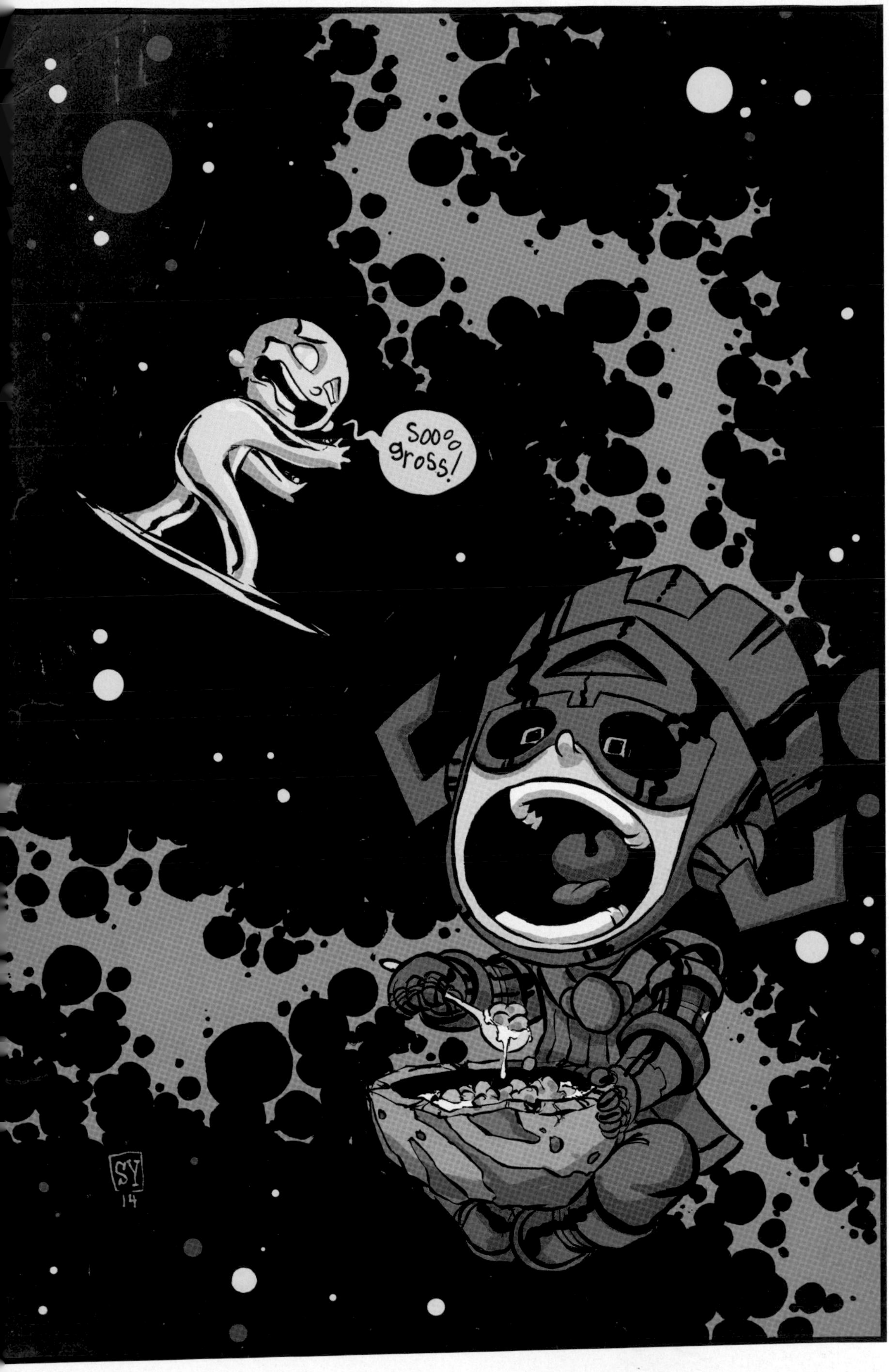
SOOoo gross!
SY 14

#1 VARIANT BY SKOTTIE YOUNG

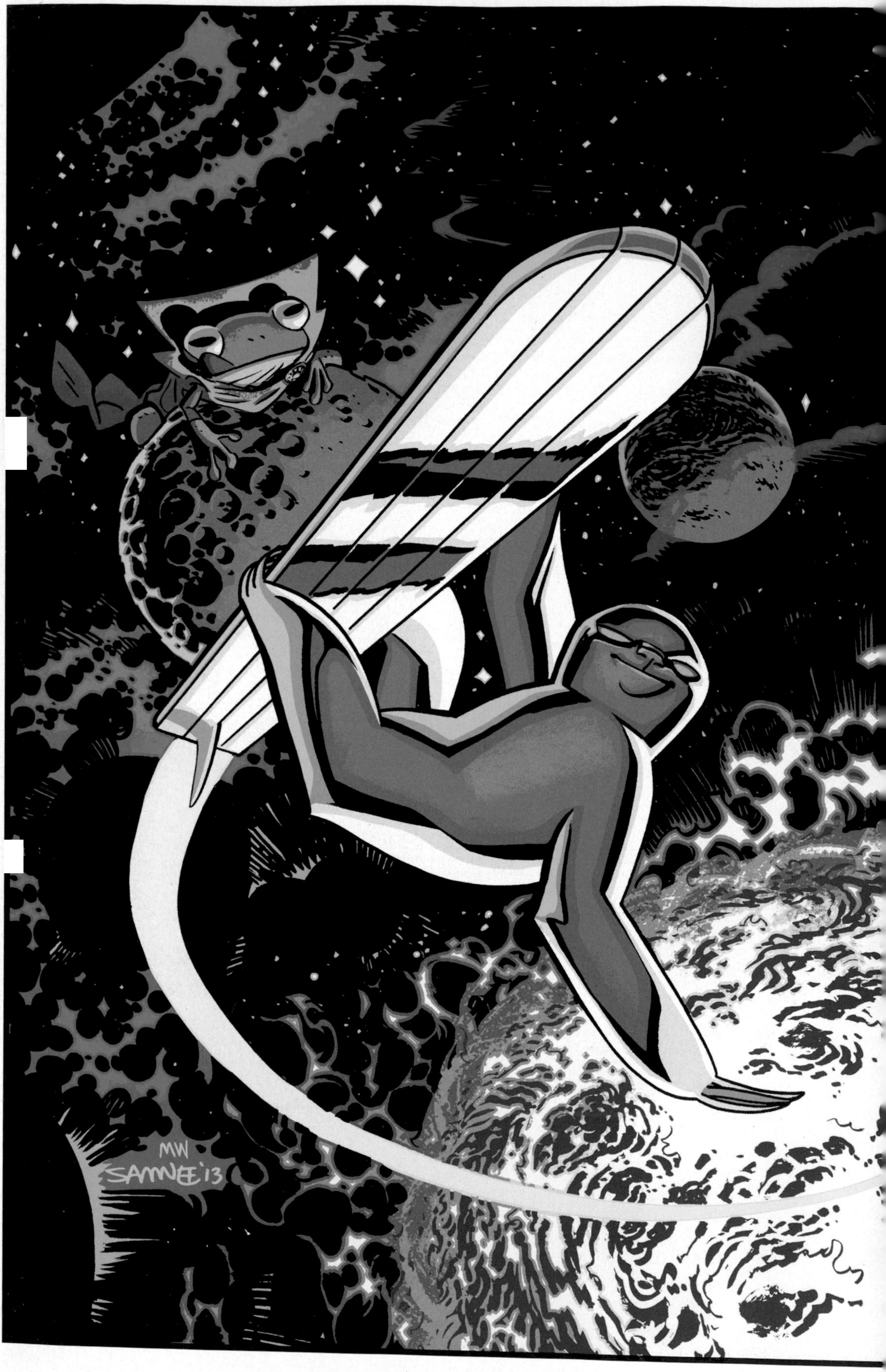
MW
SAMNEE '13

#1 ANIMAL VARIANT BY CHRIS SAMNEE & MATTHEW WILSON

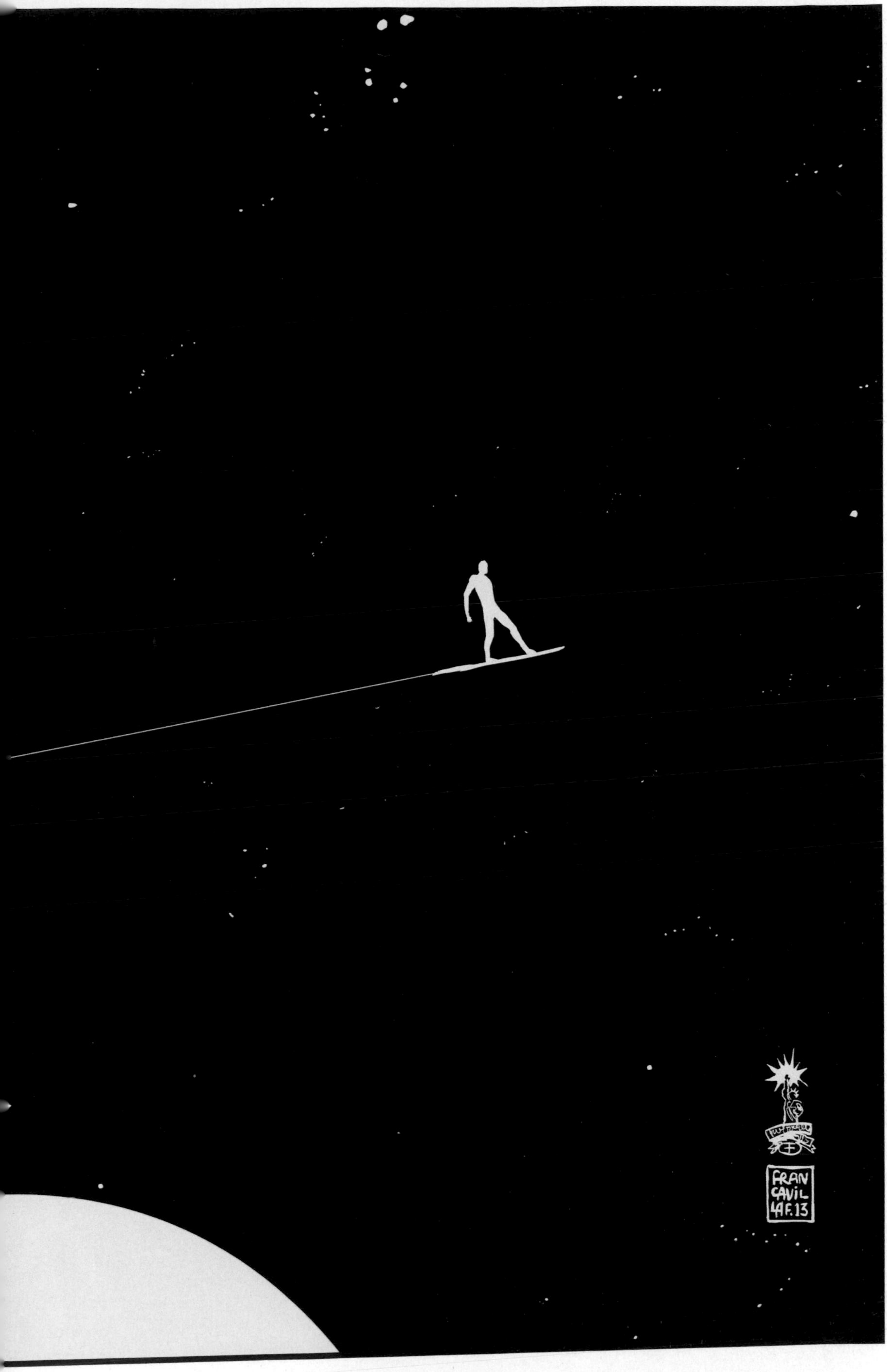
FRAN
CAVIL
LA F.13

#1 VARIANT BY FRANCESCO FRANCAVILLA

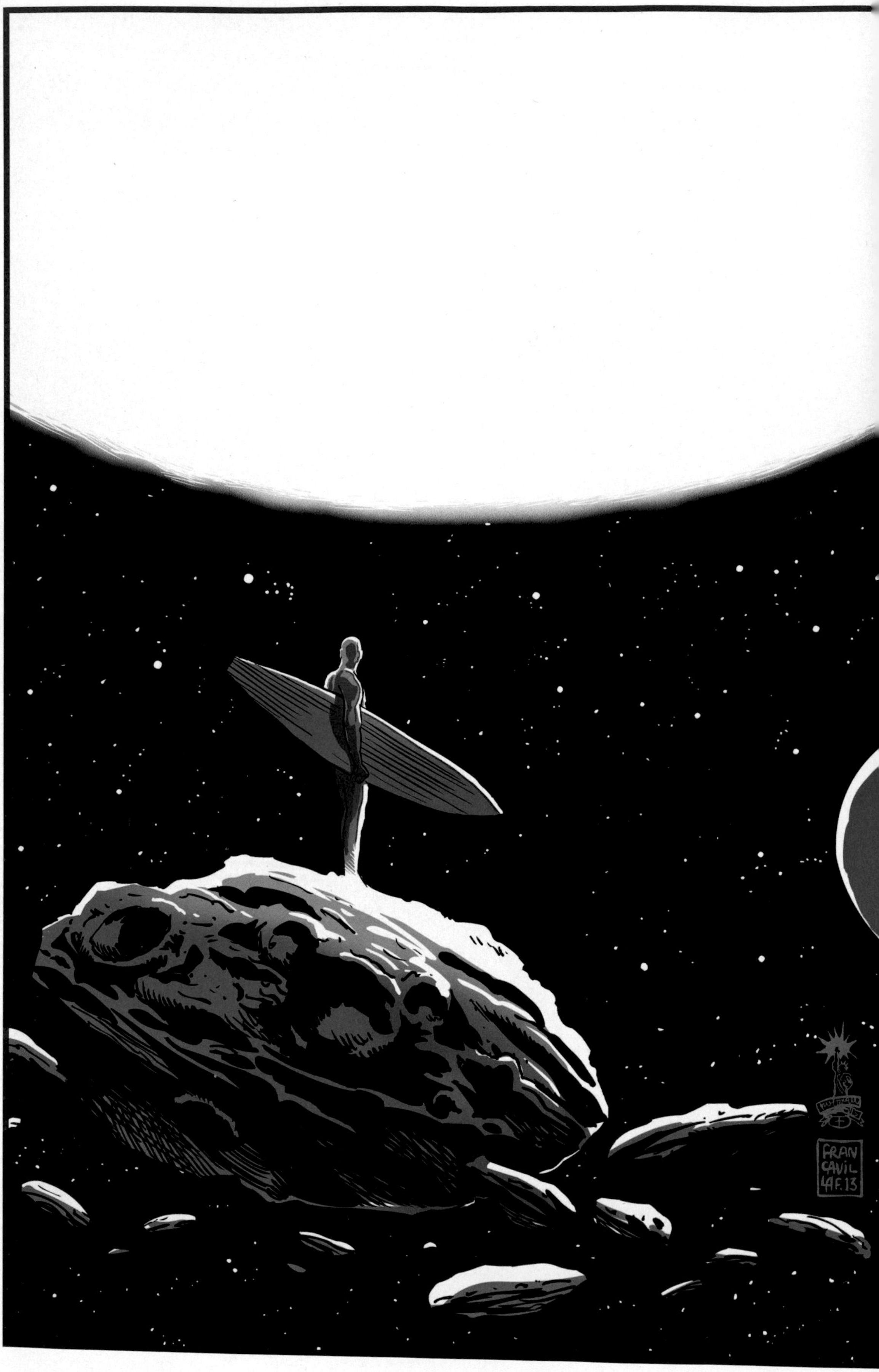
FRAN
CAVIL
LA F.13

#2 VARIANT BY FRANCESCO FRANCAVILLA

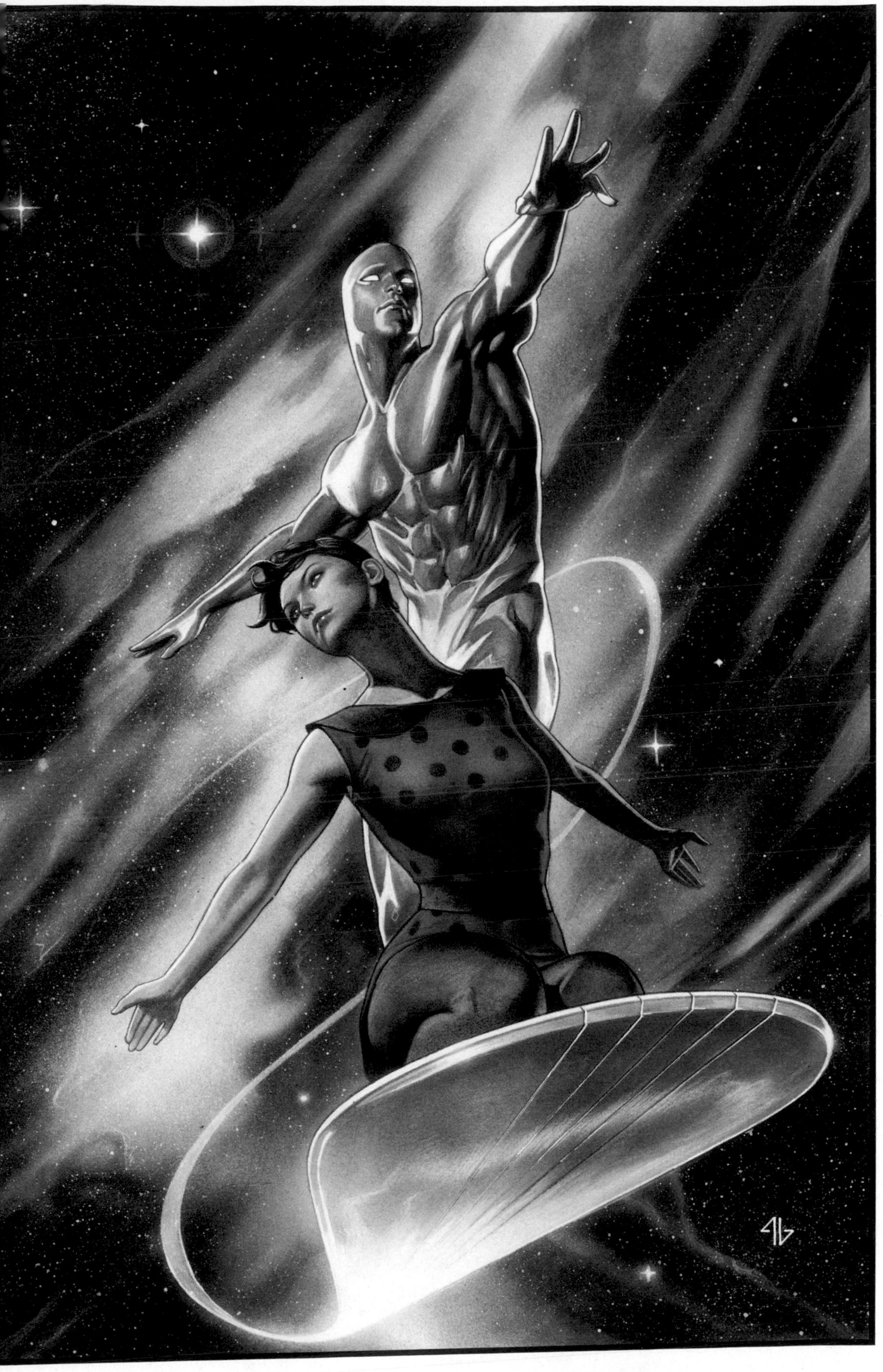

#3 VARIANT BY ADI GRANOV

DAWN DESIGNS BY MICHAEL ALLRED

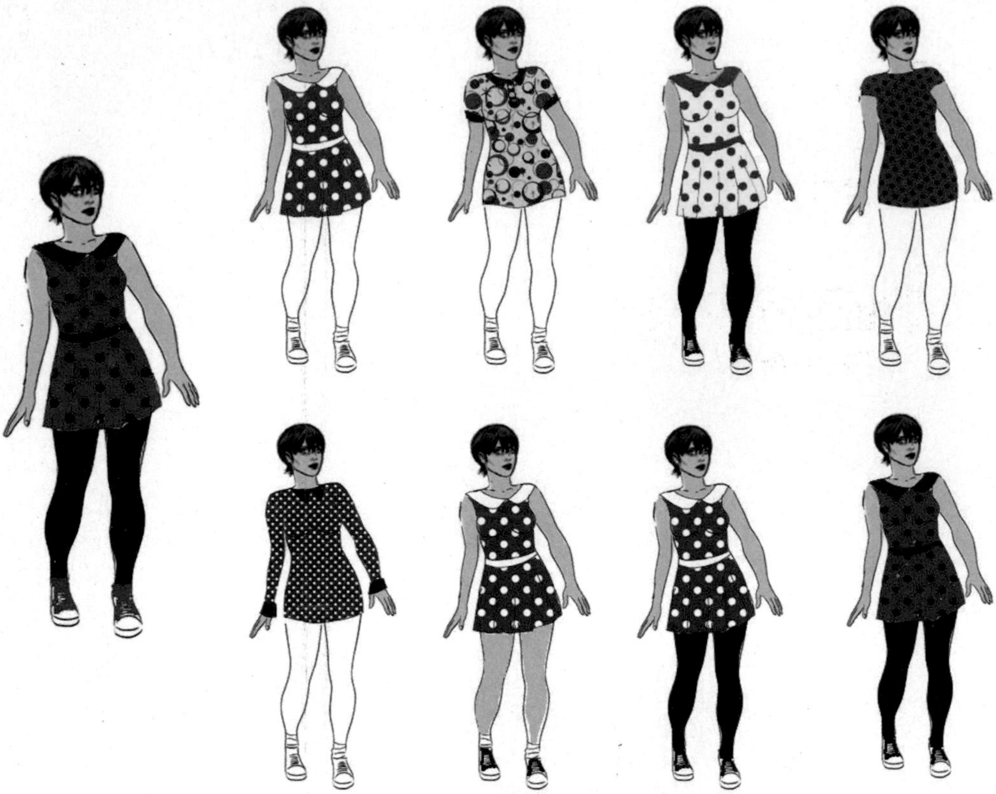

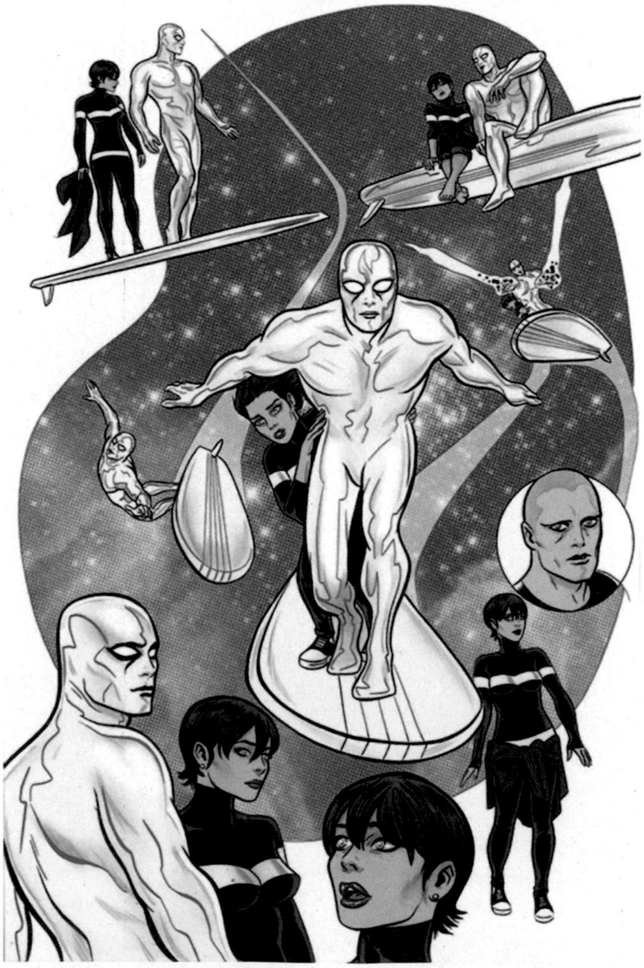